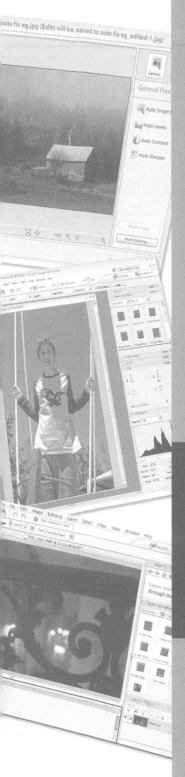

Adobe Photoshop Elements 3.0

A visual introduction to digital imaging

Philip Andrews

AMSTERDAM • BOSTON • HEIDELBERG • LONDON • NEW YORK • OXFORD
PARIS • SAN DIEGO • SAN FRANCISCO • SINGAPORE • SYDNEY • TOKYO

Focal Press is an imprint of Elsevier

Focal Press

Focal Press
An imprint of Elsevier
Linacre House, Jordan Hill, Oxford OX2 8DP
30 Corporate Drive, Burlington MA 01803

First published 2005

British Library Cataloguing in Publication Data
A catalogue record for this book is available from the British Library

Library of Congress Cataloguing in Publication Data
A catalogue record for this book is available from the Library of Congress

ISBN   0 240 51958 2

For information on all Focal Press publications visit our website at: www.focalpress.com

Printed and bound in Italy

Layout and design by the author in Adobe InDesign CS

Picture credits
With thanks to the great guys at www.ablestock.com and Hamera for their generous support in supplying the cover picture and the tutorial images for this text. Copyright © 2005 Hamera and its licensors. All rights reserved.

All other images and illustrations by the author © Philip Andrews 2005. All rights reserved.

Working together to grow
libraries in developing countries

www.elsevier.com | www.bookaid.org | www.sabre.org

ELSEVIER   BOOK AID International   Sabre Foundation

Contents

4 Simple Image Changes · 65

10 Preparing Images for the Web or Email — 219

11 Preparing Images for Printing — 247

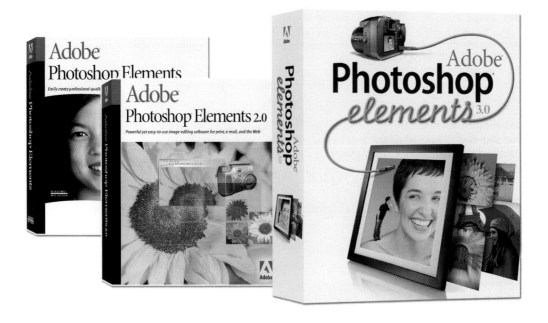

Foreword

In the mid-eighties a group of professional photographers, including myself, were invited to attend an early demonstration of the Quantel Graphics Paintbox system in action at a digital retouching house in Covent Garden, London. We all sat spellbound as we saw our scanned images instantly transformed by the magic of this new computer system. This was my first glimpse of the future of photography in a digital age. From that day forward I had always wanted to have my own computer retouching system and take control of the magic pen myself. However, I was soon brought back down to earth when I was told how much one of these systems would have cost. Back in those days digital retouching services were the preserve of an elite number of businesses such as advertising agency clients, as these were the only people who could afford to pay the equivalent of a good week's salary for an hour of electronic retouching time.

A few years later, Photoshop made its first appearance – an image editing program that was designed to run on a desktop computer. From these humble beginnings Adobe Photoshop has grown to become the leading image editing computer program used by graphic designers, artists, web designers and photographers from all around the world. Millions of people are now able to scan, capture and retouch their own photographs on desktop computers both at home and at work – in fact, I have heard all sorts of people from the bank manager to my hairdresser describe the amazing things they have been able to do to their pictures using a computer.

FOREWORD

Whenever I present seminars on Photoshop techniques, I am always pleased to note the mixed age range and makeup of the audiences who attend these events. Digital image editing has been truly democratized now that everyone can afford to play. I use the word play deliberately, because even after all the years I have been using Photoshop, I still get a buzz whenever I am sitting at the computer transforming my pictures.

Photoshop Elements is essentially a cut-down version of Photoshop, yet it contains nearly all the image manipulation power of the parent program, but in an easy-to-use interface. Although Adobe have limited the range of some of the more advanced Photoshop features and functions, they have included a host of cool features such as the File Browser and Photomerge commands. Adobe Photoshop Elements is therefore an exciting program in its own right and it's going to be fun to use as well, but it is also a powerful tool, capable of handling a number of professional tasks.

Philip Andrews is a skilled and enthusiastic teacher and here he has produced a very well-written book that will help you, the reader, to quickly get to grips with all aspects of the program. The book is clearly illustrated throughout and you will find that Philip has thoughtfully included a number of practical tips on how to capture better photographs. On top of this, he shows you more than how to operate the program – he also demonstrates how to use Photoshop Elements with examples of practical assignments, such as the production of a school newsletter or an illustrated restaurant menu. In my experience I have found that readers always find it much easier to understand a program when they are provided with project examples that have a logical purpose to them. Philip's book is in every respect refreshingly direct and easy to understand.

Whatever your interest, I am sure that you are going to get a lot of interesting use out of Photoshop Elements. Whether you are into manipulating photographs, wishing to build better websites or producing better looking prints, this book will help you to master all the necessary tools contained in the program.

The learning curve has just got shallower!

Martin Evening

www.martinevening.com
www.photoshopforphotographers.com

Introduction

Here at Adobe, we believe that we make great software but just as a car manufacturer would never consider publishing a street index, we rely on gifted authors to provide our users with directions and guidelines on how to make the most of our products.

This task is not a simple one. It requires a good understanding of the product, the digital imaging environment and most of all, the user. Philip Andrews is unique in that he is an author who possesses all these qualities. He has an on-going professional photographic practice, holds a position as a senior lecturer in Imaging and Photography in Australia and has authored over 100 articles and 10 books worldwide.

With these credentials you would imagine that his texts are informative but a little stuffy and academic – not true! In this, the third edition of his best selling Photoshop® Elements book, he again uses a very comfortable and easy to understand style that leads the reader carefully through the basics and then onto the more advanced techniques needed to edit and enhance their digital images. He not only provides 'must have' information about Photoshop Elements and how to use it, but also introduces the reader to important general digital concepts that puts the package firmly in the context of current imaging technology.

The book is dotted with great illustrations and pictures and via the download section of the associated website, readers have the opportunity to follow the step-by-step techniques using many of these same images that are featured in the text. In addition, a whole chapter of real life projects shows how you can use Photoshop Elements to enhance your digital photography projects at home, at work, on vacation or at school.

I believe that with Philip providing you with such a good 'street index' to our Photoshop Elements 3.0 software you will be creating fantastic digital images in next to no time at all.

Good luck and have fun with your image making.

Judith Salonga

Marketing Manager, Pacific

Adobe Systems

ACKNOWLEDGEMENTS

Acknowledgements

Always for Kassy-Lee, but with special thanks to Adrian and Ellena for putting up with a 'would-be author' for a father for the last few months. Yes it is over...till next time at least!

Thanks also to the enthusiastic and very supportive staff at Focal Press whose belief in quality book production has given life to my humble ideas – yet again! Special thanks to Marie Hooper, Christina Donaldson, Margaret Denley and Georgia Kennedy for as everyone knows, but doesn't acknowledge nearly enough, 'good book production is definitely a team effort'.

My appreciation goes to Judith Salonga for her support and kind introduction, and cheers also to Martin Evening, the 'Guru of GUI', and Mark Galer for their technical and 'pixel-based' guidance and to all the image makers who gave so freely of their time and pictures to provide practical examples of 'Real Life Digital Imaging'.

And thanks once more to Adobe for bringing image enhancement and editing to us all through their innovative and industry-leading products, and the other hardware and software manufacturers whose help is an essential part of writing any book of this nature. In particular I wish to thank technical and marketing staff at Adobe, Microsoft, Canon, Nikon, and Epson.

And finally my thanks to all the readers who continue to inspire and encourage me with their generous praise and great images. Keep emailing me to let me know how your imaging is going.

Philip Andrews

1

The Buzz of Digital Photography

The beginning – the digital photograph

Making the digital image

Quality factors in a digital image

The steps in the digital process

Where does Photoshop Elements fit into the process?

Photoshop Elements 3.0

Apart from the initial years of the invention of photography, I can't think of a more exciting time to be involved in making pictures. In fact, I believe that Fox Talbot, as one of the fathers of the medium, would have little difficulty in agreeing that over the last few years the world of imaging has changed forever. Digital photography has become the two buzz-words on everyone's lips. Increasing levels of technology coupled with comparatively affordable equipment have meant that sophisticated imaging jobs that were once the closely guarded domain of industry professionals are now being handled daily by home and business users.

This book introduces you to the techniques of the professionals, and more importantly, shows you how to use these skills to produce high quality images for yourself and your business. Centered on Adobe's Photoshop Elements package and completely revised to cover the new features in version 3.0 as well as the tools common to the previous two versions of the program, you will learn the basics of good digital production from the point of capturing the picture, through simple manipulation techniques to outputting your images for print and web. To help reinforce your understanding, you can practice with the same images that I have used in the step-by-step demonstrations by downloading them from the book's website (www. guide2elements.com). See Figure 1.1. Also, you will find real life examples throughout the text showing you how to use your new found skills to enhance your own images or create professional graphics for your business applications. Source files and instructions for these projects can also be found on the website, giving you the opportunity to practice your skills on real world tasks. See Figure 1.2.

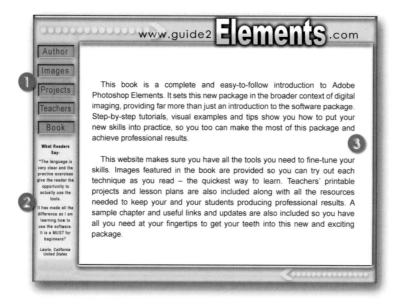

Figure 1.1 *The book's associated website contains practice images as well as downloadable projects designed to build your skills and knowledge. (1) Site buttons. (2) Reader's reviews. (3) Content window.*

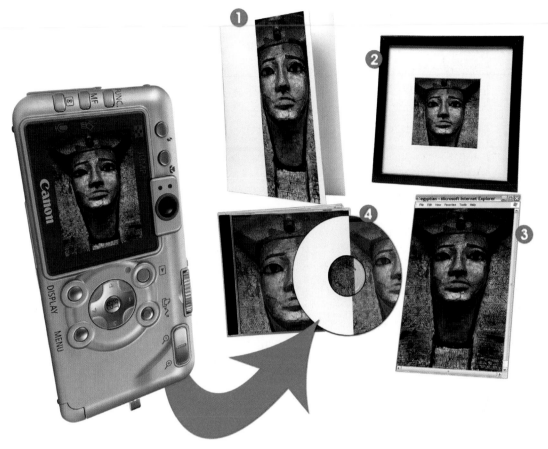

Figure 1.2 Digital imaging skills can be used to manipulate and enhance images so that they can be used in a variety of personal and business publications and products. (1) Presentation folder. (2) Framed print. (3) Web page. (4) CD artwork.

The beginning – the digital photograph

Computers are amazing machines. Their strength is in being able to perform millions of mathematical calculations per second. To apply this ability to working with images, we must start with a description of pictures that the computer can understand. This means that the images must be in a digital form. This is quite different from the way our eye, or any film-based camera, sees the world. With film, for example, we record pictures as a series of 'continuous tones' that blend seamlessly with each other. To make a version of the image the computer can use, these tones needs to be converted to a digital form. The process involves sampling the image at regular intervals and assigning a specific color and brightness to each sample. In this way, a grid of colors and tones is created which, when viewed from a distance, will appear like the original image or scene. Each individual grid section is called a picture element, or pixel. See Figures 1.3 and 1.4.

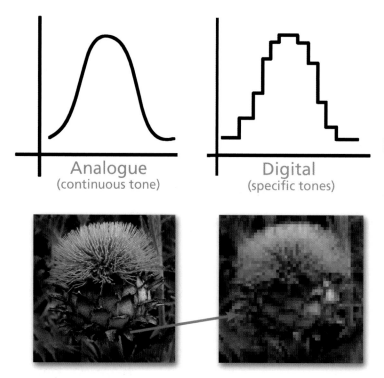

Analogue
(continuous tone)

Digital
(specific tones)

Figure 1.3 Continuous tone images have to be converted to digital form before they can be manipulated by computers.

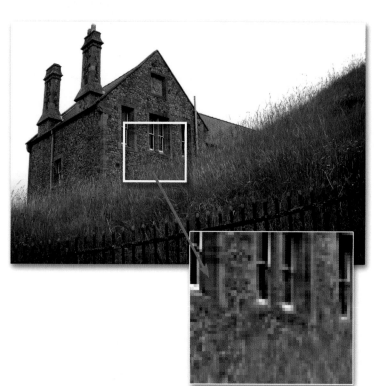

Figure 1.4 A digital picture is made up of a grid of picture elements or pixels.

Making the digital image

Digital files can be created by taking pictures with a digital camera or by using a scanner to convert existing prints or negatives into pixel form. Most digital cameras have a grid of sensors, called charge-coupled devices (CCDs), in the place where traditional cameras would have film. Each sensor measures the brightness and color of the light that hits it. When the values from all sensors are collected and collated, a digital picture results. See Figure 1.5.

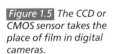

Digital SLR camera

Figure 1.5 *The CCD or CMOS sensor takes the place of film in digital cameras.*

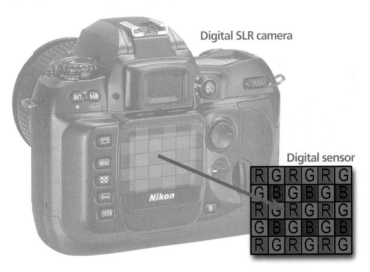

Digital sensor

Scanners work in a similar way, except that these devices use rows of CCD sensors that move slowly over the original, sampling the picture as they go. Generally, different scanners are needed for converting film and print originals; however, some companies are now making products that can be used for both. See Figure 1.6.

Quality factors in a digital image

The quality of the digital file is largely determined by two factors – the numbers of pixels and the number and accuracy of the colors that make up the image. The number of pixels in a picture is represented in two ways – the dimensions, 'the image is 900 × 1200 pixels', or the total pixels contained in the image, 'it is a 3.4 megapixel picture'.

Generally, a file with a large number of pixels will produce a better quality image overall and provide the basis for making larger prints than a picture that contains few pixels. See Figure 1.7. The second quality consideration is the total number of colors that can be recorded in the file. This value is usually referred to as the 'color or bit depth' of the image. The current standard is known as 24-bit color. A picture with this depth is made up of a selection of a possible 16.7 million colors. In practice

THE BUZZ OF DIGITAL PHOTOGRAPHY

this is the minimum number of colors needed for an image to appear photographic. In the early years of digital imaging, 256 colors (8 bit) were considered the standard. Though good for the time, the color quality of this type of image is generally unacceptable nowadays. In fact, new camera and scanner models are now capable of 36- or even 48-bit color. This larger bit depth helps to ensure greater color and tonal accuracy. See Figure 1.8.

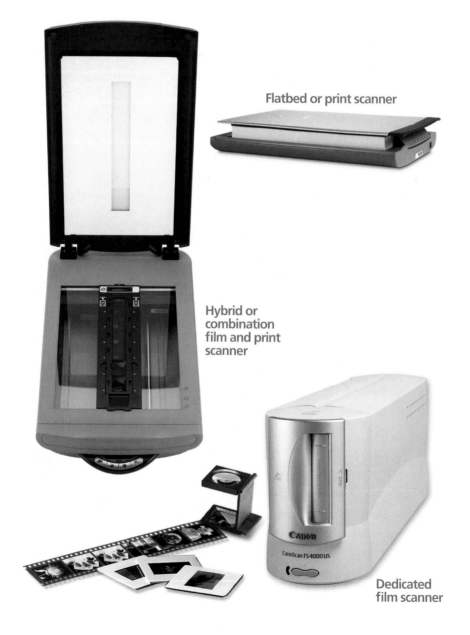

Flatbed or print scanner

Hybrid or combination film and print scanner

Dedicated film scanner

Figure 1.6 *Photographs and negatives, or slides, are converted to digital pictures using either film or flatbed scanners.*

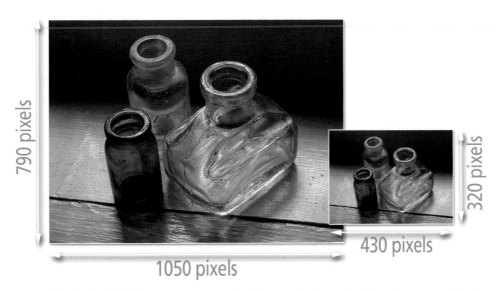

790 pixels

320 pixels

430 pixels

1050 pixels

Figure 1.7 *The size of a digital image is measured in pixels. Images with large pixel dimensions are capable of producing big prints and are generally better quality.*

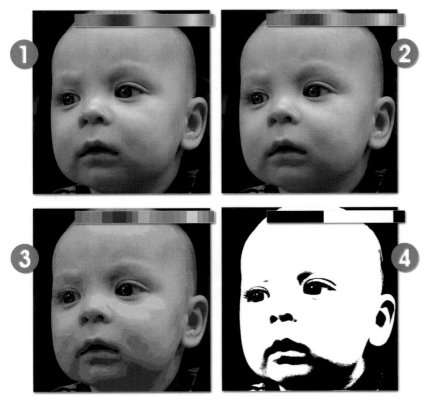

Figure 1.8 *Color or bit depth determines the number of colors possible in a digital file. (1) 24-bit color (16.7 million colors). (2) 8-bit color (256 colors). (3) 4-bit color (16 colors). (4) 1-bit color (two colors).*

The steps in the digital process

The digital imaging process contains three separate steps – capture, manipulate and output. See Figure 1.9. Capturing the image in a digital form is the first step. It is at this point that the color, quality and detail of your image will be determined. Careful manipulation of either the camera or scanner settings will help ensure that your images contain as much of the original's information as possible. In particular, you should ensure that delicate highlight and shadow details are evident in the final image.

If you notice that some 'clipping', or loss of detail, is occurring in your scans, try reducing the contrast settings. If your camera pictures are too dark, or light, adjust the exposure manually to compensate. It is easier to capture the information accurately at this point in the process than try to recreate it later.

Manipulation is where the true power of the digital process becomes evident. It is here that you can enhance and change your images in ways that are far easier than ever before. Altering the color, contrast or brightness of an image is as simple as a couple of button clicks. Changing the size or shape of a picture can be achieved in a few seconds and complex manipulations like combining two or more images together can be completed in minutes not the hours, or even days, needed with traditional techniques. See Figure 1.10. Manipulation gives digital illustrators the power to take a base image and alter it many times so that it can be used in a variety of situations and settings. Once changed, it is possible to output this same image in many ways. It can be printed, used as an illustration in a business report, become part of a website, be sent to friends on the other side of the world as an email attachment or projected onto a large screen as a segment in a professional presentation.

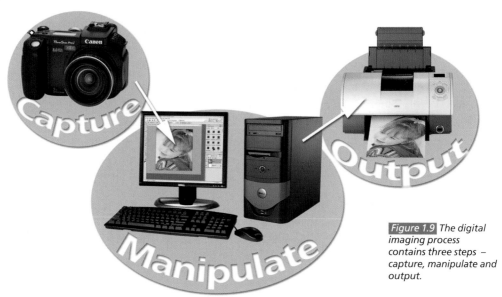

Figure 1.9 The digital imaging process contains three steps – capture, manipulate and output.

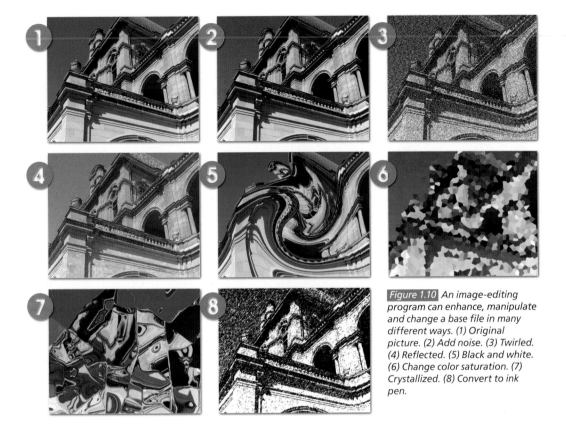

Figure 1.10 An image-editing program can enhance, manipulate and change a base file in many different ways. (1) Original picture. (2) Add noise. (3) Twirled. (4) Reflected. (5) Black and white. (6) Change color saturation. (7) Crystallized. (8) Convert to ink pen.

Where does Photoshop Elements fit into the process?

Photoshop Elements is a program that can be used for enhancing, manipulating, printing and, in version 3.0 of the software, organizing your digital photographs. Put simply, this means that it is the pivot point for the whole digital imaging process. See Figure 1.11. Its main job is to provide the tools, filters and functions that you need to manage, change and alter your pictures. Elements is well suited for this role as it is built upon the same core structure as Adobe's famous professional-level program Photoshop CS. Many of the functions found in this industry-leading package are also present in Elements, but unlike Photoshop, Adobe has made Elements easier to learn and, more importantly, easier to use than its professional cousin. In this way, Adobe has thankfully taken into account that although a lot of users need to produce professional images as part of their daily jobs, not all of these users are, or want to be, imaging professionals. See Figure 1.12. In addition, Elements contains features designed to download digital pictures from your camera, or scanner, directly into the program, as well as functions that allow you to output easily your finished images to web or print. When used in conjunction with other programs, like desktop publishing packages, it is also possible to include Elements' enhanced images in professionally prepared brochures, advertisements and reports.

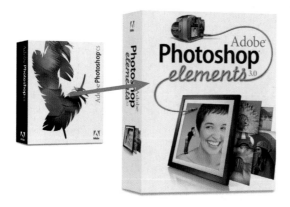

Figure 1.11 *Photoshop Elements is built on the same editing engine as its professional cousin Photoshop.*

Photoshop Elements 3.0

Rather than sitting back and basking in the reflected glory of the success of the first two releases of Elements (versions 1.0 and 2.0), Adobe has been hard at work improving what was already a great product. Version 3.0, just like the releases before it, is a state-of-the-art image-editing program full of the features and functions that digital photographers and desktop image makers desire the most. Far from being overshadowed by the power and dominance of its bigger brother Photoshop CS, Elements has quickly become the editing and enhancement 'weapon of choice' by many who count picture making as their passion. Completely revised to cover all versions of the program, this book will help you learn about the core technology and functions that are shared by Photoshop and Elements, and will also introduce you to the great range of features that are unique to Elements.

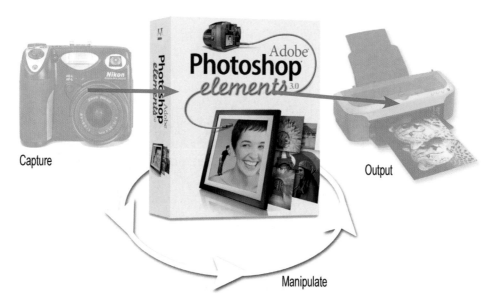

Capture

Output

Manipulate

Figure 1.12 *Elements is the center of the imaging process, providing the ability to import, manipulate and output digital pictures.*

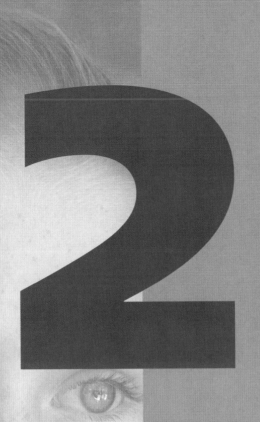

2

Introducing Photoshop Elements 3.0

Adobe Photoshop Elements 3.0 – new tools and features

The Photoshop Elements 3.0 workflow

The interface

The Macintosh difference

Photoshop Elements is the type of software tool that photographers, designers and illustrators use daily to enhance and change their photos. There are many companies who make programs designed for this purpose and in this field Adobe has a substantial advantage over most of its competitors because it also produces the flagship for the industry – Photoshop. Now in its eighth version, this product, more than any other, has forged the direction for image editing and enhancement software worldwide. In fact, the tools, functions and interface that are now standard to graphics packages everywhere owe a lot to earlier versions of Photoshop.

With the release of Elements, Adobe has recognized that not all digital imaging consumers are the same. Professionals do require a vast array of tools and functions to facilitate almost any type of image manipulation, but there is a significant, and growing, number of users that want the robustness of Photoshop but don't require all the 'bells and whistles'. This makes Elements sound like a cut-down version of Photoshop, and to some extent it is, but there is a lot more to this package than a mere subset of Photoshop's features. Adobe has taken the time to listen to its customers, and has designed and included in Elements a host of extra tools and features that are not available in Photoshop. It's this combination of proven strength and new functions that makes Elements the perfect imaging tool for digital camera and scanner owners who need to produce professional level graphics economically.

Adobe Photoshop Elements 3.0 – new tools and features

The release of version 3.0 of the program builds upon the firm foundation and following that 1.0 and 2.0 secured. The revision contains a variety of new tools and features that I predict will fast become regularly used favorites. In addition, the Windows version adds the extra organization and management features that were originally part of the Photoshop Album package. Some of the new or upgraded features can also be found in Photoshop CS, others are only available in Elements. Table 2.1 details some of the changes that are 'New for 3.0' and compares them with features found in previous versions of Photoshop and Elements.

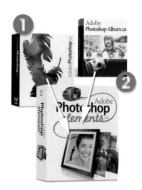

Figure 2.1 Photoshop Elements 3.0 for Windows combines many of the advanced editing features contained in Photoshop CS (1) along with the management tools of Photoshop Album (2).

These new or revised features are also highlighted throughout the book with the 'New for 3.0' symbol. As in previous versions of the program, the majority of the features and tools in Photoshop Elements are common to both Macintosh and Windows editions of the package. On the whole, they appear and function in precisely the same way irrespective of the operating system that the program is running on, but this doesn't mean that there are no differences. In fact, Photoshop Elements 3.0 for Windows does contain organizational and project features that do not appear in the Macintosh release. To help make the distinction between the two products more apparent I have also included a Macintosh and Windows symbol next to the features that are included in each release of the program.

Table 2.1 *Summary of features of different versions of Adobe Photoshop Elements and Adobe Photoshop.*

Feature	ELEMENTS			PHOTOSHOP		
	v3.0	v2.0	v1.0	CS	v7.0	v6.0
• RAW file support	✓	✗	✗	✓	✗	✗
• 16-bit file support	✓	✗	✗	✓	✓	✓
• Shadow/Highlights control	✓	✗	✗	✓	✗	✗
• Cookie Cutter cropping tool	✓	✗	✗	✗	✗	✗
• Quick Fix editor	✓	✗	✗	✗	✗	✗
• Smart fix auto enhance feature	✓	✗	✗	✗	✗	✗
• Spot Healing Brush	✓	✗	✗	✗	✗	✗
• Photo Browser with Date View	✓ WIN	✗	✗	✗	✗	✗
• Photo/Palette/Organize Bin	✓	✗	✗	✗	✗	✗
• Color Variations	✓	✓	✓	✗	✗	✓
• Hints palette	✓	✓	✓	✗	✗	✗
• PDF slide show	✓	✓	✗	✓	✗	✗
• Save for Web option	✓	✓	✓	✓	✓	✓
• Recipes (How to) palette	✓	✓	✓	✗	✗	✗
• Photomerge panoramic stitching tool	✓	✓	✓	✓	✗	✗
• Get Photos from mobile phone	✓ WIN	✗	✗	✗	✗	✗
• Image layers	✓	✓	✓	✓	✓	✓
• Adjustment layers	✓	✓	✓	✓	✓	✓
• Filter browser	✓	✓	✓	✓	✗	✗
• History palette	✓	✓	✓	✓	✓	✓
• Picture Package for multiple prints	✓	✓	✓	✓	✓	✓
• Web Photo Gallery wizard	✓	✗	✗	✗	✗	✗
• Tag and Collection creation	✓	✗	✗	✗	✗	✗
• Effects browser	✓	✓	✓	✗	✗	✗
• Red Eye Brush	✓	✓	✓	✓	✗	✗
• Painting tools	✓	✓	✓	✓	✓	✓
• Type tool	✓	✓	✓	✓	✓	✓
• Background eraser	✓	✓	✓	✓	✓	✓
• Web-based photo printing	✓	✓	✓	✓	✗	✗
• Save as JPEG 2000	✓	✓	✗	✓	✗	✗
• Photo Creations project wizard	✓ WIN	✗	✗	✗	✗	✗
• Selection/Mask Brush	✓	✓	✗	✗	✗	✗
• Attach to e-mail feature	✓	✓	✗	✗	✗	✗

Apart from the inclusion of a host of new features like the Photo filter, the ability to import high-quality photographs in the RAW file format and the Shadow/Highlights control, the major change to the program since version 2.0 has come in the way that your digital photographs are managed and organized. Unlike the previous versions of Elements which contained a simple, but effective, file browser, Elements 3.0 for Windows merges the powerful cataloging, tagging and search engine that was the basis of Photoshop Album with the editing prowess of Elements to create a complete system designed with the digital photographer in mind. See Figure 2.1. Not to be outdone the Macintosh version comes complete with a revamped file browser that shares much in common with the same feature in Photoshop CS. See Figure 2.4.

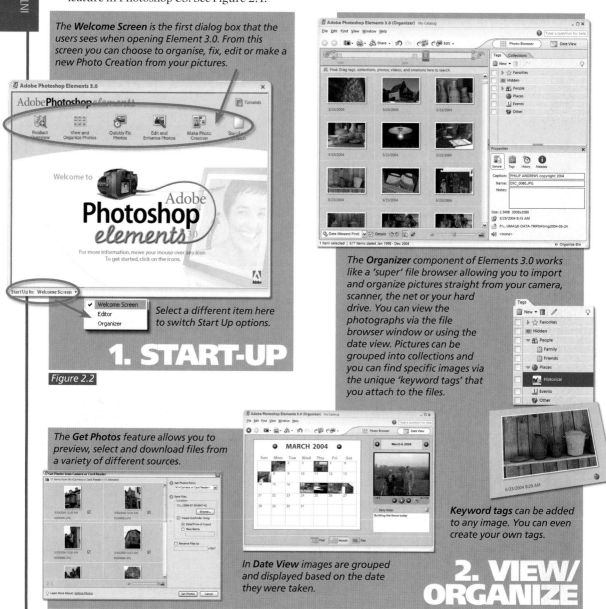

The **Welcome Screen** is the first dialog box that the users sees when opening Element 3.0. From this screen you can choose to organise, fix, edit or make a new Photo Creation from your pictures.

Select a different item here to switch Start Up options.

1. START-UP

Figure 2.2

The **Organizer** component of Elements 3.0 works like a 'super' file browser allowing you to import and organize pictures straight from your camera, scanner, the net or your hard drive. You can view the photographs via the file browser window or using the date view. Pictures can be grouped into collections and you can find specific images via the unique 'keyword tags' that you attach to the files.

The **Get Photos** feature allows you to preview, select and download files from a variety of different sources.

Keyword tags can be added to any image. You can even create your own tags.

In **Date View** images are grouped and displayed based on the date they were taken.

2. VIEW/ORGANIZE

Book resources at: **www.guide2elements.com**

The Photoshop Elements 3.0 workflow

In effect, Elements 3.0 provides a workflow solution from the moment you download your files from camera, scanner or the net, through organization and manipulation phases and then onto printing or outputting the pictures electronically (web gallery, email attachments) or as print. Understanding how the various components in the system fit together will help you make the most of the software and its new powerful features. See Figure 2.2.

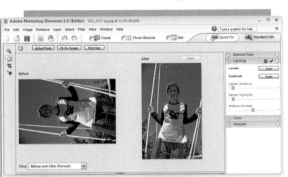

The **Quick Fix** editor provides a series of one-click or semi-automatic fixes for common problems with lighting, contrast, color and sharpness. All the controls are contained in the one screen for speed.

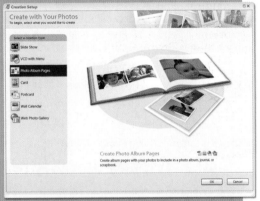

Photo Creations are a new way of grouping special output options in Elements. A step-by-step approach is used to create slide shows, VCD presentations, photo album pages, post and greeting cards, calenders and web photo galleries.

4. PHOTO CREATIONS

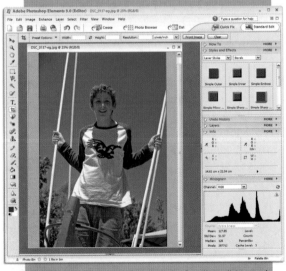

The **Standard** editor contains all the familiar editing and enhancement tools that Elements users have come to expect. It is here that you can take full control over the manipulation and fine-tuning of your pictures. You can also add text, play with layers, create multi-picture composites and combine all manner of special effects with your original photo.

3. EDIT/ ENHANCE

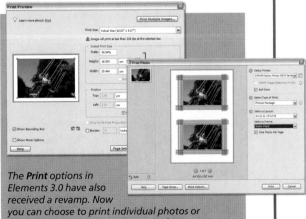

The **Print** options in Elements 3.0 have also received a revamp. Now you can choose to print individual photos or multiple pictures on a single sheet of paper. As an added bonus decorative frames can be added to the images right from the print dialog box.

5. PRINT

The interface

The program interface is the link between the user and the software. Most graphics packages work with a system that includes a series of menus, tools, palettes and dialog boxes. These devices give the user access to the features of the program. The images themselves are contained in windows that can be sized and zoomed. In this regard Elements is now different. The package is available for both the Macintosh and Windows platforms and the interface for the Standard Editor of each system is very similar, with the only differences being the result of the underlying operating system of each computer. See Figures 2.3 and 2.4.

For most editing and enhancement functions you will be using the Standard Editor component of Photoshop Elements, so over the next few pages we will look at the various parts of this screen and how they are used to allow you to interact with and change your pictures. Later on in the chapter we will also examine the interface of other parts of the Elements system such as the Organizer (Windows), Quick Fix editor and the Photo Creations wizard (Windows).

A totally new way of looking at Elements

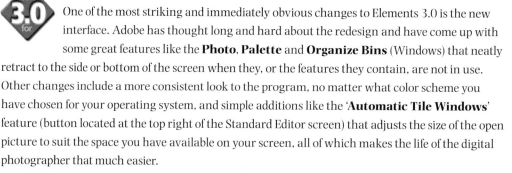

One of the most striking and immediately obvious changes to Elements 3.0 is the new interface. Adobe has thought long and hard about the redesign and have come up with some great features like the **Photo**, **Palette** and **Organize Bins** (Windows) that neatly retract to the side or bottom of the screen when they, or the features they contain, are not in use. Other changes include a more consistent look to the program, no matter what color scheme you have chosen for your operating system, and simple additions like the '**Automatic Tile Windows**' feature (button located at the top right of the Standard Editor screen) that adjusts the size of the open picture to suit the space you have available on your screen, all of which makes the life of the digital photographer that much easier.

New tools and features

Not to be content with cosmetic changes alone, Adobe has also chosen to include a range of new tools and features in the release. These include the fast and efficient **Quick Fix** editor (a grown-up version the Quick Fix dialog found in version 2.0), the **Cookie Cutter** tool used for cropping photos in specific shapes, the **Spot Healing** and **Healing Brush** tools which are great retouching spots and marks, and the **Shadow/Highlights** control which replaces both the Adjust Backlighting and Fill Flash features that we saw in previous versions of the program.

But Elements 3.0 doesn't just have new bells and whistles, it has more power too. You can now load and work with pictures with loads more colors in **16-bit** mode and even import high quality RAW files directly from your camera with the sophisticated **RAW file import dialog**. Though not fully listed here, each of the new tools and features (and their working) will be covered in detail throughout the text.

Tool bar – *displays icons of the tools available, can also be displayed in 2 column view*

Options bar – *displays the options for the currently selected tool*

Menu bar – *contains features grouped in menu and sub-menus*

Shortcuts bar – *buttons for commonly used functions*

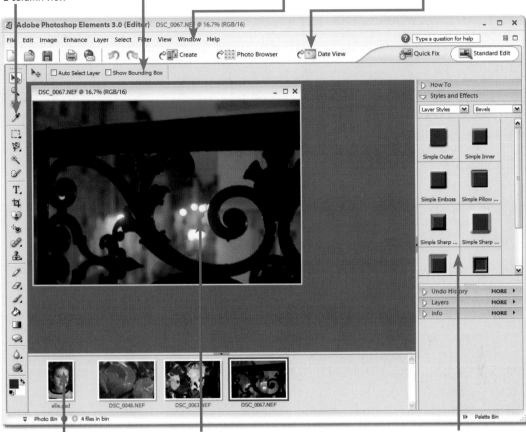

Photo Bin – *for storing pictures when minimized*

Image window – *displays the open picture in Elements, can be maximized, minimized and cancelled using the corner buttons*

Palette Bin – *for storing palettes similar to the Palette Well in v1.0, 2.0*

Figure 2.3 *The new interface for the Elements 3.0 Standard Editor as seen in Windows XP.*

Figure 2.4 *The Elements 3.0 interface as it appears when running on the Macintosh platform.*

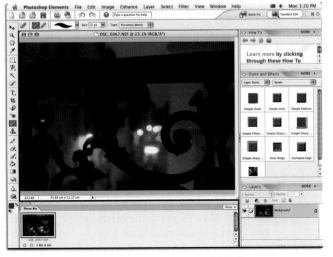

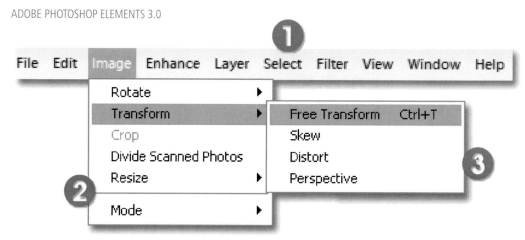

Figure 2.5 *The menu bar provides access to the major features and commands in the program. (1) Main menu bar. (2) Menu. (3) Sub-menu.*

Menus

Most programs contain a menu bar with a range of choices for program activities. In addition to the standard File, Edit, View, Window and Help menus, Elements contains five other specialist headings designed specifically for working with digital pictures. See Figure 2.5.

The **Image** menu contains features that change the shape size, mode and orientation of the picture. Version 3.0 contains an extra option, Divide Scanned Photos, which is used for separating groups of photographs that have been scanned as one picture. Grouped under the **Enhance** heading are a range of options for altering the color, contrast and brightness of images, as well as the new Smart Fix feature in both auto and manual forms. All functions concerning image layers and selections are contained under the **Layer** and **Selection** menus. The special effects that can be applied to images and layers are listed under the **Filter** menu.

Selecting a menu item is as simple as moving your mouse over the menu, clicking to show the list of items and then moving the mouse pointer over the heading you wish to use. With some selections a second menu (sub-menu) appears, from which you can make further selections. See Figure 2.5.

Some menu items can also be selected using a combination of keyboard strokes called shortcuts. The key combinations for these features are also listed next to the item in the menu list. For example, the Free Transform can be selected using the menu selections Image > Transform > Free Transform or with the key combination of Ctrl + T (the Control key and the letter T).

Because Photoshop Elements 3.0 has several different workspaces that you can work within, I will indicate the workspace first before the menu sequence required to select a feature. For instance, to select the Free Transform feature (as pictured in Figure 2.5) from inside the Standard Editor space the notation would be **Editor: Image > Transform > Free Transform**.

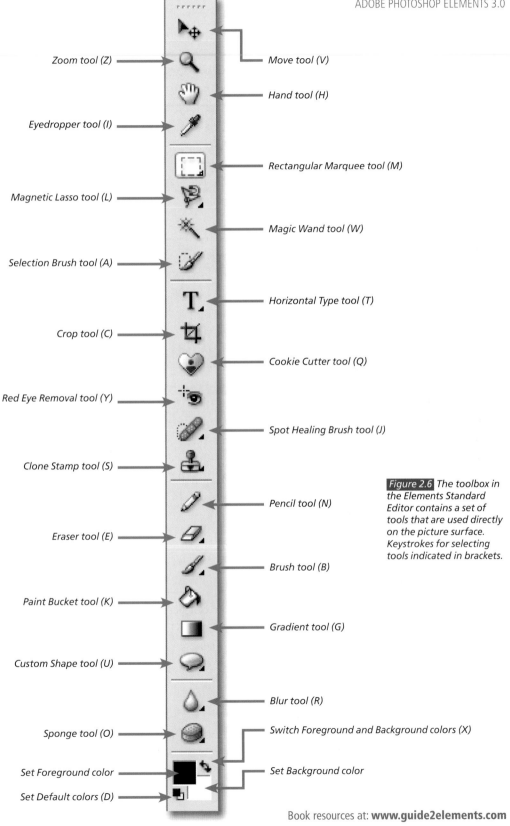

Zoom tool (Z)

Eyedropper tool (I)

Magnetic Lasso tool (L)

Selection Brush tool (A)

Crop tool (C)

Red Eye Removal tool (Y)

Clone Stamp tool (S)

Eraser tool (E)

Paint Bucket tool (K)

Custom Shape tool (U)

Sponge tool (O)

Set Foreground color

Set Default colors (D)

Move tool (V)

Hand tool (H)

Rectangular Marquee tool (M)

Magic Wand tool (W)

Horizontal Type tool (T)

Cookie Cutter tool (Q)

Spot Healing Brush tool (J)

Pencil tool (N)

Brush tool (B)

Gradient tool (G)

Blur tool (R)

Switch Foreground and Background colors (X)

Set Background color

Figure 2.6 *The toolbox in the Elements Standard Editor contains a set of tools that are used directly on the picture surface. Keystrokes for selecting tools indicated in brackets.*

Tools

Unlike menu items, tools interact directly with the image and require the user to manipulate the mouse to define the area or extent of the tools' effect. Over the years the number and types of tools found in digital photography packages have been distilled to a common few that find their way into the toolbox of most programs. Amongst these familiar items are the Magnifying Glass or Zoom tool, the Brush, the Magic Wand, the Lasso and the Cropping tool. See Figure 2.6. In addition to these few, each company produces a specialist set of customized tools that are designed to make particular jobs easier. Of these, Elements users will find the Red Eye Brush, Custom Shape, the Selection Brush and the new Healing Brush tools particularly useful.

Some tools contain extra or hidden options which can be viewed by clicking and holding the mouse key over the small triangle in the bottom right-hand corner of the tool button. Alternatively the sub-menu may list a variety of tools related to the one currently selected. Selecting a new option from those listed will replace the current icon in the toolbox with your new choice. To switch back simply reselect the original tool. See Figure 2.7.

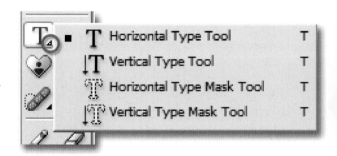

Figure 2.7 Click and hold the triangle in the bottom right of the tool icon to reveal the tool's other options or related tool choices.

Tool types

The many tools available in Photoshop Elements can be broken into several different groups based on their function or the task that they perform.

Selection tools

Selection tools are designed to highlight or isolate parts of an image. This can be achieved by drawing around a section of the picture using either the Marquee or Lasso tools or by using the Magic Wand tool to define an area by its color. The new Selection Brush tool allows the user to select an area by painting the selection with a special brush tool. Careful selection is one of the key skills of the digital imaging worker. Often, the difference between good quality enhancement and a job that is coarse and obvious is based on the skill taken at the selection stage. See Figure 2.8.

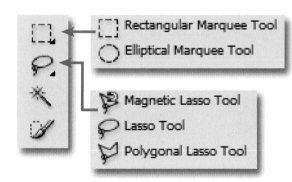

Figure 2.8 Selection tools are used to isolate a specific area in a picture. This can be achieved by drawing around the picture part or you can create the selection based on color.

Book resources at: **www.guide2elements.com**

Painting/drawing tools

Although many photographers and designers will employ Elements to enhance images captured using a digital camera or scanner, some users make pictures from scratch using the program's drawing tools. Illustrators, in particular, generate their images with the aid of tools such as the Paint Bucket, Airbrush and Pencil. This is not to say that it is not possible to use drawing or painting tools on digital photographs. In fact, the judicious use of tools like the Brush can enhance detail and provide a sense of drama in your images.

Also included in this grouping is the Eraser tool which comes in handy for cleaning up drawn illustrations and photographs alike, the Gradient tool used for filling areas with a blend from one color to another and the Custom Shape tool. Unlike the other tools in this group the Custom Shape tool creates vector-based or sharp edge graphics. This tool is especially good for producing regularly shaped areas of color which can be used as backgrounds for text. See Figure 2.9.

Enhancement tools

These tools are designed specifically for use on existing pictures. Areas of the image can be sharpened or blurred, darkened or lightened and smudged using features like the burning or dodging tool. The Red Eye Brush is great for removing the 'devil'-like eyes from flash photographs and the Clone Stamp tool is essential for removing dust marks, as well as any other unwanted picture details.

Add to these favorites the new Spot Healing tool, which works like and advanced version of the Clone Stamp, and you have a set of features more than capable of most enhancement jobs. See Figure 2.10.

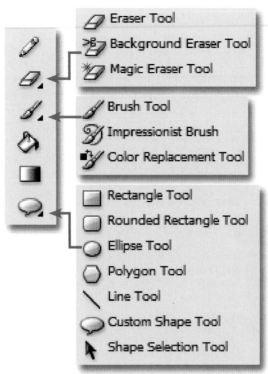

Figure 2.9 *Painting and drawing tools are used to add details to existing images or even create whole pictures from scratch.*

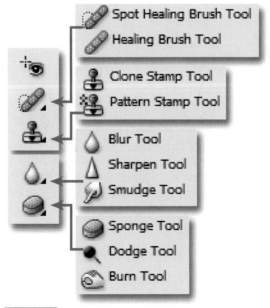

Figure 2.10 *Enhancement tools are used to alter existing images to improve their overall appearance.*

Move and view tools

The Hand tool helps users navigate their way around images. This is especially helpful when the image has been 'zoomed' beyond the confines of the screen. When a picture is enlarged to this extent it is not possible to view the whole image at one time; using the Hand tool the user can drag the photograph around within the window frame.

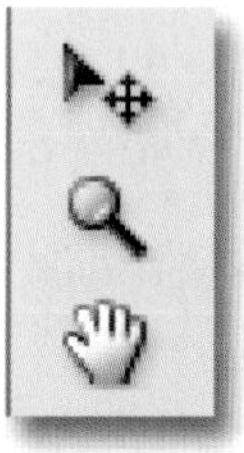

The Zoom tool allows you to get closer to, or further away from, the picture you are working on and the Move tool is used to select, and move, individual picture parts within the picture itself. See Figure 2.11.

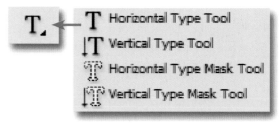

Figure 2.11 *The Hand tool is used to navigate around enlarged pictures, whereas the Zoom tool alters the magnification of the image on screen.*

Text tools

Combining text with images is an activity that is used a lot in business applications. Elements provides the option to apply text horizontally across the page, or vertically down the page. In addition, versions 2.0 and 3.0 of the program provide two special text masking options that can be used in conjunction with images to produce spectacular effects. See Figure 2.12.

T Horizontal Type Tool
T Vertical Type Tool
T Horizontal Type Mask Tool
T Vertical Type Mask Tool

Figure 2.12 *The Text tool is used to add type and type masks to images.*

Cropping tools

The final group of tools is designed for removing unwanted sections of the image. Using the standard and familiar Crop tool we can drag a marquee around the part of the picture that we wish to keep and then double click inside the frame to remove the image areas outside the selection. The new Cookie Cutter tool takes the idea further by providing the ability to crop your picture to a specific shape (not rectangular). See Figure 2.13.

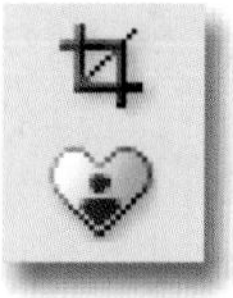

Figure 2.13 *The Crop and Cookie Cutter tools are used for changing the shape of your pictures and removing unwanted edge sections.*

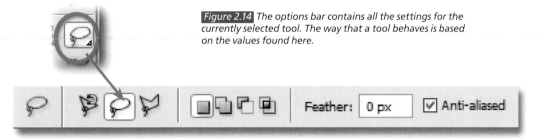

Figure 2.14 *The options bar contains all the settings for the currently selected tool. The way that a tool behaves is based on the values found here.*

Options bar

Each tool and its use can be customized by changing the values in the options bar. See Figure 2.14. It is located below the shortcuts bar at the top of the screen. The default settings are displayed automatically when you select the tool. Changing these values will alter the way that the tool interacts with your image. For complex tools like the Brush, more settings can be found by selecting the More button located to the extreme right of the bar.

Palettes

Palettes are small windows that help the user enhance their pictures by providing extra information about images or by listing a variety of modification options. See Figure 2.15. Palettes can be docked in the Palette Bin (Palette Well for versions 1.0 and 2.0) or dragged and dropped onto the main editing area. Commonly used functions can be grouped by dragging each palette by their tab onto a single palette window. To save space only have open those palettes that you need for the editing or enhancing job at hand. Close the remaining palettes by clicking the Close button ☒ in the top of the palette window or drag them to the retractable Palette Bin so that they are out of the way.

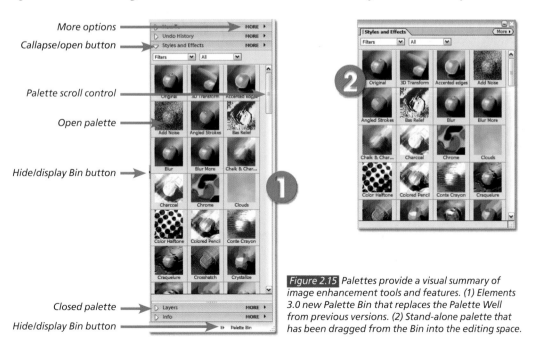

More options
Callapse/open button
Palette scroll control
Open palette
Hide/display Bin button
Closed palette
Hide/display Bin button

Figure 2.15 *Palettes provide a visual summary of image enhancement tools and features. (1) Elements 3.0 new Palette Bin that replaces the Palette Well from previous versions. (2) Stand-alone palette that has been dragged from the Bin into the editing space.*

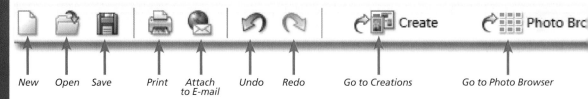

New   Open   Save   Print   Attach   Undo   Redo   Go to Creations   Go to Photo Browser
                                to E-mail

Figure 2.16 *Shortcuts are button versions of commonly used menu items. The palette well is used to store palettes when not in use.*

Shortcuts bar

The shortcuts bar in the Standard editor contains button versions of commonly used commands. See Figure 2.16. The same commands can also be accessed via the menu bar. To the right of this section of the bar are two buttons that allow you to switch between Quick Fix and Standard modes. This spot was occupied by the Palette Well in previous versions of the program. The Palette Bin now performs the same function as the Palette Well allowing the open palettes to be stored away from the main editing space providing more screen area for image windows.

The Quick Fix editor

The Quick Fix tool (Enhance > Quick Fix) first introduced in version 2.0 of Elements cleverly combined a variety of commonly used enhancement and correction tools into a single image control center. With this feature the user no longer needed to access each individual tool or menu item in turn, rather all the options are available in one place. See Figure 2.17.

The feature proved so popular that Elements 3.0 now contains a completely new editing option called Quick Fix. The component is accessed from the Welcome or start-up window, or via the Quick Fix shortcut button in the editor component. See Figure 2.18.

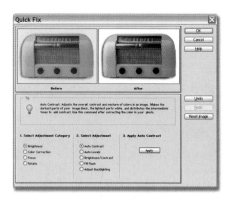

Figure 2.17 *The Quick Fix multi-dialog, as it appeared in version 2.0 of the program, cleverly brought together a variety of commonly used tools and features to save users repetitive menu selections when enhancing their images.*

Keeping the same before and after layout as the original tool, the Quick Fix editor contains a reduced tool and feature set designed to facilitate the fast application of the most frequent of all enhancement activities undertaken by the digital photographer. The Zoom, Hand, Crop and Red Eye Removal tools located in a small tool bar to the left of the screen and are available for standard image-editing changes and the fixed Palette Bin, to the right, contains the necessary features to alter and correct the lighting, color, orientation (Rotate) and sharpness of your pictures.

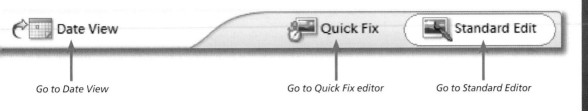

Go to Date View   Go to Quick Fix editor   Go to Standard Editor

Figure 2.18 *The new Quick Fix editor brings together all your most commonly used tools and adjustment features into one easy and quick to use work space.*

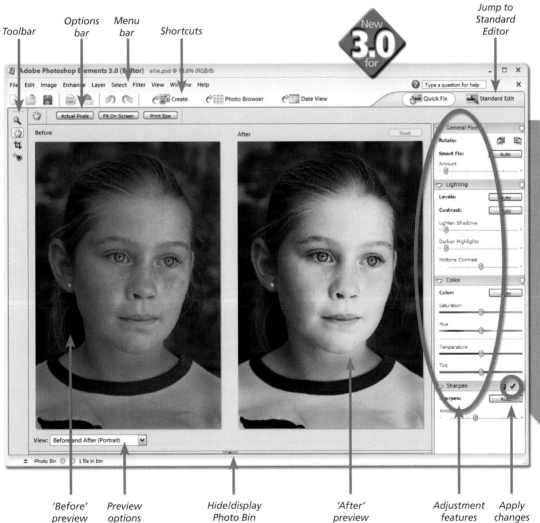

Toolbar   Options bar   Menu bar   Shortcuts   Jump to Standard Editor

ENHANCEMENT WORKFLOW

'Before' preview   Preview options   Hide/display Photo Bin   'After' preview   Adjustment features   Apply changes

One of the best aspects of this new editing option is the fact that the user can choose to apply each image change automatically, via the Auto button, or manually using the supplied sliders. This approach provides both convenience and speed when needed with the option of a manual override for those difficult editing tasks. The adjustment features are arranged in a fashion that provides a model ehancement workflow to follow – simply move from the top to the bottom of the tools starting with picture rotation, working through lighting and color alterations and lastly, applying sharpening.

The Organizer feature (Photo Browser)

Along with the new Quick Fix editor, Elements 3.0 for Windows has incorporated the sophisticated Organizer browser, first introduced in Photoshop Album, into its digital photography system. Though the older File Browser feature (Editor: File > Browse Folders) is still available in editor mode and will adequately provide a quick way to visually locate your images, it doesn't contain the range of search, tag and display options that the Organizer can boast. See Figures 2.19 and 2.20.

Once the picture files have been imported (Organizer: File > Get Photos) into the browser they can be viewed by date taken, their associated tags and even their folder location. Pairs of pictures can be viewed side by side with the View > Photo Compare feature to help choose the best shot from a series of images taken of the same subject. Instant slide shows of whole collections, or just those pictures selected from the browser, can be created and displayed using the View > Photo Review feature.

Simple editing tasks, such as the automatic adjustment of levels, contrast and/or sharpness along with simple orientation and crop changes can be performed directly from inside the browser with the Auto Fix feature. Finding your favorite pictures has never been easier as you can search by date, caption, filename, history, media type, tag and color similarity (to already selected photos).

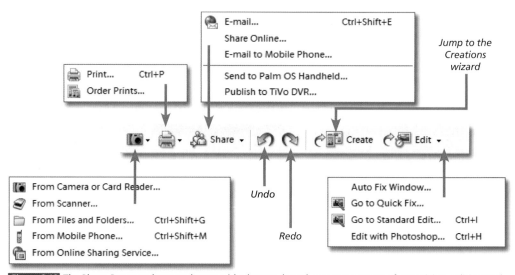

Figure 2.19 *The Photo Browser shortcuts bar provides button-based access to a range of organizing, editing and sharing options for selected thumbnail images.*

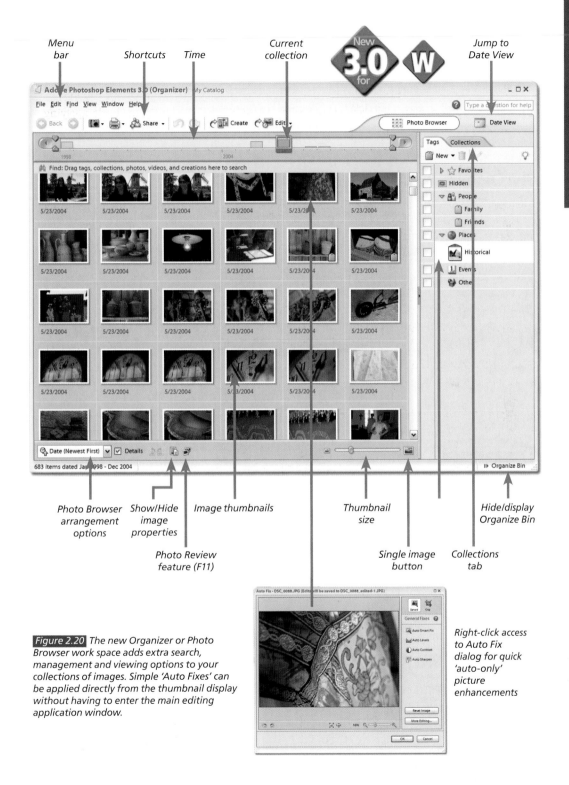

Menu bar

Shortcuts   Time

Current collection

Jump to Date View

Photo Browser arrangement options

Show/Hide image properties

Image thumbnails

Thumbnail size

Hide/display Organize Bin

Photo Review feature (F11)

Single image button

Collections tab

Figure 2.20 The new Organizer or Photo Browser work space adds extra search, management and viewing options to your collections of images. Simple 'Auto Fixes' can be applied directly from the thumbnail display without having to enter the main editing application window.

Right-click access to Auto Fix dialog for quick 'auto-only' picture enhancements

INTRODUCING PHOTOSHOP ELEMENTS

The Photo Creations feature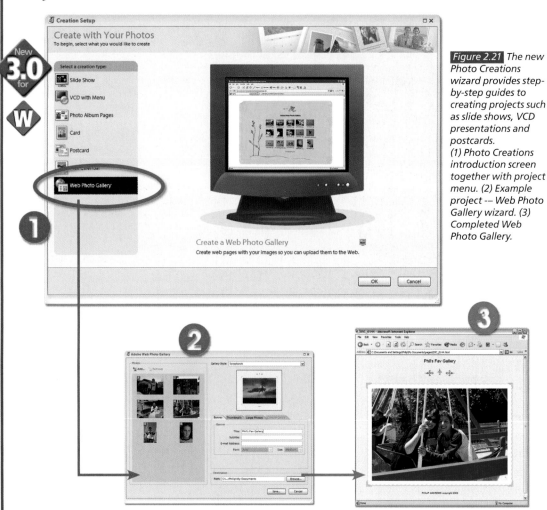

Also new to Elements 3.0 is the addition of the Photo Creations wizard. See Figure 2.21. Designed to act as a step-by-step guide to creating great projects with your pictures. This is the starting point for the production of slide shows, greeting and postcards, calendars, web photo galleries, album pages and Video CD (VCD) presentations. Whole catalogs, or even several individually selected files from the Photo Browser, can be used as a basis for the projects in the Photo Creations feature.

You can start the feature from the Photo Browser (Organizer), either of the two image editors (Quick Fix and Standard), using the 'Create' shortcut button or from the initial Welcome or start-up screen by selecting the 'Make Photo Creation' option. The pictures to include in the project can be selected in the browser prior to opening the feature or added later using the 'Add Photos' command. The steps involved in creating the project are clear and precise with sophisticated and professional results being available in minutes rather than hours, which would be the case if manually produced.

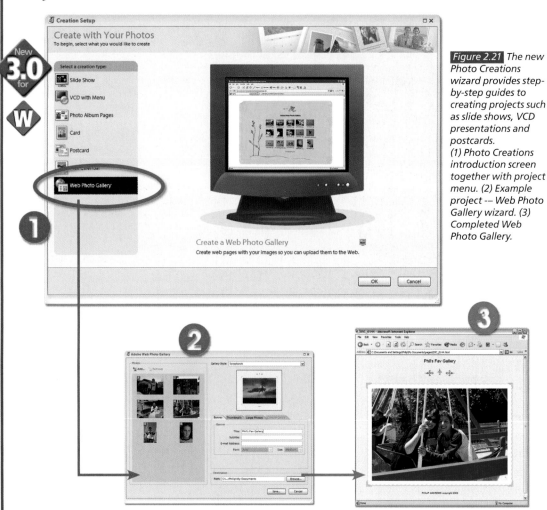

Figure 2.21 The new Photo Creations wizard provides step-by-step guides to creating projects such as slide shows, VCD presentations and postcards.
(1) Photo Creations introduction screen together with project menu. (2) Example project -- Web Photo Gallery wizard. (3) Completed Web Photo Gallery.

Book resources at: **www.guide2elements.com**

The Macintosh difference Ⓜ

Unlike previous versions of Photoshop Elements, version 3.0 has some distinct differences between the program released for Macintosh and the edition designed to run on Windows machines. The most notable changes revolve around the Photo Browser and Photo Creations work spaces which are both part of the new Windows edition of the program but are not included for Macintosh users. As we have already seen, these features were initially part of the Photoshop Album program which was only available for Windows machines and as such, the functions included with this package are more easily combined with the Windows version of Elements.

With the release of OSX, many Macintosh users found the same functionality of browsing, keyword and sorting features offered by Photoshop Album to be provided by the new Apple program iPhoto. So for this release of Elements the recommended Macintosh workflow involves combining your existing iPhoto software and library of images with the new features and functions of Elements 3.0. See Figure 2.22.

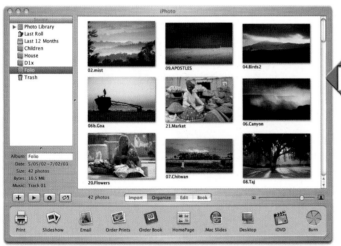

Figure 2.22 Macintosh users can obtain many of the same organizational and project features found in the Photo Browser and Photo Creations work spaces of Elements 3.0 for Windows by combining iPhoto with Photoshop Elements 3.0.

The Macintosh file browser Ⓜ

For those Macintosh users who prefer not to use iPhoto, the guys at Adobe have upgraded the basic file browser from Elements 2.0 to include many of the functions available in the Photoshop CS version of the feature. By far the most useful change in the Macintosh file browser (Editor: File > Browse Folders) for digital photographers is the ability to access a range of automated features such as the Picture Package and Contact Sheet features directly from the browser window. This means no more opening the pictures and selecting the feature or even having to store all your pictures in the one folder before starting the process, simply multi-select the very images you want to include in your Web Photo Gallery from inside the browser itself and then choose the feature from the automation drop-down menu.

Impressive as this is, it is only when you add the extensive sort and searching capabilities, the options to add and edit Keywords (called Tags in the Windows version) assigned to your pictures and the newly enhanced speed of the browser itself that you realize this is definitely not the same browser that existed in version 2.0. See Figure 2.23.

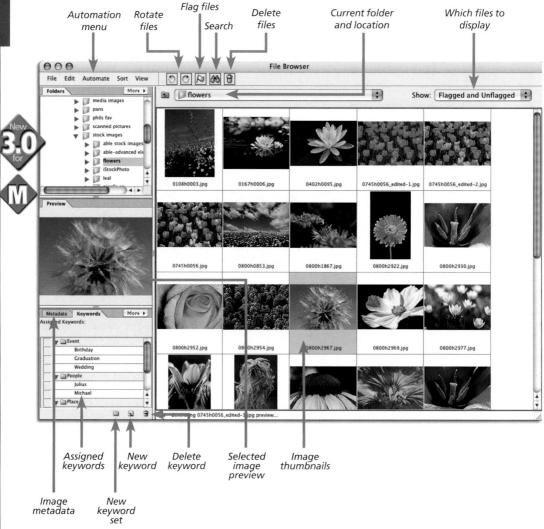

Figure 2.23 *The updated file browser in Photoshop Elements 3.0 for Macintosh contains many new features including the ability to multi-select the files that are to be used in automated functions such as the make Web Photo Gallery feature. Pictures are selected from within the browser first and then the featured is picked from the Automated menu list in the browser itself.*

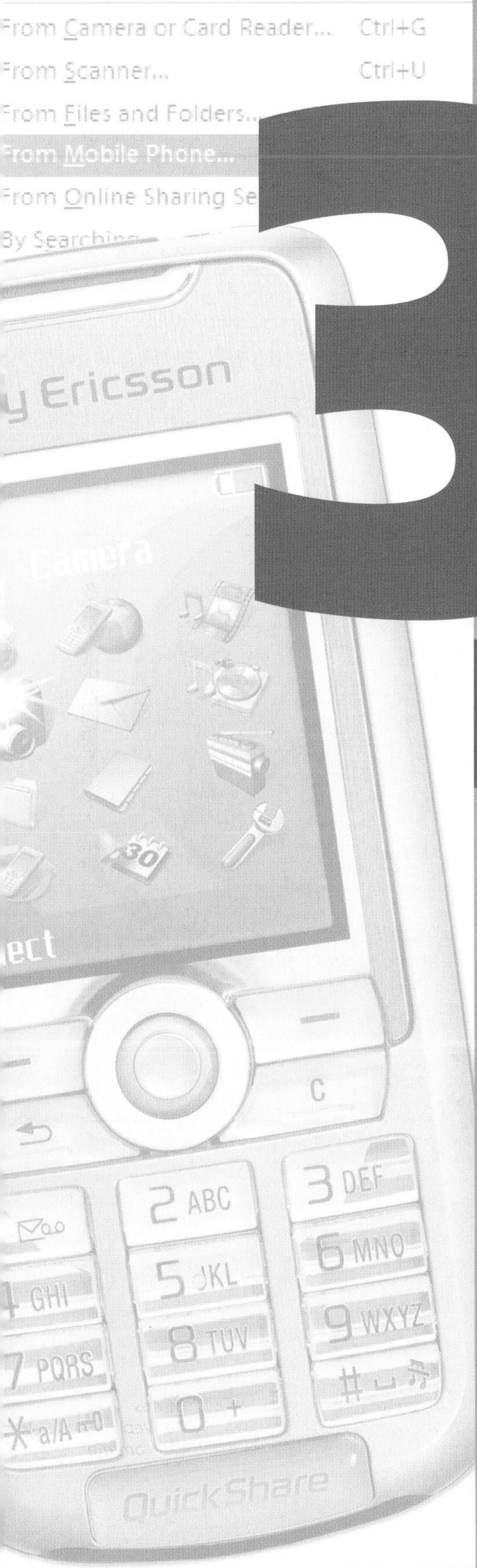

From _C_amera or Card Reader...   Ctrl+G

From _S_canner...   Ctrl+U

From _F_iles and Folders...

From _M_obile Phone...

From _O_nline Sharing Se

By Searching

3

First Steps

The welcome screen

Step 1: Getting your pictures into Elements

Creating new documents

Step 2: Viewing your pictures

Step 3: Image rotating

Step 4: Cropping and straightening

Step 5: Automatic corrections

Step 6: Printing

Step 7: Saving

As a simple introduction to the program, this chapter will take you through the first basic steps involved in digital photography from downloading your pictures from your camera to the computer to holding an enhanced print in your hand.

We won't get involved in any manual or complex editing or enhancement techniques, there will be plenty of time for these in the next couple of chapters, instead we will look at the various ways that you can get your images from your camera or scanner into the program and see how you can manage the pictures once they are there. Then we will select an individual photograph, rotate and crop the image, save the changed file and finally print the picture. So let's get started.

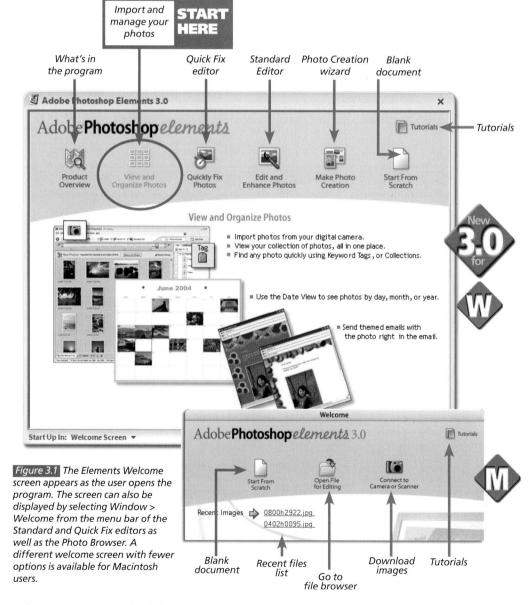

Figure 3.1 *The Elements Welcome screen appears as the user opens the program. The screen can also be displayed by selecting Window > Welcome from the menu bar of the Standard and Quick Fix editors as well as the Photo Browser. A different welcome screen with fewer options is available for Macintosh users.*

The Welcome screen

When Elements is first opened, the user is presented with a Welcome screen containing several options. See Figure 3.1. The selections are broken into different types of imaging activities and depending on where you are in the workflow, will determine your entry point into the program. So to start let's overview the options in the Welcome screen.

Product Overview – This selection provides you with a description of how Photoshop Elements can be used to enhance and improve your digital photographs. It also contains and introductory movie and details of the differences between this and other versions of Photoshop Elements.

View and Organize Photos – Designed as the first point of call for downloading your pictures from cameras, scanners and mobile phones, this selection takes you to the Photo Browser component of the Elements system. Start here when first introducing your pictures into Elements.

Quickly Fix Photos – This selection takes you directly to the Quick Fix component of the Photoshop Elements system. This editing window provides more manual control than what is available with the Auto Fix Window but less than that found in the more sophisticated Standard Editor.

Edit and Enhance Photos – Click here to take you to the Standard Editor. This window provides you with the most powerful enhancement and editing tools and features available in Elements. Users undertaking complex, multi-step alterations to their photographs should proceed directly to this work space.

Make Photo Creation – This button takes you to the step-by-step interface that guides you through the production of items such as slide shows, album pages, greetings and postcards, web galleries, wall calendars and menu driven VCD presentations.

Start From Scratch – As an alternative to commencing the editing process with an existing image you can select this option to create a new blank document in the editor work space. This is a good place to start if you need to construct a picture from several other images or if you need to create a document of a specific size and format.

Tutorials – Select this option if you want to access the Photoshop Elements help resources. This includes the How To Recipes, Help topics grouped around common activities, a glossary and an index.

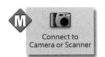

Connect to Camera or Scanner – Mac users select this option to display a dialog that you can use to select an Import Source. From here you can download files from your cameras or scanners.

Open File for Editing – This option takes Mac users directly to the File Browser where they can select a file for editing.

Step 1: Getting your pictures into Elements

One of the most significant additions to Photoshop Elements 3.0 for Windows is the Photo Browser. This feature provides a visual index of your pictures and can be customized to show them in browser mode, date mode or sorted by keyword tags or collection. Unlike the standard file browsers (Editor: File > Browse Folders) which create the thumbnails of your pictures the first time that the folder is browsed, the Photo Browser, or Organizer as it is also called, creates the thumbnail during the process of adding your photographs to a collection.

To start your first collection simply select the View and Organize option from the Welcome screen and then proceed to the File > Get Photos menu option. Select one of the listed sources of pictures provided and follow the steps and prompts in the dialogs that follow.

Organizer: File > Get Photos > From Camera or Card Reader

To start we will download photographs from a memory card or camera. This will probably be the most frequently used route for your images to enter the Elements program. See Figure 3.2. Select the From Camera or Card Reader option from the File > Get Photos menu. Next you will see the Adobe Photo Downloader dialog. After finding and selecting the source of the pictures (the card reader) you will then see a series of thumbnail size pictures of the files stored on your camera card.

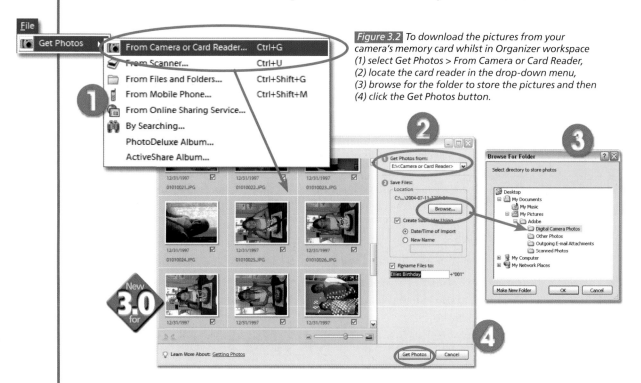

Figure 3.2 To download the pictures from your camera's memory card whilst in Organizer workspace (1) select Get Photos > From Camera or Card Reader, (2) locate the card reader in the drop-down menu, (3) browse for the folder to store the pictures and then (4) click the Get Photos button.

By default all pictures on the card will be selected ready for downloading and cataloging. If for some reason you do not want to download all the images then you can deselect them by unchecking the tick box at the bottom right-hand of the thumbnail.

Next browse for the folder where you want the photographs to be stored and check the tick box if you want a new folder to be created automatically. To help with finding your pictures you can also add a meaningful name, not the labels that are attached by the camera, to the beginning of each of the images by ticking the Rename Files To option and typing a new prefix. Finally click the Get Photos button to import the pictures. After the process is complete Elements will tell you that the files have been successfully imported and ask you if you want to delete the files from the memory card. Selecting No at this point will preserve the originals on the card, the Yes option will remove the images from the card freeing up the memory and preparing the card for further use. See Figure 3.3.

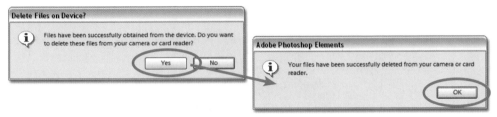

Figure 3.3 *After downloading your pictures from the memory card or the camera itself, you are given the option to delete the original files. This frees up the memory space on the card readying it for further use.*

Organizer: File > Get Photos > From Scanner Ⓦ

The Get Photos > From Scanner option enables users to obtain images directly from the scanners they have connected to their computers. A dialog asking the user to 'Select an input source' may appear if your scanner is not automatically detected. To continue, select the device from the list and click OK. Next the driver window that was supplied with the scanner will be displayed. In this dialog you can preview the picture, and adjust the settings that will govern the scanning process. See Figure 3.4.

Start by performing a Preview scan (some scanners handle this step automatically). This will produce a quick low-resolution picture of the print or negative. Using this image as a guide, select the area to be scanned with the Marquee or Cropping tool. Next, adjust the brightness, contrast and color of the image to ensure that you are capturing the greatest amount of detail possible. Now input your scan sizes, concentrating on ensuring that the final dimensions and resolution are equal to your needs. As a rough guide, remember that if your original print or film frame is small you will need to scan at a high resolution in order to produce a reasonable file size. Large print originals, on the other hand, can be scanned at lower resolutions to achieve the same file size. Sound a little confusing? It can be, but most scanner software is designed to help you through the maze.

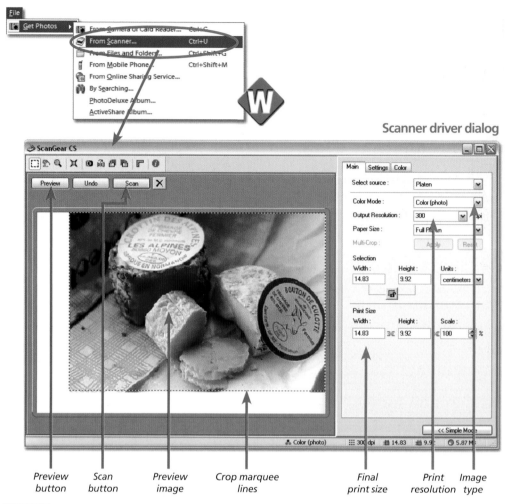

Scanner driver dialog

| Preview button | Scan button | Preview image | Crop marquee lines | Final print size | Print resolution | Image type |

Figure 3.4 *Scanner driver software contains settings to vary the output size and resolution of your images as well as controls for changing the brightness, contrast and color of your scans.*

The scanner driver dialog is designed and supplied by the same company that manufactures the scanner itself. When the Organizer: File > Get Photos > From Scanner option (Macintosh – Connect to scanner or camera from the welcome screen) is selected the Elements program goes in search of this driver software and displays it in a separate window on screen. When you alter settings you are controlling the scanning process only. All of this process happens outside of Elements and once completed, the scanned file is then passed to the Elements program. This is the reason why after scanning you sometimes need to close the control dialog to see the finished image waiting in the Elements work space behind. The driver dialog detailed above is supplied with Canon scanners. Your own scanner control may appear different from this one but all but the most basic machines will have options for changing size, resolution, contrast, brightness and color. Look to your manual or the online help option for your model to locate the controls.

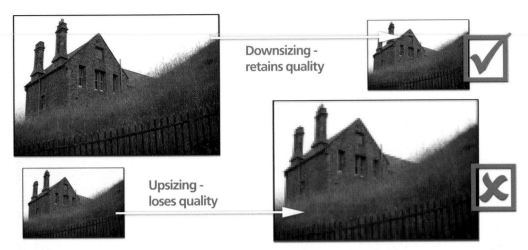

Downsizing - retains quality

Upsizing - loses quality

Figure 3.5 *Downsizing images is acceptable but enlarging always produces a final picture that is poor in quality. It is better to rescan the original if you need to print it bigger. Only enlarge a small picture as a last resort.*

Ensuring enough pixels for the job

When you capture an image using a print or film scanner you are creating a digital file. Unlike the situation with most digital cameras, where the largest pixel dimensions of the file are fixed by the size of the sensor, images made via a scanner can vary in size depending on the settings used to create them. To make sure that you have enough pixels for your requirements, it is important to remember that the quality of the image, and the size that it can be printed, is determined, in part, by its pixel dimensions. It is therefore good practice to choose the pixel dimensions for your image based on what that picture will be used for. An image that is destined to become a poster will need to have substantially more pixels than one needed for a postage stamp. 'Just how many more pixels are needed?' is a good question. The answer can be found in the numbers you input in the scanner dialog.

The final dimensions of your digital picture should be input directly into the 'Width' and 'Height' boxes of the control. Next, the output resolution that you will use when printing your picture is placed in the 'Resolution' box. The scanner driver will usually handle the rest, working out the exact file size needed to suit your requirements.

If you are unsure what resolution to input, use the settings in the following table as a starting point.

How the image will be used	The final output resolution to select
Screen or web use only	72 dots per inch (dpi)
Draft quality inkjet prints	150 dpi
Large posters (that will be viewed from a distance)	150 dpi
Photographic quality inkjet printing	200–300 dpi
Magazine printing	300 dpi

Table 3.1

See Table 3.1. If your picture is to be printed at a variety of sizes, scan your image for the largest size first and then use the tools in Elements (Editor: Image > Resize > Image Size) to downsize the digital file when necessary. Making large images smaller preserves much of the quality of the original but the reverse is not true. Enlarging small files to create the correct resolution needed for a big print job will always produce a poor quality file, especially when it is compared to one that was scanned at the right size in the first place. See Figure 3.5.

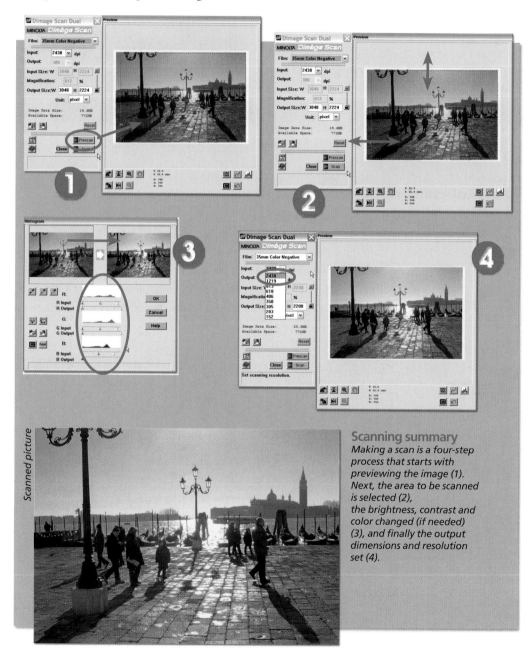

Scanning summary

Making a scan is a four-step process that starts with previewing the image (1). Next, the area to be scanned is selected (2), the brightness, contrast and color changed (if needed) (3), and finally the output dimensions and resolution set (4).

Editor: Image > Divide Scanned Photos

For those readers with many pictures to scan the new
Divide Scanned Photos feature will prove a god send. Now
you can scan several prints at once on a flatbed scanner
and then allow Elements to separate each of the individual
pictures and place them in a new document.

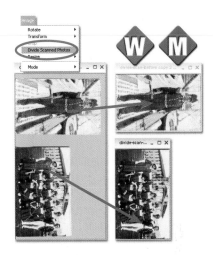

To ensure accurate division of photos place a colored
backing sheet on top of the prints to be scanned. This
helps the program distinguish where one picture starts
and the other ends.

Organizer: File > Get Photos > From Files and Folders

Acting much like the File > Open option common to most programs this selection provides you with
the familiar window that allows you to search for and open pictures that you have already saved to
your computer. Though slightly different on Windows and Macintosh machines, you generally have
the option to view your files in a variety of ways. Windows users can choose between Thumbnails,
Tiles, Icons, List and Detail views using the drop-down menu from the top of the window. See Figure
3.6. The thumbnail option provides a simplified file browser view of the pictures on your disk and
it is this way of working that will prove to be most useful for digital photographers. After selecting
the image, or images, you wish to import into the Photo Browser or Organizer, select the Get Photos
button.

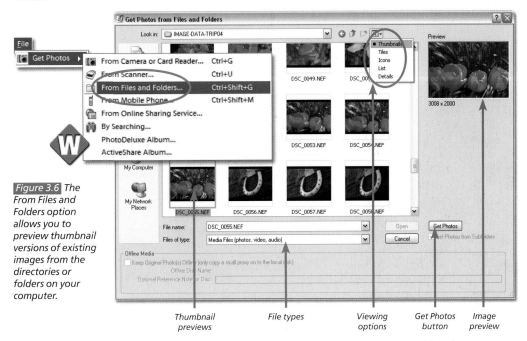

Figure 3.6 The
From Files and
Folders option
allows you to
preview thumbnail
versions of existing
images from the
directories or
folders on your
computer.

Thumbnail previews   File types   Viewing options   Get Photos button   Image preview

How to multi-select the files to import

To select several images or files at once hold down the CTRL key whilst clicking onto the pictures of your choice. To select a complete list of files without having to pick each file in turn click on the first picture and then whilst holding down the Shift key click on the last file in the group.

Organizer: File > Get Photos > From Mobile Phone

With the rise in specifications of the digital cameras built into the modern mobile phones, many photographers are finding that these cross-over devices are great for the odd snapshot, or the time when you don't have your full kit handy. It is no surprise then that Adobe has seen fit to include a new 'Get Photos > From Mobile Phone' option in the Photo Browser component of Elements 3.0. The option does not link your computer directly to your mobile phone, you will need the software that came with the unit for that, but rather watches the default folder where your phone pictures are downloaded. When new pictures are added to the folder, Elements either adds them to your catalog automatically or notifies you of the new files and asks permission to add them. See Figure 3.7.

To make sure that you can import your mobile phone pictures directly into Elements add the default download folder to the watch list first before selecting the File > Get Photos > From Mobile Phone option. Simply select File > Watch Folders and use the Add button to browse for the folder that you use to store your mobile phone pictures. At the bottom of the window you can also choose whether Elements notifies you of new files added to the watched folders or automatically imports them into the Photo Browser. See Figure 3.8.

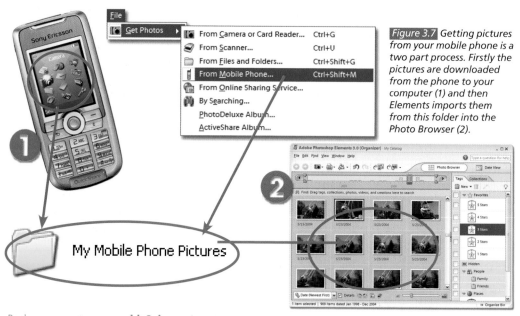

Figure 3.7 Getting pictures from your mobile phone is a two part process. Firstly the pictures are downloaded from the phone to your computer (1) and then Elements imports them from this folder into the Photo Browser (2).

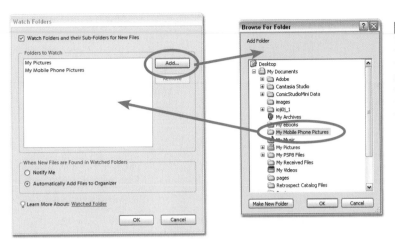

Figure 3.8 *Setting up the Photo Browser so that it watches for new files in specific folders is a good way to automatically keep your catalogs up to date. Simply add the specific folders to those listed in the File > Watch Folders window.*

Organizer: File > Get Photos > From Online Sharing Service

Elements users living in the United States of America can take advantage of the online printing and sharing opportunities provided by www.ofoto.com. After a simple, and free, sign-up procedure is completed you will be able to upload web friendly copies of your pictures directly to the service. Once stored online you can request for the files to be printed using the ofoto print service or you can choose to share the files. This 'Get Photos' option is designed to access files that have been earmarked for sharing using services like those provided by www.ofoto.com. See Figure 3.9.

Figure 3.9 *After signing up for the service images can be printed and shared online using www.ofoto.com.*

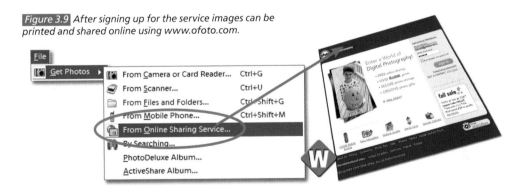

Organizer: File > Get Photos > By Searching

The Get Photos > By Searching option provides a speedy way to locate all the folders connected to your computer that contain pictures that you may want to add to your Photo Browser catalogs. After setting the search options and clicking the search button Elements will weave its way through your computer hunting down folders that contain candidate picture files. By default the program will not locate files in the GIF or PNG formats (both of which are almost exclusively used for web pages). If you are looking for these file types then you will need to use the Get Photos > From Files and Folders option. You can also choose to exclude small pictures and those images contained in system or program folders. Both these options should be selected to speed up the search process.

Once the folder list has been compiled, which usually only takes a few seconds, you can select (or multi-select) the folders whose images you wish to import. Clicking the Import Folders button will then add the pictures contained into the catalog of the Photo Browser. See Figure 3.10.

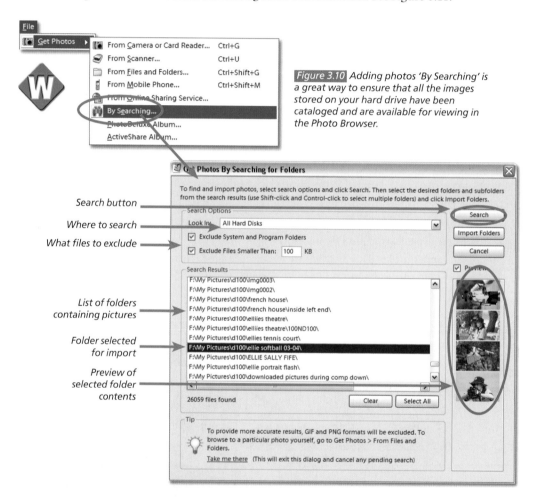

Figure 3.10 Adding photos 'By Searching' is a great way to ensure that all the images stored on your hard drive have been cataloged and are available for viewing in the Photo Browser.

Organizer: File > Get Photos > PhotoDeluxe Album and ActiveShare Album Ⓦ

Users of both PhotoDeluxe and ActiveShare products can incorporate the contents of the Albums created with these programs into their Elements Photo Browser. After selecting the appropriate option (PhotoDeluxe Album or ActiveShare Album) from the Get Photos menu, Elements will locate and list the albums found in the folder you are searching. Once selected the images are then imported into the Photo Browser and organized automatically according to date.

Other options for getting your photos into Elements

Though my recommendation is that you always import and organize your pictures via the Photo Browser and Get Photos features there will be times when you need to access existing files, or even newly photographed images, whilst in one of the Elements editor modes – Quick Fix or Standard Edit. The follow options give you just this type of access.

Editor: File > Browse Folders

This option is available for both Macintosh and Windows users and takes the user directly to the Elements File Browser, which displays thumbnail versions of images that you have created at another time and have saved to disk. Users can navigate between image directories using the folder tree in the top left-hand corner of the dialog. Camera, or scanner, settings and image information can be viewed on the bottom left of the browser in the scrollable text box. Sometimes called EXIF data, these details are stored in the picture file together with the image information. Users can add their own caption, copyright, author and title information for individual images through the File Info dialog box (File > File Info). Images can be renamed and folders added or deleted directly in the dialog using the extra options found in the menu activated by the 'More' side arrow at the top right of the box. Groups of selected images can be 'Batch Renamed' or moved to new folders. Double-clicking a thumbnail in the browser will open the selected image directly into the program. See Figure 3.11.

Editor: File > Open

Working in much the same way as the Get Photos > From Files and Folders option, selecting File > Open presents you with the standard Windows file browser. From here you can navigate from drive to drive on your machine before locating and opening the folder that contains your pictures. You can refine the display options by selecting the specific file type (file ending) to be displayed and as we have already noted you can also choose the way to view the files. In the example the thumbnail view was selected so that it is possible to quickly flick through a folder full of pictures to locate the specific image you are after. See Figure 3.12.

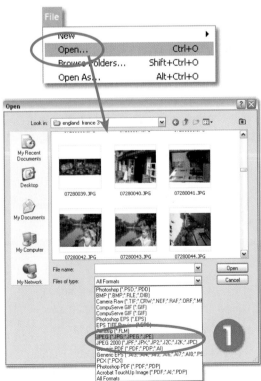

Figure 3.11 *Selecting File > Open displays the standard Windows open dialog. (1) You can alter the range of files displayed by selecting the specific file format to show.*

Editor: File > Open As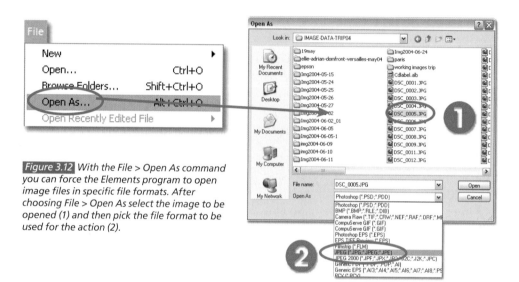

On the odd occasion that a specific file won't open using the File > Open command you can try to open the file in a different format. Do this by selecting the File > Open As option and then choosing the file you want to open. After making this selection pick the desired format from the Open As pop-up menu, and click the Open button. This action forces the program to ignore the file format it has assumed the picture is saved in and treat the image as if it is saved as the file type you have selected. If the picture still refuses to open, then you may have selected a format that does not match the file's true format, or the file itself may have been damaged when being saved. See Figure 3.12.

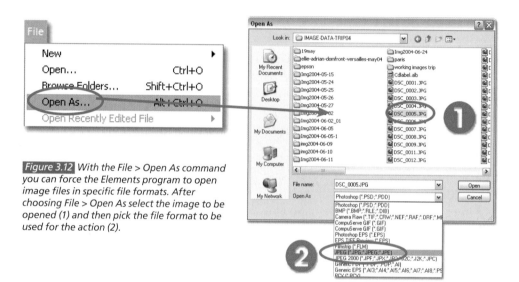

Figure 3.12 With the File > Open As command you can force the Elements program to open image files in specific file formats. After choosing File > Open As select the image to be opened (1) and then pick the file format to be used for the action (2).

Editor: File > Open Recently Edited File

As you browse open and edit various pictures from your folders Elements keeps track of the last few files and lists them under the File > Open Recently Edited Files menu item.

This is a very handy feature as it means that you can return quickly to pictures that you are working on without having to navigate back to the specific folder where they are stored.

By default Photoshop Elements lists the last 10 files edited. You can change the number of files kept on this menu via the 'Recent file list' setting in the Edit > Preferences > Saving Files window. Don't be tempted to list too many files as each additional listing uses more memory.

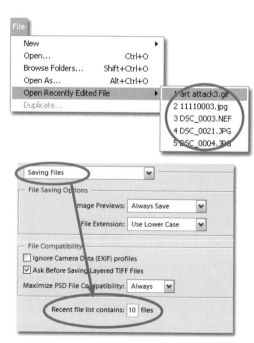

Creating new documents

Editor: File > New > Blank File

The New > Blank File option creates an Elements picture from the settings selected in the New dialog box. The box has sections for the image's name, width, height, resolution and mode. The background content of the image can be chosen from the list at the bottom of the box and you can also choose an existing template from a range of document types from the drop-down Preset menu. See Figure 3.13.

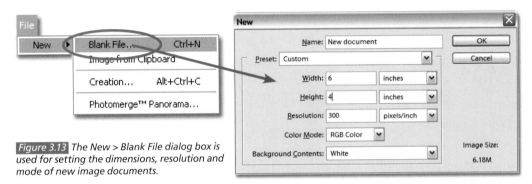

Figure 3.13 *The New > Blank File dialog box is used for setting the dimensions, resolution and mode of new image documents.*

At this stage it is important to remember that the quality of the image, and the size that it can be printed, is determined, in part, by its pixel dimensions. As we saw in the scanner section earlier in the chapter, you should choose your image's pixel dimensions based on what you intend to use the picture for. Small prints need fewer total pixels than those images intended for large posters. To ensure that your document will suit your end purpose, input the final dimensions of your product directly into the 'Width' and 'Height' boxes. Next, add the resolution that you will use when outputting your image in the 'Resolution' box. Be sure to check that the resolution unit is set to pixels/inch not pixels/cm; inadvertently picking the wrong option here will have you creating huge images needlessly. If you are unsure what print resolution to input, use the guide in Table 3.1.

Editor: File > New > Image from Clipboard

Many programs contain the options to copy (Edit > Copy) and paste (Edit > Paste) information. For the most part, these functions occur within a single piece of software, but occasionally the process can also be used to copy an image, or some text, from one program and place it in another. Previous versions of Elements provided different pathways for making a new file from pictures stored in the computer's memory, but version 3.0 uses a specialist 'Image from Clipboard' item that can be found under the File > New menu. Once a picture has been copied to memory selecting the New > Image from Clipboard option automatically creates a new document of the correct size to accommodate the copied content and pastes the picture in as a new layer. There is no need to guess the size of the copied picture as Elements automatically determines this when it creates the new document.

It is worth noting that if there is no image stored in memory then this option will be 'grayed out' (unavailable) in the menu list. See Figure 3.14.

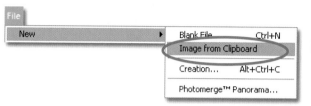

Figure 3.14 *The New > Image from Clipboard dialog box is used for pasting already copied pictures as a layer in a new Elements document.*

Editor: File > New > Creation

As we have already seen in earlier chapters the Photo Creation set of step-by-step wizards is a new addition to Elements having been acquired from the highly successful Photoshop Album software.

Including the Creation option in the File > New menu for Windows users means that you can jump from the editing program directly into the Photo Creation process. As most of the creations products (slide shows, web gallery, album pages) use several images as a basis for their projects it is no surprise that after selecting the File > New > Creation option the Photo Browser window is displayed. After all, it is here that you will make your selection of images to include in the project before proceeding to the Creations window. See Figure 3.15.

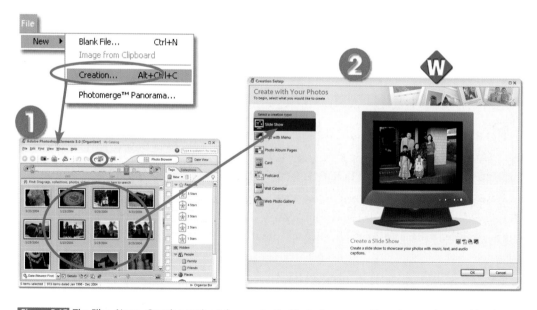

Figure 3.15 *The File > New > Creation option takes you to the Photo Browser or Organizer work space (1), where you can select the images to include in your creation. Next you click on the Create shortcut button to transfer the selected files to the Creations work space and main menu screen (2).*

Editor: File > New > Photomerge Panorama

One of the most popular features of all those included in Elements is the special panoramic stitching tool called Photomerge. In fact the tool was valued so highly by digital photographers the world over that many who already owned Photoshop purchased its smaller brother just so that they could use it. Now that Photomerge is included in Photoshop CS, the latest version of the program, there is no need for the Photoshop users to lust any more.

Selecting the New > Photomerge Panorama option takes you directly to the Photomerge Add Files dialog. Use the Browse button to locate the pictures that you want to include in the stitched panorama and then click OK. The selected images are transferred to the Photomerge work space and the program attempts to sequence, arrange and blend the individual images to form a single wide angle photograph. See Figure 3.16. For more details on how to use the Photomerge feature see Chapter 9 Creating Great Panoramas.

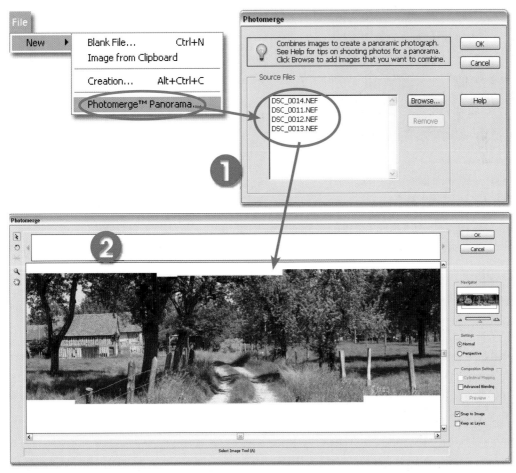

Figure 3.16 *Choosing the File > New > Photomerge Panorama option starts the panorama stitching process by displaying the Add Files dialog first (1). After browsing for and locating the pictures to include in the composition you click OK to proceed to the main Photomerge work space (2). From here you can fine tune the stitching process and produce the final panoramic photograph.*

Editor: File > Import > Frame From Video

Almost hidden from view in a new position on the File > Import menu is the Frame From Video option. With the increase in popularity of digital video, it was a great move on Adobe's part to include this feature in version 2.0 of the program. The option gives the users the opportunity to capture still frames from a variety of stored video formats. The Frame From Video dialog employs familiar video player buttons to play, rewind and fast forward the selected footage. The Grab button snatches still frames from the playing video and places them into Elements ready for editing. Though images captured in this fashion are rarely of equal quality to those sourced from a dedicated stills camera or scanner, there are occasions when a feature such as this fits the bill. See Figure 3.17.

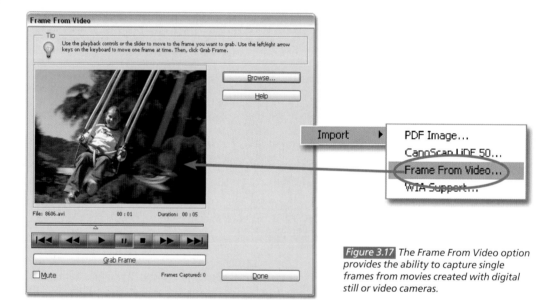

Figure 3.17 *The Frame From Video option provides the ability to capture single frames from movies created with digital still or video cameras.*

Step 2: Viewing your pictures

After importing your pictures into the Photo Browser Windows users can then choose to display them in browse or date mode. Files can be tagged with appropriate keywords, to help when searching for specific pictures later, or grouped into collections of images with similar subjects. Although this is not the place to undertake major editing tasks you can apply simple enhancements (mostly automatic) using the options in the Auto Fix Window (Edit > Auto Fix Window). We will look at these in step 5 of this 'First Steps' introduction.

To apply more complex changes to your photographs you can jump from the browser directly to both the Quick Fix and Standard editor windows. In the same way you can also use selected pictures or collections as the basis for producing one of the many Photo Creations options available. But don't think that Photo Browser's prowess ends there, the images you select can also be printed, emailed to your friends, shared online and even sent to a mobile phone all from this one window.

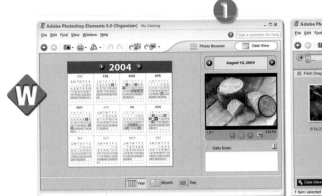
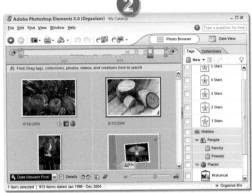

Figure 3.18 *Windows users can view their cataloged pictures in the Organizer work space in two different ways. (1) Date view – photos organized according to the date they were shot. (2) Photo Browser view – based on a thumbnail view with an associated timeline at the top.*

Organizer: View > Photo Review

The Photo Review features provides an instant slide show of the files that you have currently displayed in the Photo Browser. Seeing the photos full size on your machine is a good way to edit the shots you want to keep from those that should be placed in the 'I will remember not to do that next time' bin. Using the provided menu you can play, pause, or advance to next or last photos, using the VCR-like controls. You can enlarge or reduce the size that the picture appears on screen with the magnification slider (Zoom Level control). For quick magnification changes there are also 'Fit to Window' and 'Actual Pixels' buttons. But the real bonus of the feature is the list of actions that you can perform to pictures you review. You can automatically enhance, add and remove tags, mark the file for printing and add the file to a chosen collection using the choices listed under the Action menu. Specific picture properties such as the tag, history, and metadata are available by hitting the Alt + Enter keys to display the properties window. See Figure 3.19.

As well as showing all the photos currently in the browser you can also multi-select the images to include in the review session before starting the feature, or even limit those pictures displayed to a particular collection. The Photo Review preferences can be set when the feature is first opened or accessed via the last item on the action menu.

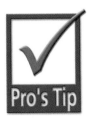

First stop Photo Review

All together, the options available in the Photo Review feature make this a great place to check the results of a day's shooting. You can flick through the images that you have recorded, sorting the good ones into a newly created collection and deleting the not so good examples of your photographic prowess. If you prefer to keep all the images together and just add keyword tags to selected files then this is easily achieved here as well.

Figure 3.19 *The View > Photo Review feature is a great way to check and organize your photos after they have been downloaded into Elements.*

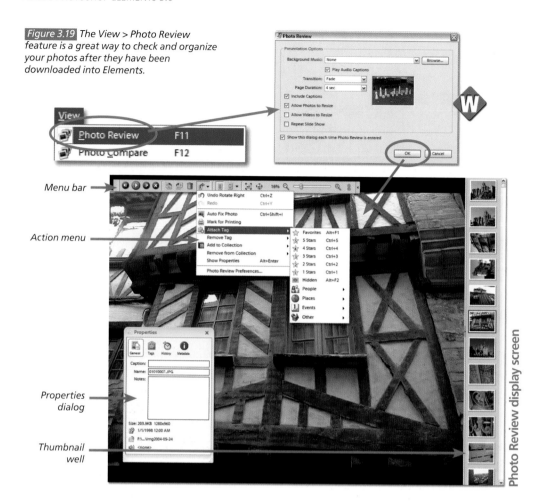

Menu bar

Action menu

Properties dialog

Thumbnail well

Photo Review display screen

Organizer: View > Photo Compare ⓦ

Closely linked to the Review feature detailed above is the Photo Compare option which allows Windows users to display two similar pictures side by side. This is a great way to choose between several images taken at the same time to ensure that the best one is used for printing or passed onto the editor for enhancement. See Figure 3.20.

To select the images to show click onto one of the compare work spaces (left or right in the example) and then click on a thumbnail. Now select the other work space and click the

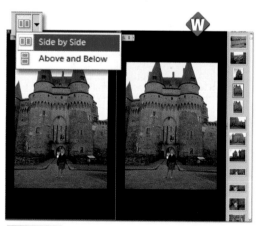

Figure 3.20 *The Photo Compare feature provides a side-by-side view of two images giving the user a chance to compare similar photos.*

comparison image thumbnail. All the Photo Review adjustment and organizational controls are available in the Compare feature, including the Zoom Control which provides the ability to examine candidate files more closely.

Comparing apples with apples

Pro's Tip

Clicking the Sync Pan and Zoom button (chain icon) will magnify both pictures to the same zoom level when either picture is changed. The feature also scrolls both pictures in unison allowing the same specific areas of a photograph to be examined without the need to independently move each image.

Editor: View > Zoom In and Zoom Out

Images displayed in the editor work space can be viewed at a variety of different magnifications. To alter the size of the picture on screen, use either the menu option View > Zoom In or Zoom Out, or the Zoom tool. Clicking on a photo with the tool selected will enlarge the picture and clicking with the Alt key (Windows) or Option key (Macintosh) held down will reduce the size. Clicking and dragging will draw a marquee, which will then enlarge the selected part to fill your window. Double-clicking the Zoom tool automatically displays the image at 100%. See Figure 3.21.

View > Zoom In/Zoom Out

Zoom tool

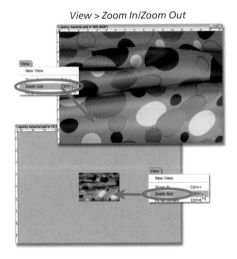
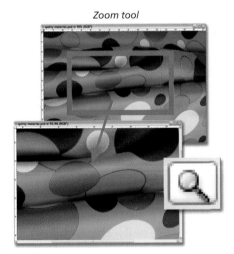

Figure 3.21 Images can be enlarged or reduced on screen by using either the Zoom In or Out feature (View > Zoom In or Out) or the Zoom tool.

Editor: Window > Navigator

When the picture is enlarged beyond the boundaries of the window, you will only be able to see a small section of the image at one time. To navigate around the picture, use the Hand tool to click and drag the picture within the box. Alternatively, Elements contains a special Navigator window, where you can interactively enlarge and reduce image size, as well as move anywhere around the image boundaries. See Figure 3.22.

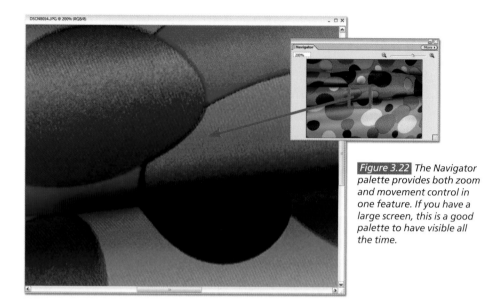

Figure 3.22 *The Navigator palette provides both zoom and movement control in one feature. If you have a large screen, this is a good palette to have visible all the time.*

Step 3: Image rotating

One of the first tasks to undertake on pictures that you have downloaded from your camera or scanner is to correct their orientation. This, of course, is only true for those images that were taken with the camera on the side, or prints that were inadvertently scanned the wrong way up.

You can rotate your pictures back to their rightful orientation in the Photo Browser or Photo Review features or in any of the Elements editor work spaces. Use the steps below to reorientate your photos depending on the work space you have open.

Photo Browser: Select the thumbnail of the picture that needs rotating and then select Edit > Rotate 90° Left or Right. See Figure 3.23.

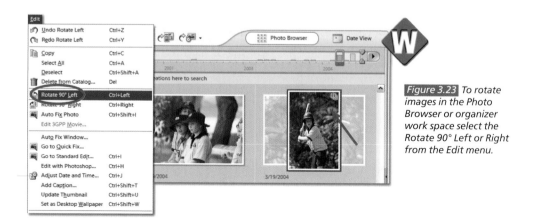

Figure 3.23 *To rotate images in the Photo Browser or organizer work space select the Rotate 90° Left or Right from the Edit menu.*

Photo Review: Either wait until the image you need to rotate is displayed on the main screen, or select it from the Thumbnail well on the left of the window, and then click one of the rotate buttons located in the tool bar.

Standard Editor: To rotate the whole picture using the Image > Rotate > 90° Left or Right options. Rotating the photo 180° will turn the picture upside down. Flipping the canvas provides a mirror image of the original. The other options in the Rotate menu are for rotating separate layers in an image. For more information on layers, see Chapter 6.

Quick Fix Editor: As well as using the same menu commands detailed for the Standard Editor above, you can also click on the rotate buttons displayed in the General Fixes > Rotate section of the editor's Palette well.

Step 4: Cropping and straightening

Cropping

Cropping a picture can help add drama to an image by eliminating unneeded or unwanted detail. It can also be a good method for altering the orientation of a crooked scan. Again there are several different ways of cropping your pictures depending on which Elements work space you are using, but all are dependent on selecting the portion of the image you wish to retain, using either the Marquee or Crop tools, to function.

Quick Fix and Standard Editors: With the first approach you need to select the Marquee tool and then click and drag the tool over the image to define a selection (of the area you wish to keep). Then to apply the crop choose Image > Crop from the menu bar. See Figure 3.24.

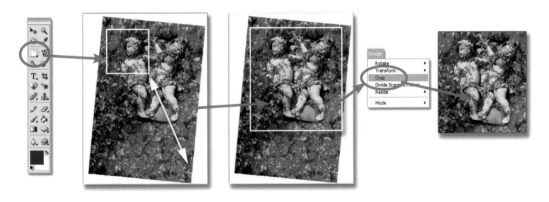

Figure 3.24 *The Marquee tool is used to select an area that is then cropped using the menu option Image > Crop.*

If you want a little more control then try using the specialist Crop tool. Looking like a set of darkroom easel arms, it is present in both editors' tool bars. Once selected, click and drag on the image surface. You will see a marquee-like box appear. The box can be resized at any time by dragging the handles positioned at the corners or sides. When you are satisfied with the changes, crop the image by either clicking the OK button in the options bar or double-clicking inside the crop marquee. See Figure 3.25.

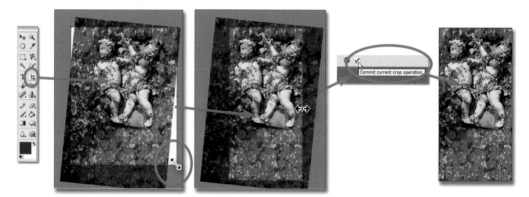

Figure 3.25 *The Crop tool allows adjustment of the selection via the handles positioned at the corners and sides of the bounding box.*

Photo Browser: There is no cropping tool directly available in the main Photo Browser window but if you select the Edit > Auto Fix Window feature you will be able to select the Crop option from the Editing tools on the left of the window. Unlike the crop options above this tool enables you to crop to specific formats to suit the paper you will be printing on, such as 6 × 4 inches, by simply selecting the required size from the list in the Aspect Ratio drop-down menu. Click the Apply button to proceed with the crop. See Figure 3.26.

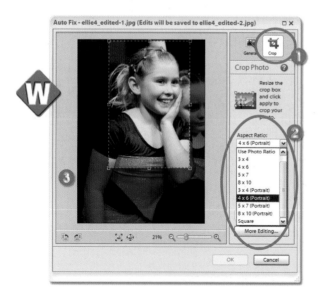

Figure 3.26 *The Crop tool in the Edit > Auto Fix Window feature (Photo Browser) gives you a choice of a customized crop or a preset crop that is designed to suit the format of specific printing papers.*
(1) Crop tool.
(2) Preset crop formats.
(3) Crop and image preview.

Straightening

The crop marquee, in the editor work spaces, can also be rotated to suit an image that is slightly askew. You can rotate the selection box by clicking and dragging the mouse pointer outside the edges. Now when you click the OK button the image will be cropped and straightened. See Figure 3.27. If this all seems a little too complex, Elements also supplies automatic 'Straighten Image' and 'Straighten and Crop Image' functions. Designed especially for people like me, who always seems to get their print scans slightly crooked, these features can be found at the bottom of the Image > Rotate menu. See Figure 3.28.

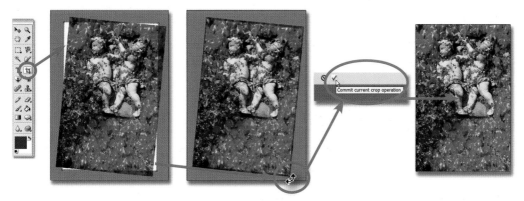

Figure 3.27 *Rotating the Crop tool's selection provides the option for straightening crooked images.*

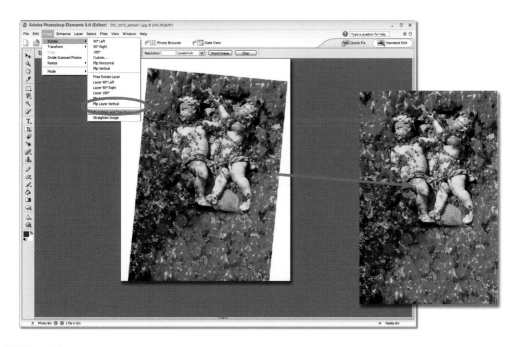

Figure 3.28 *Elements also provides automated straightening and cropping options.*

Step 5: Automatic corrections

First some background

One of the real strengths of the Elements program is that the editing and enhancement capabilities of the software are built upon the industry standard Photoshop platform. But as most people who have had a play with Photoshop will tell you, this 'killer' application it is not an easy beast to tame, let alone master. This is where Elements steps in. It combines the majority of the editing abilities of Photoshop with an easier interface and therefore a much simpler learning curve. Version 3.0 continues this tradition by providing a variety of enhancement and editing options for the digital photographer. They are skillfully arranged from the automatic, 'press this button now' type tools that provide quick and accurate results for the majority of pictures, through to the more sophisticated and user controlled features required for completion of more complex, professional level, correction tasks. See Figure 3.29.

In this First Steps section of the book, we will take a look at the quick and automatic correction tools that are part of the Photo Browser work space only. These tools will provide a good starting point for the majority of changes that you will want to make to your digital photographs and, somewhat more importantly, they will give you good results quickly without having to understand too much about the underlying theory of how the tool works and how best to use it.

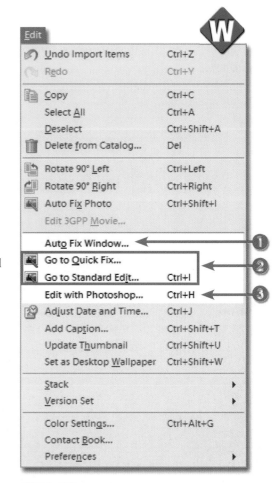

Figure 3.29 *Photoshop Elements 3.0 for windows contains a range of editing and enhancement features grouped according to complexity and degree of user control. These editing options are available from the Photo Browser either through the menu structure or by right clicking a selected image thumbnail.*
(1) The Auto Fix Window provides automatic corrections from within the Photo Browser.
(2) The image is sent to Elements' Quick Fix or Standard Editor work spaces.
(3) The image is sent to Photoshop to be edited.

As your skills develop, however, you will probably want to take a little more control over the editing and enhancement process and for this reason Chapters 4 and 5 of the book will introduce you to the range of more sophisticated tools and features that are part of the Quick Fix and Standard editor work spaces. The editing and enhancement options presented in the later chapters are capable of results that rival the professionals. But that's coming up; for the moment let's look at the changes we can make using the tools available in the Photo Browser.

Photo Browser: Edit > Auto Fix Window 〔W〕

The Auto Fix Window feature is made up of two different sections – General fixes and Crop controls (see Step 4 for cropping details). Four general fixes are available with the resultant changes being reflected in the preview image. See Figure 3.30.

Auto Smart Fix – This command corrects general color problems and also adjusts shadow and highlight areas of the picture.

Auto Levels – Use this button to increase the overall contrast of the picture and correct any color cast present in the image. The feature tries to diagnose and correct color casts by balancing the color components of the picture. For the majority of average photographs this approach will give good

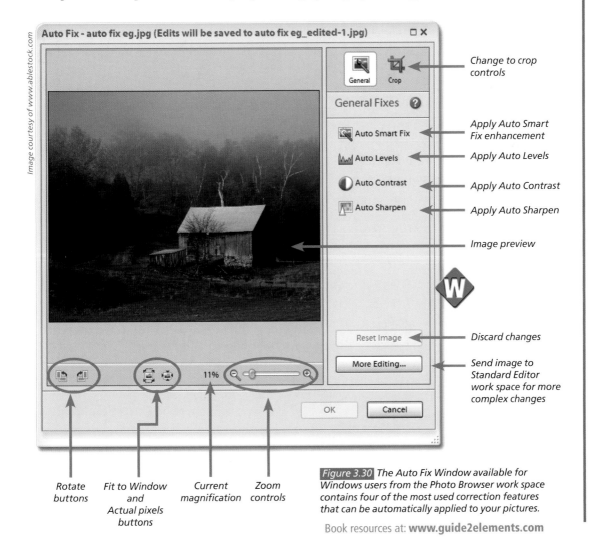

Image courtesy of www.ablestock.com

Change to crop controls

Apply Auto Smart Fix enhancement

Apply Auto Levels

Apply Auto Contrast

Apply Auto Sharpen

Image preview

Discard changes

Send image to Standard Editor work space for more complex changes

Rotate buttons

Fit to Window and Actual pixels buttons

Current magnification

Zoom controls

Figure 3.30 *The Auto Fix Window available for Windows users from the Photo Browser work space contains four of the most used correction features that can be automatically applied to your pictures.*

results, but in some cases the color problem may be exasperated or overcorrected creating more problems rather than solving them. If this occurs simply click the Reset Image button to discard the Auto Levels changes.

Auto Contrast – This command limits the changes to the picture to contrast only and ignores any color cast present in the photograph. Apply Auto Contrast to pictures whose contrast needs improving but have a strong color tint that you wish to retain. This is also a good option if Auto Levels creates more color cast problems than it corrects.

Auto Sharpen – Applies a general sharpening of all the details in the picture. This is equivalent to applying a sharpening filter to your photograph. This 'fix' should be applied once and as a last enhancement step before saving and printing.

To improve your pictures using these features try each of the first three fixes at a time checking the results in the preview image as you go. To remove unwanted changes, click the Reset Image button. Apply the Auto Sharpen command as the last step in the process when you are happy with the other picture alterations and then click OK to apply the changes to the photograph.

Version sets

The changed file is not saved over the top of the original, instead a new version of the image is saved with a file name that is appended with the suffix '_edited' attached to the original name. This way you will always be able to identify the original and edited file. The two files are 'stacked' together in the Photo Browser with the latest file displayed on top. The stack of photos representing different editing stages in the picture's history is called a Version Set and is identified with an icon in the top left of the picture showing a pile of photos. To see the other images in the version stack simply right-click the thumbnail image and select Version Set > Reveal Photos in Version Set. See Figure 3.31.

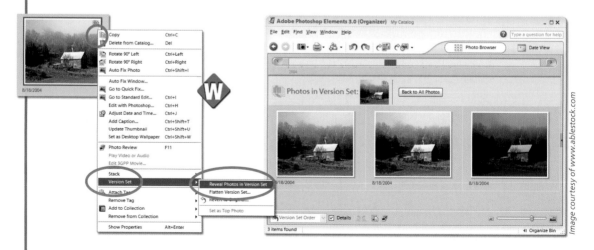

Image courtesy of www.ablestock.com

Figure 3.31 *The Photo Browser keeps separate versions of your edited files and groups them in Version Sets.*

Using the other options available in this pop-up menu the sets can be expanded or collapsed, the current version reverted back to its original form or all versions flattened into one picture. Version Set options are also available via the Photo Browser Edit menu.

Undo, Revert and Undo History

With so many options available for changing images, it's almost inevitable that occasionally you will want to reverse a change that you have made. One way to step back through your changes is to select and earlier permutation of your picture via the Version Sets feature as detailed above, but Elements also provides several other methods to achieve this.

The Undo control, Edit > Undo, will successfully take your image back to the way it was before the last change. The Undo command is available in all Elements' work spaces. If you are unhappy with all the alterations you have made since opening the file, you can use the Revert feature, File > Revert to Saved, to exchange the saved version of your file with the one currently on screen. Revert options are available in the editing work spaces in Elements. See Figure 3.32.

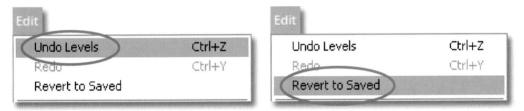

Figure 3.32 Image changes can be reversed by using either the Undo (Edit > Undo) feature or Revert options (File > Revert).

The Undo History palette (Window > Undo History) provides complete control over the alterations made to your image. Each action is recorded as a separate step in the palette. Reversing any change is a simple matter of selecting the previous step in the list. See Figure 3.33.

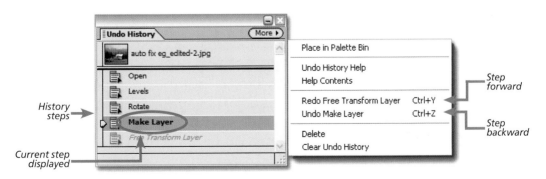

Figure 3.33 The Undo History palette provides the facility to step backwards through the most recent image changes.

Step 6: Printing

The falling price of quality inkjet printers means that more and more people are now able to output photographic quality prints right at their desktop. To get you started quickly we will look at the print options available from the Photo Browser but keep in mind that these features are also available from the editing work spaces as well. For more details on printing from Photoshop Elements see Chapter 11.

Elements 3.0 for Windows contains a brand new Print Selected Photos feature that provides users with a common place to start the print process. This feature largely replaces the Print Preview option found in earlier versions of the program. To display the feature you can select the Print item from the File menu or select the same option from the pop-up menu displayed when you click the Print shortcut button. See Figure 3.34.

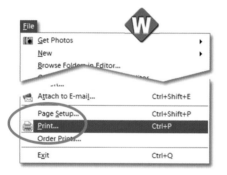
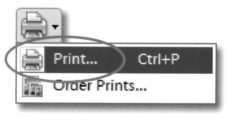

Figure 3.34 *The Elements Print option, which can be accessed via the File menu or the icon on the shortcut bar, displays a brand new Print Selected Photos dialog.*

Before accessing the feature select the image or images that you want to print. Don't worry if you need to add more pictures when you are in the dialog as the great guys at Adobe have kindly added an Add photos button at the bottom left of the screen. The process for creating a print project is as easy as setting the options in sections 1, 2 and 3 of the dialog.

Section 1: Start by selecting the printer that will output the image from those listed for your computer. At this stage you should also check that the actual settings for the printer match the type of image you are printing and the media (paper) you are using. Do this by adjusting the settings in the Printer Preferences window which can be displayed by clicking the button next to the printer drop-down menu.

Print options for Macintosh users

Mac users do not have access to the Print Selected Photos feature but do have a revised Print dialog and the ability to print multiple pictures using the Picture Packages and Contact Sheet features.

Images currently selected for printing

Preview of image as it will print

Print project creation steps

Printer selected for output

Display printer preferences window

Type of print menu

Extra options for print type selected

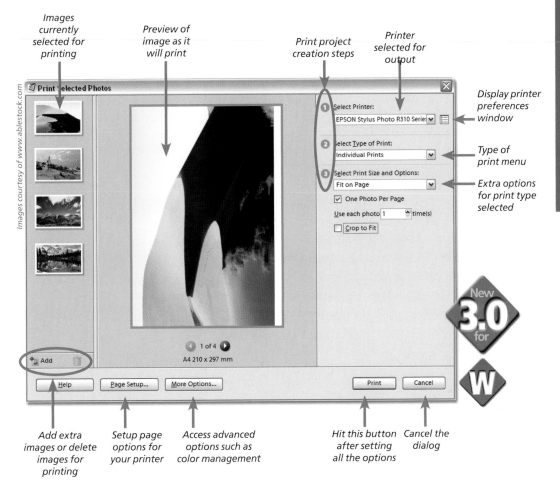

Images courtesy of www.ablestock.com

Add extra images or delete images for printing

Setup page options for your printer

Access advanced options such as color management

Hit this button after setting all the options

Cancel the dialog

Figure 3.35 Windows users can use the new Print Selected Photos dialog as the pivot point for all your printing activities. From this one spot you can output individual photos, contact sheets, picture packages, and label sets. See Chapter 11 for more details on advanced printing tasks.

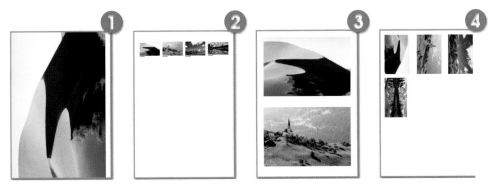

Figure 3.36 You can select a range of different print types from the Print Selected Photos dialog. The options include (1) Individual Prints, (2) Contact Sheets, (3) Picture Packages with a variety of images per page templates and (4) Labels to suit standard sheet label sizes and shapes.

Section 2: Next choose the type of print you wish to create. See Figure 3.36. There are four options to select from:

• Individual Prints – designed for printing a single photograph per page,
• Contact Sheets – used for creating a sheet of small thumbnails of a group of selected pictures,
• Picture Packages – is ideal for putting several larger photos on a single page using templates, and
• Labels – creates a page of label-sized pictures that match commercially available label sheets.

Section 3: The options available in this section change according to the print type that you selected in the previous step. For instance when you select Individual Print you can then choose the size that you want the image to be on the page, the number of times the same picture will be repeated, the number of photos to print on each page and whether to allow the program to crop the picture in order to fill the full page. See Figure 3.37.

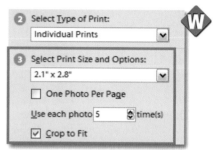

Figure 3.37 The options available in section 3 are determined by the Print type in section 2.

After adjusting the settings in each of the sections of the Print Selected Photos dialog click the Print button to output your photograph. Now sit back and enjoy your first digital photograph.

More printing options
See Chapter 11 for fuller details on the array of print options available to both Macintosh and Windows Photoshop Elements users.

Step 7: Saving

Whilst you are making changes to your photos, the picture is stored in the memory (RAM) of the computer. With the alterations complete, the file should then be saved to a hard drive or disk. In previous versions of Elements the user needed to perform this saving step habitually after completing editing, and this still remains the case for images edited in the Standard and Quick Fix editor work spaces. But as we have already seen, for the changes made directly from the Photo Browser, Elements automatically saves the edited file and the original together in a version set. These auto-save actions are terrific for the new user as it reduces the chance of overwriting the original file or losing changes that have taken valuable time to complete.

Editor: File > Save

Saving images edited in either the Quick Fix or Standard editor is a three-step process that starts by choosing File > Save from the menu bar. With the Save dialog open, navigate through your hard drive to find the directory or folder you wish to save your images in. Next, type in the name for the file and select the file format you wish to use. To include the edited file in a Version Set with the original click check the Save in Version Set with Original box at the bottom of the dialog. See Figure 3.38.

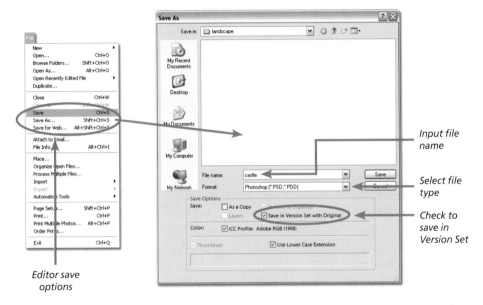

Editor save options

Input file name

Select file type

Check to save in Version Set

Figure 3.38 *Saving images is an important part of the imaging process, as it is this step that commits all changes permanently to memory. For most users the Photoshop or PSD format should be used. Other file types have characteristics, like compression, that make them a better choice when sharing files, especially across the Internet. Use the File > Save As option to save your picture in other formats.*

Editor: File > Save As

For most images you should use the Photoshop or PSD format. This option gives you a file that maintains all of the specialized features available in Elements. This means that when you next open your image you will be able to continue to use items like layers and editable text. If, on the other hand, you want to share your images with others, either via the web or over a network, then you can choose to save your files in other formats, like JPEG or TIFF. Each of these options can provide more compact files than PSD, but don't support all of Elements' advanced features.

To save a file in a format other than the PSD file type select the File > Save As option selecting a different option from the drop-down format menu.

'The formats I use'

Elements, like its industry-leading brother Photoshop, can open and save files in a multitude of different file formats. It's great to have such a choice, but the big question that most new digital photographers ask is 'What format should I use?'

And like most of the big questions in life there is no single answer to this query. The best way to decide is to be clear about what you intend to use the image for. Knowing the 'end use' will help determine what file format is best for your purposes. Until we look more closely at format characteristics like compression, use the way I work as a starting point. My approach is outlined below.

At the *scanning*, or *image capture*, stage, I tend to favor keeping my files in a TIFF or RAW format. The save options in most scanning software will usually give you the option to save as a TIFF straight after capture and many digital cameras offer the option to store pictures as either RAW or TIFF files. If I need to use JPEG with my camera to increase the number of shots I can fit on my compact flash cards, I change the format to TIFF when I download the pictures to my computer. This way, I don't have to be concerned about any further loss of image quality derived from opening and saving JPEG files, but I still get the advantages of good compression. As an added bonus I can also use the files on both Mac and IBM platforms.

When *manipulating* or *adjusting images*, I always use the PSD or the Photoshop and Photoshop Elements format, as this allows me the most flexibility. I can use, and maintain, a number of different layers which can be edited and saved separately. Even when I share my work, I regularly supply the original PSD file so that last minute editing or fine-tuning can continue right up to going to press. If, on the other hand, I don't want my work to be easily edited, I supply the final image in a TIFF format, which can be opened by both Mac and Windows machines.

If the final image is to be used for *web*, then I use GIF, PNG or JPEG depending on the numbers of colors in the original and whether any parts of the image contain transparency. There is no firm rule here. A balance between size and image quality is what is important, so I will try each format and see which provides the best mix. See Table 3.2.

Table 3.2 *For tasks the Photoshop Elements or PSD file format should be used. Other file types have characteristics, like compression, that make them a better choice when sharing files across the Internet.*

File Type	Compression	Color Modes	Layers	Metadata	Uses
Photoshop (.PSD)	X	RGB, CMYK, Indexed color, Grayscale	✓	✓	Desktop publishing (DTP), Internet, publishing, photographic work
GIF (.GIF)	✓	Indexed color	X	X	Internet
JPEG (.JPG)	✓	RGB, CMYK, Grayscale	X	✓	DTP, Internet, publishing, photographic work
TIFF (.TIF)	✓	RGB, CMYK, Indexed color, Grayscale	✓	✓	DTP, Internet, publishing, photographic work
PNG (.PNG)	✓	RGB, Indexed color, Grayscale	X	X	Internet

Organizer: File > Backup Ⓦ

As well as the save options detailed above, Adobe has also introduced a Backup feature in the Windows version of the program that is designed for copying your pictures (and catalog files) onto DVD or CD for archiving purposes. Follow the steps in the wizard to make a copy or backup of all the photos you have currently listed in your Photo Browser.

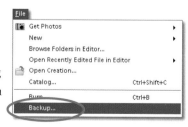

4

Simple Image Changes

ADOBE PHOTOSHOP ELEMENTS 3.0

65

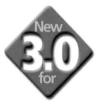

Three levels of editing

As we started to see in the last chapter, Elements 3.0 provides a variety of edit and enhancement options for users to change and alter their digital photographs. The options for Windows users can be grouped around three different approaches to the task:

1 The simplest tools are almost always fully automatic with the user having little control over the final results. These are the types of color, contrast and brightness controls that are available in the Photo Browser (via the Edit > Auto Fix Window). This is the place to start if you are new to digital photography and want good results quickly and easily.

2 The second level of features sits in the middle ground between total user control and total program control over the editing results. The tools in this group are primarily available in the Quick Fix editor but also encompass some of the more automatic or easy-to-use controls

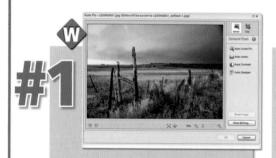

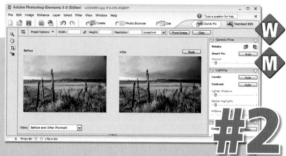

- Simple control using the Auto Fix Window
- Most changes applied automatically
- New users start here for good, quick results
- Control of: cropping, rotation, contrast, color, shadow and highlight detail, and sharpening
- See Chapter 3 for details

- Middle-level control using the Quick Fix and Standard editors
- Some changes applied automatically, others via a user controlled slider
- New users progress here with experience and understanding
- Control of: cropping, rotation, contrast, color (saturation, hue, temperature, tint, shadow and highlight detail, red-eye, midtone contrast and sharpening
- See Chapter 4 for details

Book resources at: **www.guide2elements.com**

available in the Standard Editor work space. Move to these tools once you feel more confident with the digital photography process as a whole (downloading, making some changes, saving and then printing) and find yourself wanting to do more with your pictures.

3 The final group of tools are those designed to give the user professional control over their editing and enhancement tasks. Many of the features detailed here are very similar to, and in some cases exactly the same as, those found in the Photoshop program itself. These tools provide the best quality changes available with Elements, but they do require a greater level of understanding and knowledge to use effectively. The extra editing and enhancement power of these tools comes at a cost of the user bearing all responsibility for the end results. Whereas the automatic nature of many of the features found in the other two groups means that bad results are rare, misusing or overapplying the tools found here can actually make your picture worse. This shouldn't stop you from venturing into these waters, but it does mean that it is a good idea to apply these tools cautiously rather than with a heavy hand.

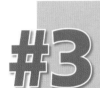

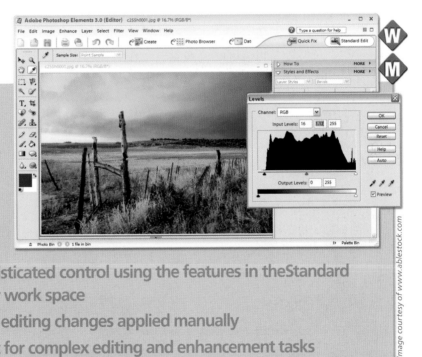

Image courtesy of www.ablestock.com

- Sophisticated control using the features in theStandard Editor work space
- Most editing changes applied manually
- Great for complex editing and enhancement tasks performed by more experienced users
- The most control of all the major editing and enhancing of your digital photographs
- See Chapter 5 for details

Figure 4.1 *Photoshop Elements 3.0 has three different levels of editing and enhancement tools available to users. This means that you will have features that suit your skills level no matter how much digital photography experience you have.*

Including three levels of editing features is Adobe's way of providing digital photographers with exactly the tools they need irrespective of their experience level and understanding. It also means that users can progress to more sophisticated tools as their confidence and knowledge grow. This said, it can be a little confusing for those of you who are new to the program to know 'what tool to use when'. For this reason I have broken the features into the three categories detailed above and have separated their introduction into separate chapters in the book. See Figure 4.1.

Setting up your screen for Elements

In the previous chapter we looked at how to download, crop, rotate, auto-enhance, print and save images directly from the Photo Browser or Organizer work space. Now you can try your hand at some simple changes courtesy of the editor components of Elements 3.0. It is here that you will start to see the power of the digital process. With a few clicks of the mouse you can perform basic picture adjustments and enhancements easier than ever before. This chapter will take you step by step through these changes and also show you how to use these techniques.

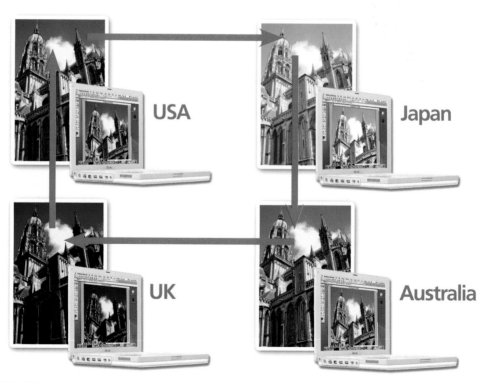

Figure 4.2 *Even with exactly the same file and editing program, images can appear very different on several machines.*

Popularity can be a problem

One of the truly amazing features of digital imaging is the diversity of people using the technology. Many individuals in various occupations, using various brands of equipment, in different countries across the world use computer-based picture making as part of their daily work or personal life. The popularity of the system is both its strength and, potentially, one of its weaknesses. On the positive side it means that an image I make in Australia can be viewed in the United Kingdom, enhanced in the United States and printed in Japan. Each activity would involve importing my picture into a different computer, with a different screen, running an image-editing package like Elements. This is where problems can occur. Even though the program and image are exactly the same, the way that the computer is set up can mean that the picture will appear completely different on each machine. On my computer the image exhibits good contrast and has no apparent color casts. In the UK though, it might look a little dark, in the USA slightly blue and in Japan too light and far too green. See Figure 4.2.

Before you start

To help alleviate this problem, Adobe has built into its imaging programs a color management system that will help you set up your machine so that what you see will be as close as possible to what others see. For this reason, it is important that you set up your computer using the system before starting to make changes to your images. The critical part of the process is the calibration of your monitor. To achieve this, use the following steps:

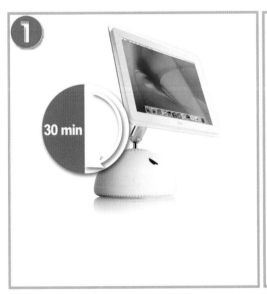

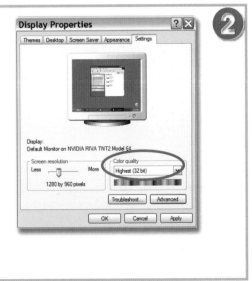

To start the calibration process make sure that your monitor has been turned on for at least 30 minutes.

Check that your computer is displaying thousands (16-bit color) or millions (24- or 32-bit color) of colors.

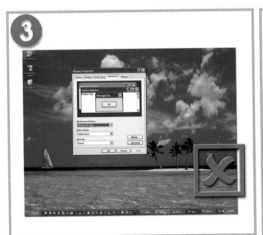

Remove colorful or highly patterned backgrounds from your screen, as this can affect your color perception.

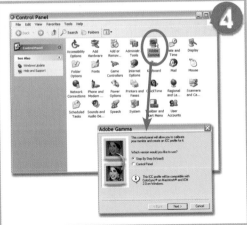

Start the Adobe Gamma utility.
In Windows, this is located in the Control Panel. For Macintosh users, use Apple's own Display Calibrator Assistant, as Adobe Gamma is not used with the new system software.

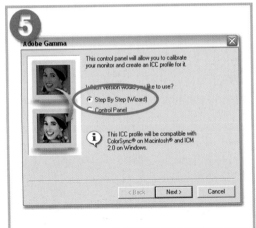

Use the step-by-step Wizard to guide you through the setup process. If a default profile was not supplied with your computer, contact your monitor manufacturer or check their website for details.

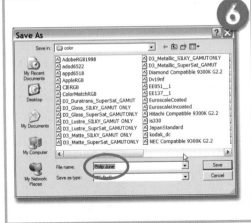

Save the profile, including the date in the file name. As your monitor will change with age, you should perform the Gamma setup every couple of months. Saving the setup date as part of the profile name will help remind you when last you used the utility.

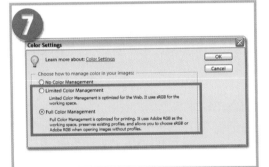

Now that your screen is correctly calibrated you need to ensure that the Photoshop Elements program is set to use the results of your hard work. Got to Photo Browser: Edit > Color Settings or Editor: Edit > Color Settings and make sure that either the Limited or Full Color Management option is selected. With this option activated the pictures you create will be color managed throughout the whole digital photography process.

Calibrate all screens and use color management wherever possible

Keep in mind that for the color management to truly work, all your friends or colleagues who will be using your images must calibrate their systems as well.

Brightness and contrast changes

As we saw in Chapter 1, a digital picture is made up of a grid of pixels, each with a specific color and brightness. The brightness of each pixel is determined by a numerical value between 0 and 255. The higher the number, the brighter the pixel will appear; the lower the value, the darker it will be. The extremes of the scale, 0 and 255, represent pure black and white, and values around 128 are considered midtones. In a correctly exposed image with good brightness and contrast, the tones will be spread between these two extremes. If an image is underexposed, then the picture will appear dark on screen and most of its pixels will have values between 128 and 0. In contrast, images that have been overexposed appear light on screen and the majority of their pixels lie in the region between 128 and 255. See Figure 4.3.

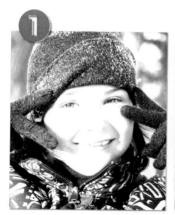
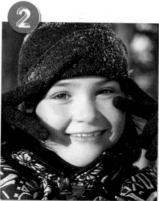
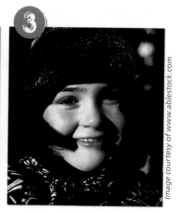

Image courtesy of www.ablestock.com

Figure 4.3 *A well-exposed photograph (2) will have good brightness and contrast and will display a good spread of tones between black and white or shadow and highlight. An underexposed image (3) appears dark on screen where as an overexposed image (1) appears light on screen.*

The best method for correcting these situations is for you to recapture the picture, changing the settings on your scanner or camera to compensate for the exposure problem. Good exposure not only ensures a good spread of tones, but also it gives you the chance to capture the best detail and quality in your photographs. It is a misunderstanding of the digital process to excuse poor exposure control by saying 'it's okay, I'll fix it in Elements later'. You will not get the best quality pictures possible if you use Elements to correct shooting or scanning mistakes as images that are too dark or light are pictures where vital detail has been lost forever. See Figure 4.4. Sometimes though, a reshoot is not possible or a rescan not practical. In these circumstances, or in a situation where only slight changes are necessary, Elements has a range of ways to change the brightness and contrast in your photos.

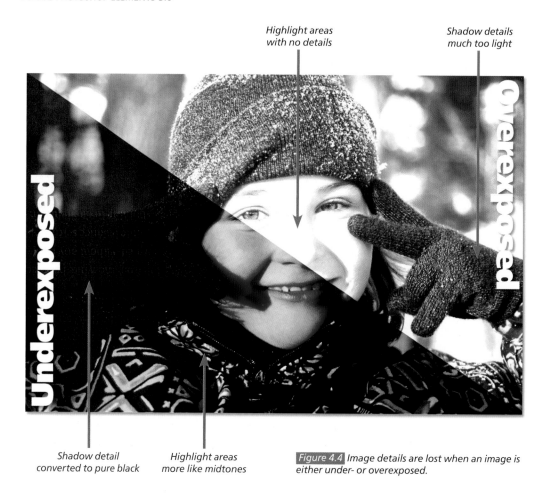

Highlight areas
with no details

Shadow details
much too light

Shadow detail
converted to pure black

Highlight areas
more like midtones

Figure 4.4 Image details are lost when an image is
either under- or overexposed.

Editor: Enhance > Adjust Lighting > Brightness/Contrast

Version 2.0: Enhance > Adjust Brightness/Contrast > Brightness/Contrast
Version 1.0: Enhance > Brightness/Contrast > Brightness/Contrast

The Brightness/Contrast command helps you make basic adjustments to the spread of tones within
the image. When opened you are presented with a dialog containing two slider controls. Click
and drag the slider to the left to decrease brightness or contrast, to the right to increase the value.
Keep in mind that you are trying to adjust the image so that the tones are more evenly distributed
between the extremes of pure white and black. Too much correction using either control can result
in pictures where highlight and/or shadow details are lost. As you are making your changes, watch
these two areas in particular to ensure that details are retained. See Figure 4.5.

1 Select Enhance > Adjust Lighting > Brightness/Contrast.

2 Move sliders to change image tones.

3 Left to decrease brightness/contrast, right to increase.

4 Click OK to finish.

FEATURE SUMMARY

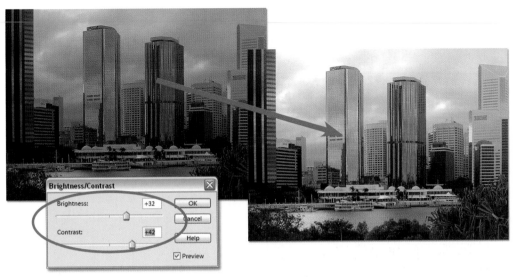

Figure 4.5 *The Brightness/Contrast feature is located under the Adjust Brightness/Contrast section of the Enhance menu. After adjusting the brightness and contrast of an image, the picture will appear clearer and its tone will be spread more evenly.*

Editor: Enhance > Auto Contrast

Version 1.0/2.0: Enhance > Auto Contrast

The Auto Contrast command can be used as an alternative to the Brightness/Contrast sliders. In this feature, Elements assesses all the values in an image and identifies the brightest and darkest tones. These pixels are then converted to white and black, and those values in between are spread along the full tonal range. Auto Contrast works particularly well with photographic images. See Figure 4.6.

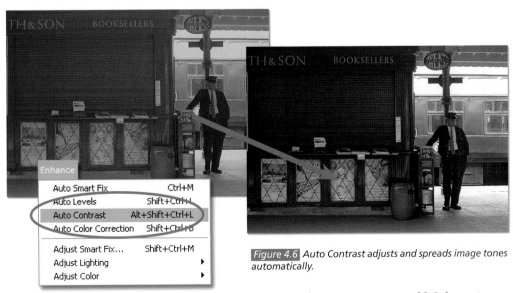

Figure 4.6 *Auto Contrast adjusts and spreads image tones automatically.*

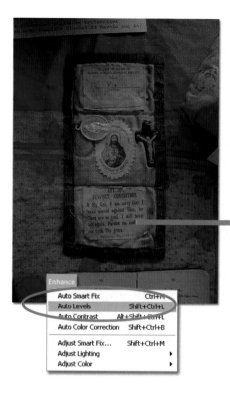

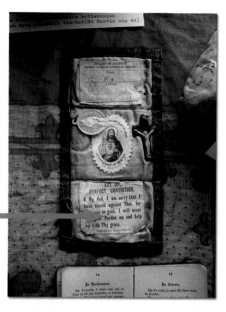

Figure 4.7 Auto Levels adjusts and spreads the tones of each individual color channel. In some pictures, this feature can help to reduce color casts.

Editor: Enhance > Auto Levels

Version 1.0/2.0: Enhance > Auto Levels

The Auto Levels command is similar to Auto Contrast in that it maps the brightest and darkest parts of the image to white and black. It differs from the previous technique because each individual color channel is treated separately. In the process of mapping the tones in the Red, Green and Blue channels, dominant color casts can be neutralized. See Figure 4.7. This is not always the case; it depends entirely on the make-up of the image. In some cases the reverse is true; when Auto Levels is put to work on a neutral image a strong cast results. If this occurs, undo (Edit > Undo) the command and apply the Auto Contrast feature instead.

Editor: Enhance > Auto Smart Fix

The new Auto Smart Fix feature enhances both the lighting and color in your picture automatically. The command is used to balance the color and improve the overall shadow and highlight detail. Most images are changed drastically using this tool. In some cases the changes can be too extreme. In which case, the effect should be reversed using the Edit > Undo command and the more controllable version of the tool – Adjust Smart Fix – used instead. See Figure 4.8.

Editor: Enhance > Adjust Smart Fix

The Adjust Smart Fix version of the feature provides the same control over color, shadow and highlight detail but with the addition of a slider control that determines the strength of the enhancement changes. Moving the slider from left to right will gradually increase the amount of correction applied to your picture. This approach provides much more control over the enhancement process and is a preferable way to work with all but the most general photos. The Auto button, also located in the dialog, automatically applies a fix amount of 100% and provides a similar result to selecting Enhance > Auto Smart Fix. See Figure 4.8.

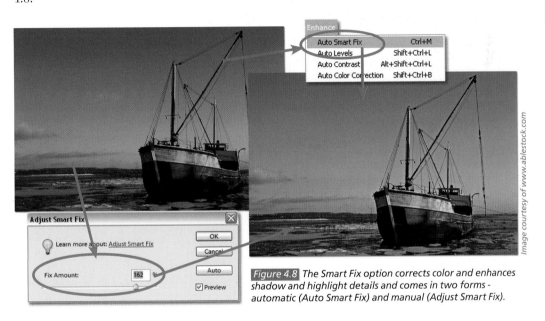

Image courtesy of www.ablestock.com

Figure 4.8 *The Smart Fix option corrects color and enhances shadow and highlight details and comes in two forms - automatic (Auto Smart Fix) and manual (Adjust Smart Fix).*

The Quick Fix editor – 'the new quick change central'

The Quick Fix editor is home for many of the automatic or 'quick and easy' enhancement tools. You can access and apply the features via the menu system or take advantage of the controls displayed in the Palette Bin.

Here you will find features that will enable you to quickly and easily adjust lighting, color, sharpening and, with the Smart Fix tool, highlight and shadow detail as well. You can let the program apply the changes for you by pressing the Auto button, or you can take control of the changes you apply by using the slider controls. And the best thing of all you can see the before and after results of your changes on screen via the zoomable previews.

There is no doubt that for making speedy adjustments of your favorite images in Elements 3.0, the Quick Fix editor is the best place to start. See Figure 4.9.

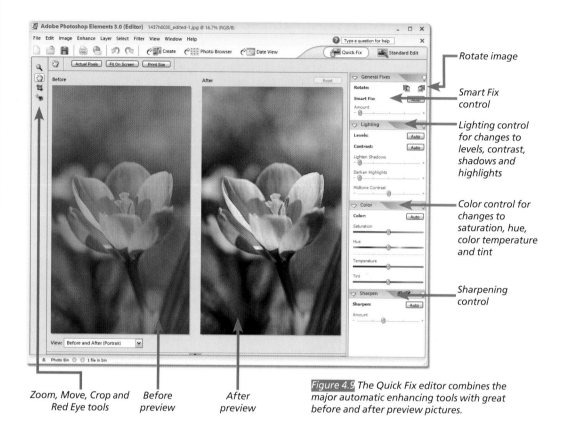

Rotate image

Smart Fix control

Lighting control for changes to levels, contrast, shadows and highlights

Color control for changes to saturation, hue, color temperature and tint

Sharpening control

Zoom, Move, Crop and Red Eye tools

Before preview

After preview

Figure 4.9 *The Quick Fix editor combines the major automatic enhancing tools with great before and after preview pictures.*

Altering a few tones only

Now that we have changed the brightness and contrast of the image so that the tones are more evenly spread between black and white, we can start to look at individual areas or groups of tones that need special attention.

For instance, when you are taking pictures on a bright sunny day, or where the contrast of the scene is quite high, the shadows in the image can become so dense that important details are too dark to see. A traditional method used by photographers to lighten the shadows is to capture the scene using a combination of existing light and a small amount of extra light from a flash. The flash illuminates the shadows, in effect 'filling' them with light, hence the name 'Fill Flash'. This is a great solution for a difficult problem.

Similarly, if the foreground or center section of a scene is dark, then the exposure system in a digital camera can overcompensate and cause the surrounding area to become too light. 'No problem', you say, as you adjust the brightness so that the whole picture is darker but this action also affects the shadow and midtone areas of the picture causing them to lose detail.

So how can we alter the brightness of just the shadow or only the highlight areas? Well Adobe provided quite a clever solution to these problems in the previous versions of the program employing two previously unknown features – Fill Flash and Adjust Backlighting (see details below for their uses). In version 3.0 of the program Adobe has introduced yet another new feature called the Shadow/Highlight control. The tool combines into one dialogue two different controls that performed similar functions in previous versions of the product.

Editor: Enhance > Adjust Lighting > Shadow/Highlights

Designed as a replacement for both the Fill Flash and Adjust Backlighting controls, this one little dialog contains the same power as the previous two features in an easy-to-use format. The tool contains three sliders – the upper one is for Lightening Shadows which replaces the Fill Flash tool, the control in the middle Darkens Highlights and is a substitute for the Adjust Backlighting tool and the final slider adjusts Midtone Contrast.

Moving the Shadows control to the right lightens all the tones that are spread between the middle tones and black. Sliding the Highlights control to the right darkens those tones between middle values and white. The beauty of this feature is that unlike the Brightness/Contrast tool, these changes are made without altering other parts of the picture. To fine tune the tonal changes a third slider is also included in the dialog. Moving this Midtone control to the right increases the contrast of the middle values and movements to the left decrease the contrast making the image 'flatter'. See Figure 4.10.

FEATURE SUMMARY

1 Select Enhance > Adjust Lighting > Shadow/Highlights.

2 Move all sliders so that their values are set to 0%.

3 Move the Lighten Shadows slider to the right to lighten the dark tones.

4 Move the Darken Highlights slider to the right to darken light areas.

5 Adjust the Midtone Contrast slider to restore any lost contrast to the picture.

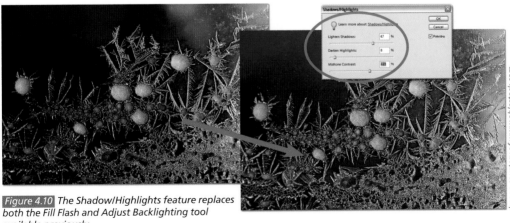

Image courtesy of www.ablestock.com

Figure 4.10 *The Shadow/Highlights feature replaces both the Fill Flash and Adjust Backlighting tool available previously.*

SIMPLE IMAGE CHANGES

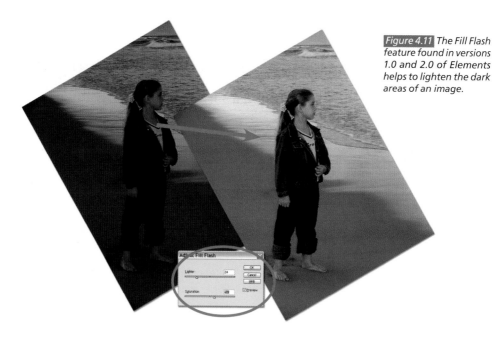

Figure 4.11 The Fill Flash feature found in versions 1.0 and 2.0 of Elements helps to lighten the dark areas of an image.

Fill Flash (not in version 3.0)
Version 2.0: Enhance > Adjust Lighting > Fill Flash
Version 1.0: Enhance > Fill Flash

Adobe took the traditional 'fill flash' technique and incorporated it as an enhancement feature into the two previous versions of Elements. You can use this command to lighten the shadow areas of contrasty images. The degree of lightening is controlled by the slider in the feature's dialog. Version 2.0 of the program included a second slider in the dialog that enabled the user to control the saturation, or color strength, of the image as well as the lightness. See Figure 4.11.

1 Select Enhance > Adjust Lighting > Fill Flash.

2 Move the Lighter slider to change image tones.

3 Move the Saturation slider to the right to increase color strength and to the left to decrease.

4 Click OK to finish.

Adjust Backlighting (not in version 3.0)
Version 2.0: Enhance > Adjust Lighting > Adjust Backlighting
Version 1.0: Enhance > Adjust Backlighting

When Adobe recognized that a specialist highlight darkening feature was needed in Elements they included the Adjust Backlighting feature into versions 1.0 and 2.0 of the program. When inside the feature's dialog moving the Darker slider will alter the strength of the highlight darkening effect. See Figure 4.12.

1 Select Enhance > Adjust Lighting > Adjust Backlighting.

2 Move the Darker slider to change image tones.

3 Click OK to finish.

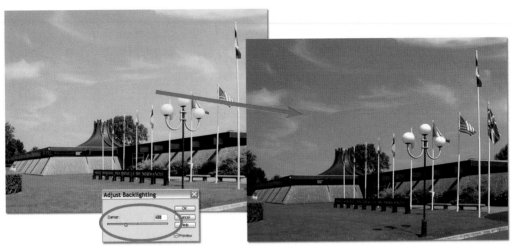

Figure 4.12 The Adjust Backlighting feature, found in previous versions of Elements, darkens the light areas of an image in traditional photographic practice.

Dodge and Burn tools

It is no surprise, given Adobe's close relationship with customers who are professional photographers, that some of the features contained in both Photoshop and Elements have a heritage in traditional photographic practice. The Dodge and Burn tools are good examples of this. Almost since the inception of the medium, photographers have manipulated the way their images have printed. In most cases this amounts to giving a little more light to one part of the picture and taking a little away from another. This technique, called 'dodging and burning', effectively lightens and darkens specific parts of the final print.

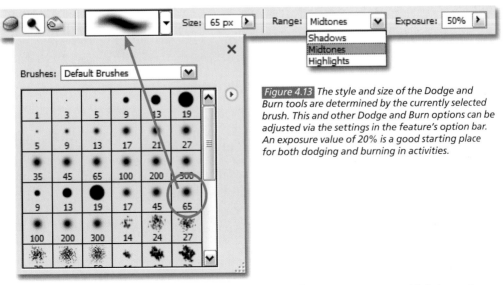

Figure 4.13 The style and size of the Dodge and Burn tools are determined by the currently selected brush. This and other Dodge and Burn options can be adjusted via the settings in the feature's option bar. An exposure value of 20% is a good starting place for both dodging and burning in activities.

Adobe's version of these techniques involves two separate tools. See Figure 4.14. The Dodge tool's icon represents its photographic equivalent, a cardboard disk on a piece of wire. This device was used to shade part of the photographic paper during exposure. Having received less exposure, the area is lighter in the final print. When you select the digital version from the Elements toolbox, you will notice the cursor change to a circle which you can click and drag over your image to lighten the selected areas. The size and shape of the circle is based on the current brush size and shape. This can be changed via the palette in the options bar. Also displayed here are other options that allow you to lighten groups of tones like shadows, midtones and highlights independently. There are also controls to change the strength of the lightening process by adjusting the exposure. See Figure 4.15.

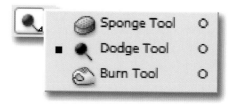

Figure 4.14 *The Dodge and Burn tools are used to lighten and darken different parts of the picture.*

1 Select Dodge tool from toolbox.

2 Choose brush size from palette in the options bar.

3 Select the group of tones to adjust – highlights, midtones or shadows.

4 Set the strength of the effect via the exposure value.

5 Click and drag cursor over image to lighten.

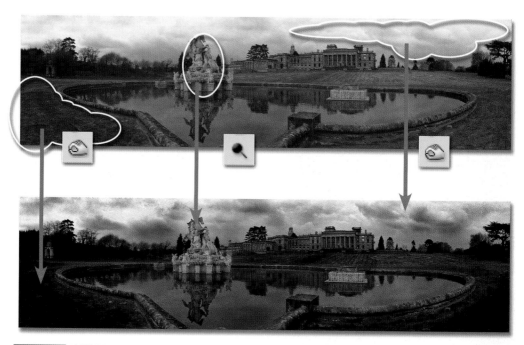

Figure 4.15 *Skillful dodging and burning can help improve the appearance of specific dark and light picture areas.*

The Burn tool's attributes are also based on the settings in the options bar and the current brush size, but rather than lightening areas this feature darkens selected parts of the image. Again, you can adjust the precise grouping of tones, highlights, midtones or shadows that you are working on at any one time. See Figure 4.16.

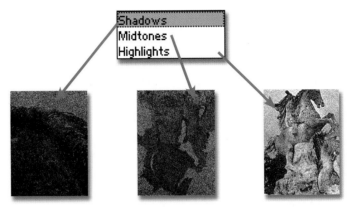

Figure 4.16 *Highlights, shadows and midtones can be dodged and burnt separately.*

1 Select Burn tool from toolbox.

2 Choose brush size from palette in the options bar.

3 Select the group of tones to adjust – highlights, midtones or shadows.

4 Set the strength of the effect via the exposure value.

5 Click and drag cursor over image to darken.

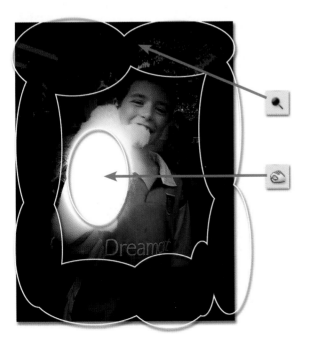

As with many digital adjustment and enhancement techniques, it is important to apply dodging and burning effects subtly. Overuse is not only noticeable, but you can also lose the valuable highlight and shadow details that you have worked so hard to preserve. See Figure 4.17.

Figure 4.17 *Too much dodging and burning is noticeable and can eventually degrade the image rather than improve it.*

Color corrections

Our eyes are extremely complex and sophisticated imaging devices. Without us even being aware, they adjust to changes in light color and level. For instance, when we view a piece of white paper outside on a cloudy day, indoors under a household bulb or at work with fluorescent lights, the paper appears white. Our eyes adapt to each different environment.

Unfortunately, digital sensors, including those in our cameras, are not as clever. If I photographed the piece of paper under the same lighting conditions, the pictures would all display a different color cast. Under fluorescent lights the paper would appear green, lit by the household bulb it would look yellow and when photographed outside it would be a little blue. See Figure 4.18.

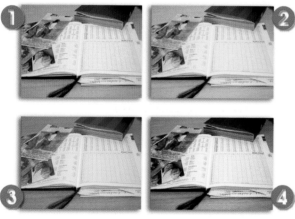

Figure 4.18 The dominant color (cast) in an image changes when it is shot under different light sources.
(1) Fluorescent.
(2) Household bulb.
(3) Candlelight.
(4) Daylight.

This situation occurs because camera sensors are generally designed to record images without casts in daylight. As the color balance of the light for our three examples is different from daylight, that is, some parts of the spectrum are stronger and more dominant than others, the pictures record with a cast. Camera manufacturers are addressing the problem by including 'auto white balance' functions in their designs. These features attempt to adjust the captured image to suit the lighting conditions it was photographed under, but even so, some digital pictures will arrive at your desktop with strange color casts. See Figure 4.19.

Figure 4.19 Some cameras include an auto white balance feature designed to compensate for different light sources.

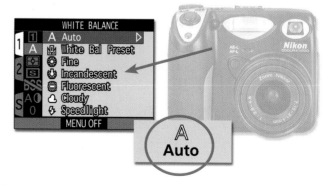

Editor: Enhance > Auto Color Correction

The Auto Color Correction feature, first seen in version 2.0 of the program, works in a similar way to tools like Auto Levels and Auto Contrast, providing a one-click fix for most color problems. As with all 'I'll let the computer decide' features, sometimes such automatic fixes do not produce the results that you expect. In these scenarios use the Undo (Edit > Undo) command to reverse the changes and try one of the manual tools detailed below. See Figure 4.20.

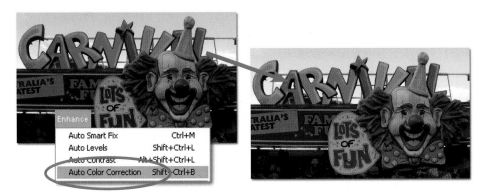

Figure 4.20 *Auto Color Correction provides a one-click correction for most cast problems.*

Editor: Enhance > Adjust Color > Remove Color Cast
Version 2.0: Enhance > Adjust Color > Color Cast
Version 1.0: Enhance > Color > Color Cast

To help provide a more selective solution to the color cast problem, Adobe included the Color Cast command in Elements. This function is designed to be used with images that have areas that are meant to be white, gray or black. By selecting the feature you can then click onto the neutral area and all the colors of the image will be changed by the amount needed to make the area free from color casts. This command works particularly well if you happen to have a white, gray or black in your scene. See Figure 4.21. Some image makers include a gray card in the corner of scenes that they know are going to produce casts in anticipation of using Color Cast to neutralize the hues later.

FEATURE SUMMARY

1 Select Enhance > Adjust Color > Remove Color Cast.

2 Use the eyedropper tool to click on a part of the image that is meant to be either a neutral white, gray or black.

3 If you are unhappy with the results, click the Reset button to start again.

4 Click OK when the cast has been removed.

Keep in mind that this command produces changes based on the assumption that what you are clicking with the eyedropper is meant to be neutral – that is, the color should contain even amounts of red, green and blue. In practice, it is not often that images have areas like this. For this reason, Elements contains another method to help rid your images of color casts.

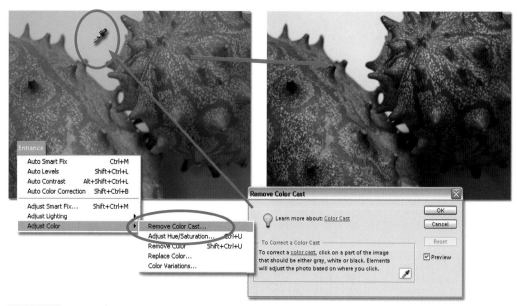

Figure 4.21 *The Remove Color Cast feature works when you select a portion of the picture that should be neutral (white, gray or black) but exhibits a cast. Elements then rebalances the rest of the hues in the image to ensure that this part of the picture is cast free.*

Editor: Enhance > Adjust Color > Color Variations

Version 2.0: Enhance > Adjust Color > Color Variations
Version 1.0: Enhance > Variations

An alternative to using the Remove Color Cast feature is the Color Variations command. Versions 2.0 and 3.0 of Elements include a revised and simplified Color Variations dialog. The color changing thumbnails have been rationalized so that users only have to make simple decisions about increasing or decreasing the red, green or blue components of their images.

This feature, as it appeared in version 1.0, was based on a color wheel, which was made up of the primary colors red, green and blue, and their complementary colors cyan, magenta and yellow. See Figure 4.22. Increasing the amount of one color in an image automatically decreases its complementary. Put simply, increasing red will decrease cyan, increasing green will reduce magenta and increasing blue will lessen yellow. Understanding this link will help you use the Color Variations command. In addition to changes to color, this feature also gives options to change the picture's brightness and saturation.

The version 3.0/2.0 Color Variations feature is divided into four parts. The top of the dialog contains two thumbnails that represent how your image looked before changes and its appearance after. The radio buttons in section 1 (middle left) allow the user to select the parts of the image they wish to alter. In this way, highlights, midtones and shadows can all be adjusted independently. The 'amount' slider in section 2 (bottom left) controls the strength of the color changes. The final part, section 3 (bottom left), is taken up with six color and two brightness preview images. These represent how your picture will look with specific colors added or when the picture is brightened or darkened. Clicking on any of these thumbnails will change the 'after' picture by adding the color chosen. To add a color to your image, click on a suitably colored thumbnail. To remove a color, click on its opposite.

FEATURE SUMMARY

1 Select Enhance > Adjust Color > Color Variations.

2 Choose the tones you want to change (shadows, midtones or highlights) or alternatively select saturation.

3 Adjust the Amount slider to set the strength of each change.

4 Click on the appropriate thumbnails to make changes to your image.

5 Click OK to finish.

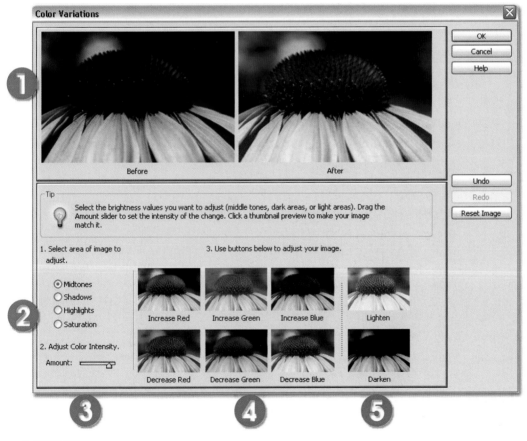

Figure 4.22 The Color Variations feature, as it appears in version 3.0, gives the user more control over color changes in the image. (1) Before and after thumbnails. (2) Image area to change. (3) Color strength or intensity. (4) Color variations thumbnails. (5) Brightness thumbnails.

The Red Eye Removal tool

Version 1.0/2.0: Red Eye Brush

Using the built-in flash in your camera is a great way to make sure that you can keep photographing in any light conditions. One of the problems with flashes that are situated very close to the lens is that portrait pictures, especially when taken at night, tend to suffer from 'red eye'. The image might be well exposed and composed, but the sitter has glowing red eyes. This occurs because the light from the flash is being reflected off the back of the eye.

Adobe recognized that a lot of small modern digital cameras have flashguns close to their lens – the major cause of this problem – and developed a specialist tool to help retouch these images. Called the Red Eye Removal tool in version 3.0 and the Red Eye Brush in previous releases, it changes the crimson color in the center of the eye for a more natural looking black.

To correct the problem is a simple process that involves selecting the tool and then clicking on the red section of the eye. Elements locates the red color and quickly converts it to a more natural dark gray. The tool's options bar provides settings to adjust the pupil's size and the amount that it is darkened. Try the default settings first and if the results are not quite perfect, undo the changes and adjust the option's settings before reapplying the tool. See Figure 4.23.

1 Select the Red Eye Removal tool from the toolbox.

2 Click on the red area of the eye to apply the color change.

3 If the results are not perfect, Edit > Undo the changes.

4 Adjust the Pupil Size and Darken Amount settings in the options bar.

5 Click on the red area to reapply the color change.

The Red Eye Removal tool is available in both the Quick Fix and Standard editing work spaces.

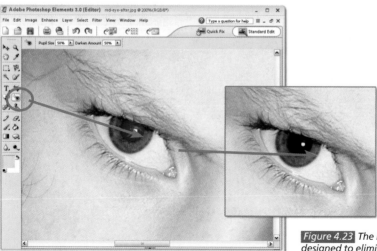

Figure 4.23 *The Red Eye Removal tool is designed to eliminate the 'devil-like' eyes that result from using the in-built flash of some digital cameras.*

To correct red eye using the Brush tool found in versions 1.0 and 2.0 of the program, pick the tool from the toolbox, select the brush size and type, and push the default colors button on the options bar and then click on the red section of the eyes. The Tolerance slider controls how similar to the current color a pixel must be before it is replaced. Low values restrict the effect to precisely the current color, higher values replace a broader range of dissimilar hues.

Using filters and effects

Editor: Filters

Version 2.0: Window > Filters
Version 1.0: Window > Show Filter Browser

The filters contained within image-editing programs are capable of producing truly stunning effects. Digital filters are based on the traditional photographic version, which is placed in front of the lens of the camera to change the way the image is captured. Now, with the click of a button it is possible to make extremely complex changes to our images almost instantaneously – changes that a few years ago we couldn't even imagine.

The filters in Adobe Photoshop Elements can be found grouped under a series of subheadings based on their main effect or feature in the Filter menu. Selecting a filter will apply the effect to the current layer or selection. Some filters display a dialog that allows the user to change specific settings and preview the filtered image before applying the effect to the whole of the picture. This can be a great time saver, as filtering a large file can take several minutes. See Figure 4.24.

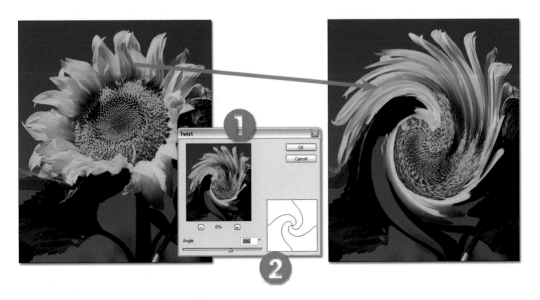

Figure 4.24 Most filters are supplied with a preview and settings dialog that allows the user to view changes before committing them to the full image. (1) Filter preview thumbnail. (2) Filter controls.

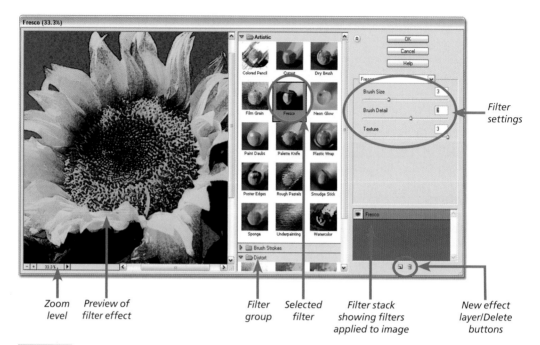

Zoom level   Preview of filter effect   Filter group   Selected filter   Filter stack showing filters applied to image   New effect layer/Delete buttons

Figure 4.25 *The new Filter Gallery feature allows users to preview filter effects, alter filter settings and even apply several different filters to the same image interactively.*

Editor: Filter > Filter Gallery

New 3.0 for

Other filters have now been incorporated into a new Filter Gallery (Filter > Filter Gallery) feature. Designed to allow the user to apply several different filters to a single image it can also be used to apply the same filter several different times. The dialog consists of a preview area, a collection of filters that can be used with the feature, a settings area with sliders to control the filter effect and a list of filters that are currently being applied to the picture.

Multiple filters are applied to a picture by selecting the filter, adjusting the settings to suit the image and then clicking the New effect layer button at the bottom of the dialog. Filters are arranged in the sequence they are applied. Applied filters can be moved to a different spot in the sequence by click-dragging them up or down the stack. Click the 'eye' icon to hide the effect of the selected filter from preview. Filters can be deleted from the list by selecting them first and then clicking the 'dustbin' icon at the bottom of the dialog.

Most of the filters that can't be used with the Filter Gallery feature are either applied to the picture with no user settings or make use of the filter preview and settings dialog detailed above. See Figure 4.25.

If neither of these preview options are available, then as an alternative, you can make a partial selection of the image using the Marquee tool first and then using this to test the filter. Remember filter changes can be reversed by using the undo feature.

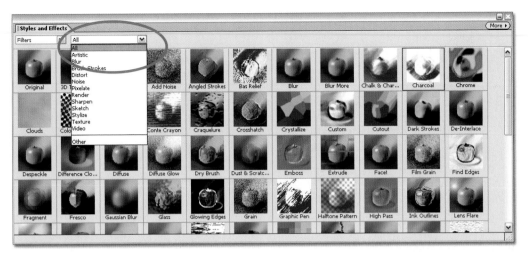

Figure 4.26 *The Filter Browser, located within the new Styles and Effects palette, gives users a good idea of the types of changes that a filter will make to an image when selecting a specific filter.*

Editor: Window > Styles and Effects

The number and type of filters available can make selecting which to use a difficult process. To help with this decision, Elements also contains a Filter Browser type feature that displays thumbnail versions of different filter effects. The browser is located with other thumbnail previews of Effects and Layer Styles in the new Styles and Effects palette (Window > Styles and Effects). Double-clicking the filter preview thumbnail will open the Filter Gallery and apply the filter changes to your picture. The selection of filters previewed at any one time can be changed by altering the selection in the pop-up menu at the top of the palette. See Figure 4.26.

Let's get filtering

To give you a head start with your filtering, the next couple of pages contain some examples of the effects of a range of filters when applied to the same base image. See Figure 4.27. The results, along with the filter preview/settings and dialogs, are printed on the next couple of pages. See Figures 4.28 and 4.29. After that, the use and control of some of the selected filters are also featured in more detail.

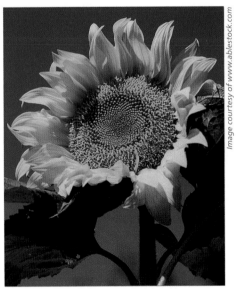

Image courtesy of www.ablestock.com

Figure 4.27 *The base image used for all filter examples over the next few pages.*

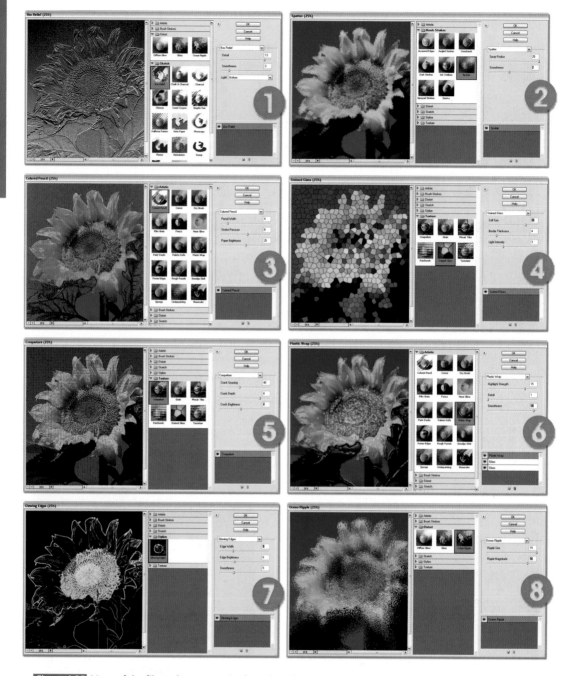

Figure 4.28 Many of the filters that you use in Photoshop Elements will open up via the Filter Gallery feature. This will give you the added ability to be able to combine filter effects and even reapply the same effect several times. Some of the filters that work with the filter gallery include: (1) Filter > Sketch > Bas Relief, (2) Filter > Brush Strokes > Spatter, (3) Filter > Artistic > Colored Pencil, (4) Filter > Texture > Stained Glass, (5) Filter > Texture > Craquelure, (6) Filter > Artistic > Plastic Wrap, (7) Filter > Stylize > Glowing Edges and (8) Filter > Distort > Ocean Ripple.

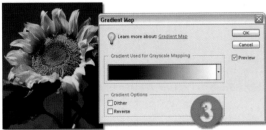

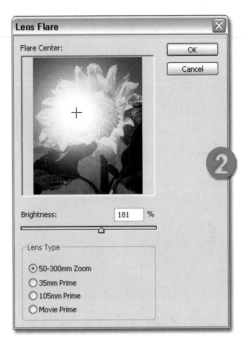

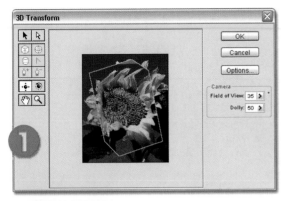

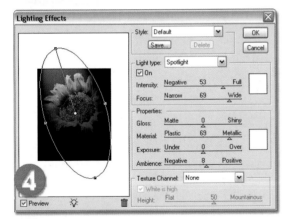

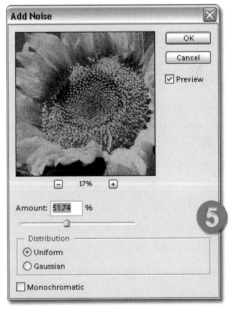

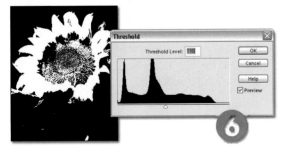

Figure 4.29 Filters that are not included in the
Filter Gallery often have their own preview and
settings dialog. These include:
(1) Filter > Render > 3D Transform,
(2) Filter > Render > Lens Flare,
(3) Filter > Adjustments > Gradient Map,
(4) Filter > Render >Lighting Effects,
(5) Filter > Noise > Add Noise and
(6) Filter > Adjustments > Threshold.

Book resources at: **www.guide2elements.com**

SIMPLE IMAGE CHANGES

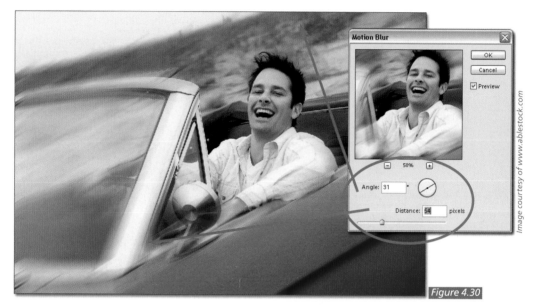

Image courtesy of www.ablestock.com

Figure 4.30

Editor: Filter > Blur > Motion Blur

The Motion Blur filter is great for putting back a sense of movement into action pictures that have been frozen by being photographed with a fast shutter speed. Used by itself, the filter produces photos that are very blurred and often lack any recognizable detail. Unless this is the effect you are looking for, it is best to apply this filter via a feathered selection to help retain sharpness in the some picture parts whilst blurring others. See Chapter 6 for more details on selection techniques.

The filter dialog contains a single slider, a preview window and a motion direction (angle) dial. The Angle dial determines the direction of the blur and should be set to simulate the natural direction of the subject. The Distance slider controls the amount of blur added to the picture – higher values create longer streaks and a more dramatic effect, smaller settings produce more subtle results.

FEATURE SUMMARY

1 Before applying the filter we need to set up some controls over where the motion blur will be applied in our picture. To do this we start by selecting the area to remain sharp. Here I have used the Lasso tool to draw a freehand selection around the driver. Next, I invert the selection (Select > Inverse) so that the entire image except the driver is now selected.

2 To soften the transition between the sharp and blurred sections of the picture I applied a large feather (Select > Feather) to the selection. This replaces the normal sharp edge of the selection with a gradual change between selected and non-selected areas. I used a feathering of about 10% (100 pixels) of the total width of the picture.

3 Next I hid the selection using the shortcut keys of CTRL + H (the selection is still active, you just cannot see the marching ants) and opened the Motion Blur dialog (Filter > Blur > Motion Blur). I adjusted the Angle and Distance settings to suit the picture. Make sure that the Preview option is selected so that you can see the results in the full image. Click OK to complete.

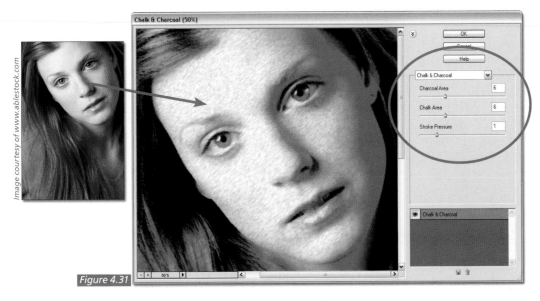

Image courtesy of www.ablestock.com

Figure 4.31

Editor: Filter > Sketch > Chalk & Charcoal

The Chalk & Charcoal filter is one of several drawing-like filters that can be found in the Sketch section of the Filter menu. The feature simulates the effect of making a drawing of the photograph with white chalk and black charcoal. The tones in the photograph that range from shadow to mid-gray are replaced by the charcoal strokes and those lighter values (from mid-gray to white) are 'drawn' in using the chalk color.

The filter dialog gives you control over the balance of the amount and placement of the charcoal and chalk areas as well as the pressure of the stroke used to draw the picture. Higher values for the Charcoal and Chalk area sliders will increase the number and variations of tones that are drawn with these colors. High settings for the Stroke Pressure slider produce crisper transitions between tones and a more contrasty result.

1 Set the foreground colors to default (foreground – black, background – white) by clicking the small black and white squares in the bottom left of the tool bar. The filter uses the foreground color as the 'charcoal' color and the background color as the 'chalk' color. If you have the same color set for background and foreground then a warning dialog will appear.

2 Select the Chalk & Charcoal filter from the Filter > Sketch menu. Using the Preview window as a guide, adjust the Charcoal and Chalk Area sliders until you have situated the two tones in the positions most suited for the image. In the example I wanted to ensure that the shadow areas remained dark but still contained detail and the skin tones were still fairly light.

3 Next move your attention to the Stroke Pressure Slider. Adjust the setting until you achieve a good balance of both detail and contrast. You may need to readjust the Chalk and Charcoal Area sliders to ensure a good spread of tones after the Pressure Slider alterations.

FEATURE SUMMARY

SIMPLE IMAGE CHANGES

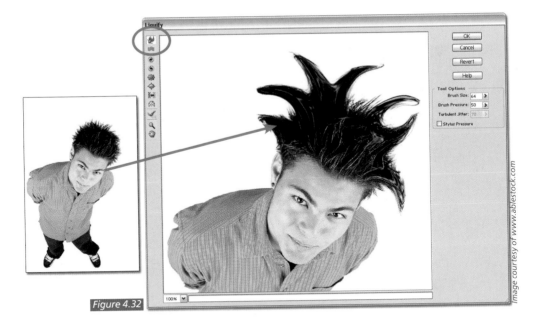

Figure 4.32

Image courtesy of www.ablestock.com

Editor: Filter > Distort > Liquify

The liquify filter is a very powerful tool for warping and transforming your pictures. The feature contains its own sophisticated dialog box complete with a preview area and no less than eight different tools that can be used to twist, warp, push, pull and reflect your pictures with such ease that it is almost as if they were made of silly putty.

1 Open an example image and then the Liquify filter (Filter > Distort > Liquify). The dialog opens and with a preview in the center, tools to the left and tool options to the right (use the Size, Pressure and Jitter options to control the effects of the tools). We will start with a simple manipulation designed to broaden the subject's smile. Select the Warp tool and drag the edge of the lips sideways and upwards. Make the brush smaller if too much of the surrounding detail is being altered as well.

2 Now let's exaggerate the perspective in the existing picture. Select the Pucker tool and increase the size of the Brush to cover the entire bottom of the figure. Click to squeeze in the subject's feet and legs. Now select the Bloat tool and place it over the upper portion of the subject, click to expand this area. If you are unhappy with any changes you can use the keyboard shortcuts for Edit > Undo (Ctrl + Z) to remove the last changes. If you want you can bloat the eyes as well.

3 To finish the caricature switch back to the Warp tool and drag some hair out and away from the subject's head. You can also use this tool to drag down the chin and lift the cheekbones. The picture can be selectively restored at any point by choosing the Reconstruct tool and painting over the changed area. Click OK to apply the changes that you have previewed to the fuller image. Depending on the size of the original this can take some time.

FEATURE SUMMARY

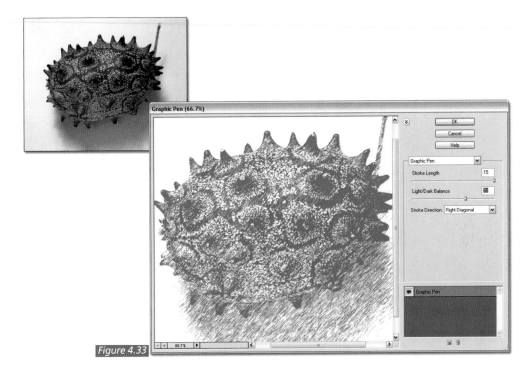

Figure 4.33

Editor: Filter > Sketch > Graphic Pen

The Graphic Pen filter is one of the group of the Sketch filters. The feature simulates the effect of making a drawing of the photograph with a thin graphic arts pen. Close, overlapping strokes are used for the shadow areas, midtones are represented by balancing strokes and with the paper color showing through and highlight details are drawn with a few sparse strokes.

The filter dialog gives you control over the balance of light and dark (paper and stroke) and the length of the pen stroke used to draw the picture. There is also a drop-down menu for selecting the direction of the pen strokes.

1 Set the foreground colors to default (foreground – black, background – white) by clicking the small black and white squares in the bottom left of the tool bar. The Graphic Pen filter uses the foreground color as the 'ink' color and the background color as the 'paper' color.

2 Select the Graphic Pen filter from the Filter > Sketch menu. Using the Preview window as a guide adjust the Stroke length, Light/Dark Balance and Stroke Direction controls. Click OK to filter the picture.

3 To add a little more color to your Graphic Pen 'drawings' select colors other than black and white for the foreground and background values. Double-click each swatch to open the color swatch palette where you can select the new color.

FEATURE SUMMARY

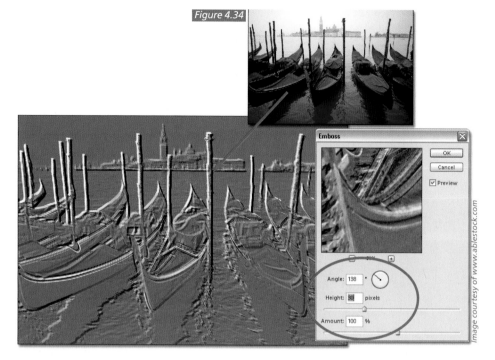

Figure 4.34

Image courtesy of www.ablestock.com

Editor: Filter > Stylize > Emboss

The Emboss filter converts your picture to flat areas of gray, fringed by lighter tones of various colors. The final result simulates an embossing effect making the picture appear as though it has been beaten into a sheet of thin metal.

The filter dialog contains two sliders, a preview window and a light direction (angle) dial. The Angle dial determines the direction of the light used to produce the shadows and highlights that create the depth of the embossing effect. The Height slider controls the size of the edge outlines and adjusting the Amount slider determines the level of picture detail used in the final result.

1 With your picture open select the Emboss filter from the Stylize group in the Filter menu.

2 With the filter dialog open make sure that the Preview option is clicked and that the preview window is set to 100%. Turn the Angle dial to adjust the lighting direction used in the effect. Next move the Height slider until the edges of the effect are the size you desire. Movements to the right increase the size of the edge lines.

3 Now turn your attention to the Amount slider. Move the control until the embossing effect is applied to the level of texture you desire. Movements to the right increase the detail in the result. If necessary, drag the visible area in the preview window to examine more closely the changes in other areas of the picture. Click OK to complete.

FEATURE SUMMARY

Third party filters

Ever since the early versions of Photoshop Elements Adobe provided the opportunity for third party developers to create small pieces of specialist software that could plug into the program. The modular format of the software means that Adobe and other software manufacturers can easily create extra filters that can be added to the program at any time. In fact, some of the plug-ins that have been released over the years have became so popular that Adobe themselves incorporated their functions into successive versions of Elements. This is how the new Photo filter, making its first appearance in Elements 3.0, came into being.

Most plug-ins register themselves as extra options in the Filter menu where they can be accessed just like any other Elements feature. The Digital SHO filter from Applied Science Fiction is a great example of plug-in technology. Designed to automatically enhance the shadow detail in digital photographs, when installed it becomes part of a suite of filters supplied by the company that are attached to the Filter menu. See Figure 4.35.

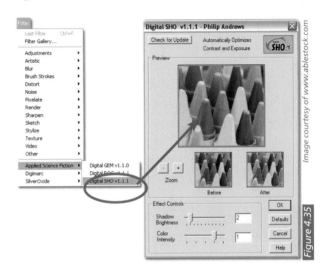

Figure 4.35

Image courtesy of www.ablestock.com

The 10 commandments for filter usage

1 Subtlety is everything. The effect should support your image not overpower it.

2 Try one filter at a time. Applying multiple filters to an image can be confusing.

3 View at full size. Make sure that you view the effect at full size (100%) when deciding on filter settings.

4 Filter a layer. For a change, try applying a filter to one layer and then using the layer opacity slider to control how strongly the filter image shows through.

5 Print to check effect. If the image is to be viewed as a print, double check the effect when printed before making final decisions about filter variables.

6 Fade strong effects. If the effect is too strong, try fading it. Apply the filter to a duplicate image layer that is above the original. Then reduce the opacity of this layer so the unfiltered original shows through.

7 Experiment. Try a range of settings before making your final selection.

8 Select then filter. Select a portion of an image and then apply the filter. In this way you can control what parts of the image are affected.

9 Different effects on different layers. If you want to combine the effects of different filters, try copying the base image to different layers and applying a different filter to each. Combine effects by adjusting the opacity of each layer.

10 Did I say that subtlety is everything?!

Getting help with Elements

In developing Elements, Adobe designed a range of learning aids that can help you increase your skills and understanding of the program. There is the usual Help menu complete with a dedicated window containing Contents, Topics, Search and Index listings for the whole program, but alongside this traditional approach Adobe also developed a couple of new help devices – namely the tool and feature Hints and the terrific How To guided tutorial system.

Hints

Version 2.0: Window > Hints
Version 1.0: Window > Show Hints

The Hints feature provides instant descriptions and help for the tool or feature that you are currently using. In versions 1.0 and 2.0 of the program the Hint details were displayed in a special Hints palette. The palette was located in the Palette Well or under the Window menu. In version 3.0 of the program the same information can be found by clicking the help or hyperlink associated with the feature or tool. See Figure 4.36.

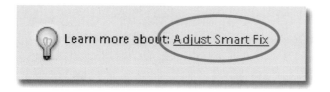 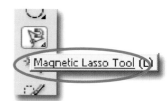

Figure 4.36 *The Hints function is an extension of the Help system and offers the user a detailed explanation of the tool, menu or feature selected and is activated by clicking the hyperlink next to the tool or displayed in the feature palette or dialog.*

The How To feature

Version 2.0: Window > How To
Version 1.0: Window > Show Recipes

The How To palette, known as the Recipes palette in version 1.0 of Elements, is an in-built tutorial system designed to take you step by step through a range of common enhancement and editing activities. Rather than just simple text-by-text instruction, the Recipes are interactive. If you are unable or unsure how to perform a specific step, then you can ask the program to 'Do this step for me'. To make best use of the feature, keep the window open whilst performing each step on your own image. See Figure 4.37.

FEATURE SUMMARY

1 Select Window > How To or click the How To tab in the Palette Well.

2 Choose a recipe category and pick the recipe to use.

3 Work through the step-by-step instructions.

4 Click the 'Do this step for me' link if you are unsure of how to proceed.

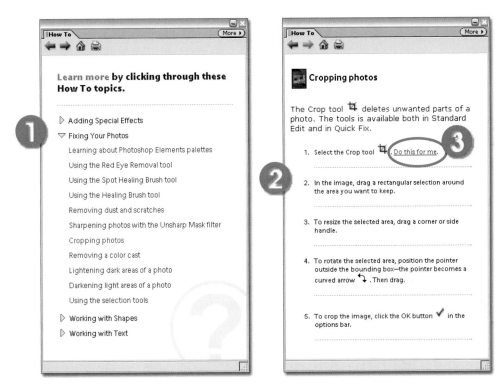

Figure 4.37 *The How To or Recipe palette provides step-by-step tutorials covering major adjustment and enhancement techniques. (1) Recipe groups. (2) Step-by-step instructions. (3) Action buttons.*

Help

The Photoshop Elements help system is centered around the Help dialog (Help > Photoshop Elements Help). See Figure 4.38. From here you can search for and more importantly locate specific information on tools, menu items and program features from the vast array of help files that accompany the program. Over the last few years more and more software companies have published the many pages that detail how their programs work in electronic form rather than weighty paper volumes that used to come with your favorite software. Having the information in this format means that you can easily search for and list all the documents that deal with a specific subject in a matter of seconds. Add to this interactive contents, index and glossary sections and you have a help system that generally supplies answers quickly and is far more efficient than the old software manual.

Forward and back Contents page Print Space to input search topic Search button

Help categories

Help topics

Go to Adobe help online

Help window

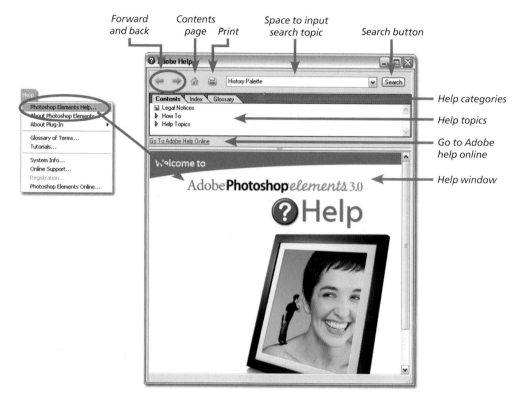

Figure 4.38 *The Help feature in Elements provides a variety of ways to access the massive amount of help files shipped with the package. You can browse through the Contents list, choose from Index headings, locate details in the Glossary or use the Search feature to hunt down the information you need.*

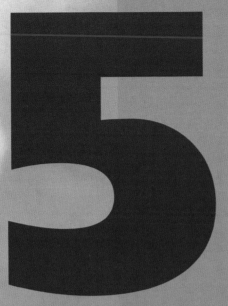

5

Advanced Techniques

Better digital capture

Professional tonal control

Advanced color control

High quality sharpening techniques

Retouching techniques

Adding texture to an image

Changing the size of your images

ADVANCED TECHNIQUES

Photoshop Elements has always been a software program that could produce professional results that go way beyond what you would expect given its modest price. I guess one of the main reasons for this is the fact that so many of the tools and features in the package are built on the same professional-level editing technology that gives Photoshop its strength. So it should come as no surprise when we come across tools and features that are very similar, and in some cases exactly the same as those found in Photoshop. It is these very features when coupled with a professional approach to their use that will get you producing high quality digital photographs just like the pros (but at a fraction of the price!).

Elements 3.0 carries on this tradition by including some great new 'highend' tools for us to play with. The most dramatic of these are the built in RAW import editor (yes just like Photoshop) and the new ability to support 16-bit color pictures. These features might not mean much to you now but this chapter will introduce these and other quality editing tools, techniques and ideas that will ensure that you produce the absolute best quality pictures possible.

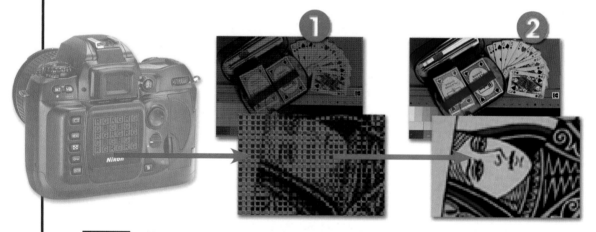

Figure 5.1 *Unlike TIFF and JPEG formats, RAW files contain the unprocessed image and shooting data. In many cameras this visual information is laid out in the Bayer pattern (1) of the original sensor. The RAW data needs to be interpolated to create the full color digital file we normally associate with camera output (2).*

Better digital capture

More and more medium to high end cameras are being released with the added feature of being able to capture and save your pictures in RAW format. Selecting the RAW format stops the camera from processing the color separated (primary) data from the sensor and reducing the image's bit depth, and saves the picture in this unprocessed file type. This means that the full description of what the camera 'saw' is saved in the image file and is available to you for use in the production of quality pictures. Many photographers call this type of file a 'digital negative' as it has a broader dynamic range, extra colors and the ability to correct slightly inaccurate exposures.

Sounds great, doesn't it? All the quality of an information-rich image file to play with, but what is the catch? Well RAW files have to be processed before they can be used in a standard image-editing application. To access the full power of these digital negatives you will need to employ a special dedicated RAW editor. Photoshop Elements 3.0 is the first version of the program to have such an editor built into the program. Designed specifically to allow you to take the unprocessed RAW data directly from your camera's sensor and convert it into a usable image file format, the Elements RAW editor also provides access to several image characteristics that would otherwise be locked into the file format. Variables such as color depth, white balance mode, image sharpness and tonal compensation (contrast and brightness) can all be accessed, edited and enhanced as apart of the conversion process. Performing this type of editing on the full high-bit, RAW data provides a better and higher quality result than attempting these changes after the file has been processed and saved in a non-RAW format such as TIFF or JPEG. See Figure 5.1.

So what is in a RAW file?

To help consolidate these ideas in your mind try thinking of a RAW file as having three distinct parts:

Camera Data, usually called the EXIF or metadata. Including things such as camera model, shutter speed and aperture details, most of which cannot be changed.

Image Data which, though recorded by the camera, can be changed in a RAW editor and the settings chosen here directly affect how the picture will be processed. Changeable options include color depth, white balance, saturation, distribution of image tones and application of sharpness.

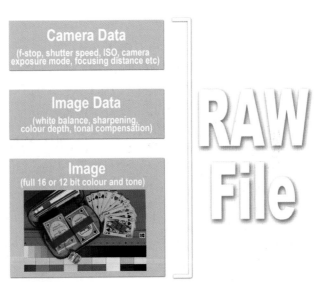

Figure 5.2 *The RAW file is composed of three separate sections: Camera Data, Image Data and the Image itself. By keeping these components separate it is possible to edit variables like white balance and color depth, which are usually a fixed part of the file format, in the RAW file editor.*

The Image itself. This is the data drawn directly from the sensor sites in your camera in a non-interpolated form. For most RAW enabled cameras, this data is supplied with a 16-bit color depth providing substantially more colors and tones to play with when editing and enhancing than found in a standard 8-bit camera file. See Figure 5.2.

RAW processing in action

When you open a RAW file in Elements 3.0 you are presented with a RAW editing dialog containing a full color, interpolated preview of the sensor data. Using a variety of menu options, dialogs and image tools you will be able to interactively adjust image data factors such as tonal distribution and color saturation. Many of these changes can be made with familiar slider controlled editing tools normally found in features like Levels and the Shadows/Highlights control. The results of your editing can be reviewed immediately via the live preview image and associated histogram graphs.

After these general image-editing steps have taken place you can apply some enhancement changes such as filtering for sharpness, removing color noise and applying some smoothing. The final phase of the process involves selecting the color depth and image orientation. Clicking the OK button sets the program into action applying your changes to the RAW file, whilst at the same time interpolating the Bayer data to create a full color image and then opening the processed file into the full Elements work space. See Figure 5.3.

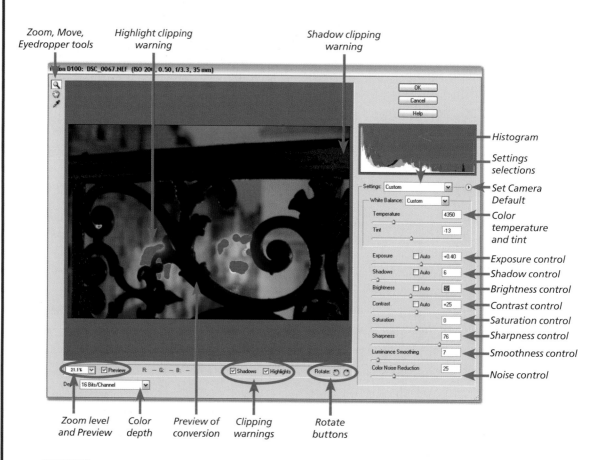

Figure 5.3 *When you attempt to open a RAW file in Elements the RAW editor or plug-in is activated. It provides a range of sophisticated controls for the enhancement and conversion of your RAW files. When you have finished making your changes, you click OK, the plug-in closes and the converted file is placed into the Elements work space.*

Book resources at: **www.guide2elements.com**

The RAW advantage

The real advantages of editing and enhancing at the RAW stage are that these changes are made to the file at the same time as the primary image data is being interpolated to form the full color picture. Editing after the file is processed (saved by the camera in 8-bit versions of the JPEG and TIFF format) means that you will be applying the changes to a picture with fewer tones and colors.

A second bonus for the dedicated RAW shooter is that actions like switching from the white balance option selected when shooting to another choice when processing are performed without any image loss. This is not the case once the file has been processed with the incorrect white balance setting, as anyone who has inadvertently left the tungsten setting switched on whilst shooting in daylight can tell you.

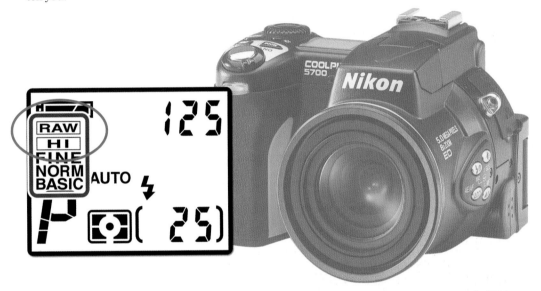

Figure 5.4 *If you want the best quality pictures always make sure that your scanner or camera captures in 16-bit per channel or 48-bit mode. On most cameras this is referred to as the tiff or raw setting.*

Color depth

Each digital file you create (capture or scan) is capable of representing a specific number of colors. This capability, usually referred to as the 'mode' or 'color depth' of the picture, is expressed in terms of the number of 'bits'. Most photos these days are created in 24-bit mode. This means that each of the three color channels (red, green and blue) is capable of displaying 256 levels of color (or 8 bits). When the channels are combined, a 24-bit image can contain a staggering 16.7 million discreet tones/hues.

This is a vast amount of colors and would be seemingly more than we could ever need, see, or print, but many modern cameras and scanners are now capable of capturing up to 16 bits per channel or 'high bit' capture in either RAW or TIFF file formats. This means that each of the three colors can have as many as 65,536 different levels and the image itself a whooping 281,474,976 million colors (last time I counted!). But why would we need to capture so many colors? See Figures 5.4 and 5.5.

More colors equals better quality

Most readers would already have a vague feeling that a high-bit file is 'better' than a low-bit alternative, but understanding why is critical for ensuring the best quality in your own work.

Here are the main advantages in a nutshell:

1 Capturing images in high-bit mode provides a larger number of colors for your camera or scanner to construct your image with. This in turn leads to better color and tone in the digital version of the continuous tone original or scene.

2 Global editing and enhancement changes made to a high-bit file will always yield a better quality result than when the same changes are applied to a low-bit image.

3 Major enhancement of the shadow and highlight areas in a high-bit image is less likely to produce posterized tones than if the same actions were applied to a low-bit version.

4 More gradual changes and subtle variations are possible when adjusting the tones of a high-bit photograph using tools like Levels than is possible with low-bit images.

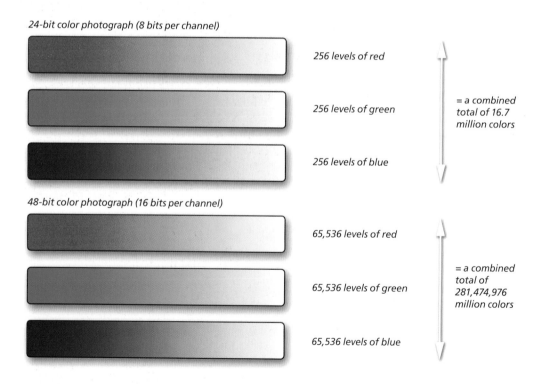

24-bit color photograph (8 bits per channel)

256 levels of red

256 levels of green

256 levels of blue

= a combined total of 16.7 million colors

48-bit color photograph (16 bits per channel)

65,536 levels of red

65,536 levels of green

65,536 levels of blue

= a combined total of 281,474,976 million colors

Figure 5.5 *The higher the bit depth of an image the more levels of tone and numbers of colors it can display.*

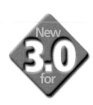

Photoshop Elements is now 16-bit enabled

But why all this talk about 16-bit files? Well Elements 3.0 is now 16-bit enabled. This means that if you have a camera or scanner that is capable of capturing in this mode you can now take advantage of the extra color and tone it provides. 'Fantastic!' you say. 'No more 8-bit tweaking for me, I'm a 16-bit fanatic from here on in.' But there is a catch (you knew there had to be).

Despite the power and sophistication of Elements 3.0, only a subset of its features is available for working on 16-bit files. Of the tools, the Rectangular and Elliptical Marquee and Lasso, Eyedropper, Move and zoom tools all function in this mode. In addition, you can rotate, resize, apply auto levels, auto contrast or auto color correct or use more manual controls such as Levels, Shadow/Highlights and Brightness/Contrast features. The Sharpen, Noise, Blur and Adjustment filter groups also work here as well. Does this mean that making enhancement changes in 16-bit mode is unworkable? No, you just need to use a different approach. Read on.

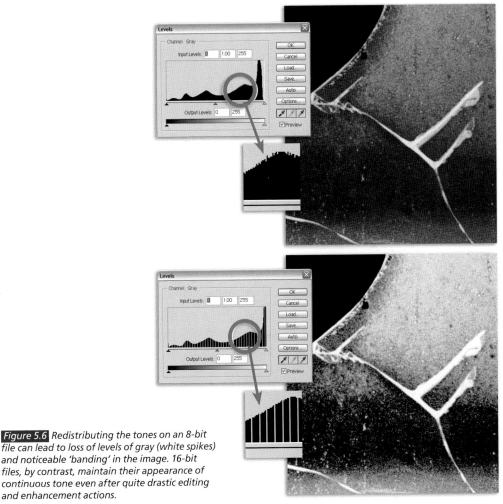

Figure 5.6 Redistributing the tones on an 8-bit file can lead to loss of levels of gray (white spikes) and noticeable 'banding' in the image. 16-bit files, by contrast, maintain their appearance of continuous tone even after quite drastic editing and enhancement actions.

Global versus local enhancement

Some digital photographers break their enhancement tasks into two different sections – global and local.

Global, or those changes that are applied at the beginning of the process and are applied to the whole picture. These include general brightness and contrast changes, some color correction and the application of a little sharpening.

Local changes are those that are more specific and are sometimes applied to just sections of the picture. They may include dodging and burning in, removal or unwanted dust and scratches, the addition of some text and the application of special effects filters.

This separation of enhancement tasks fits neatly with the way that the 16-bit support works in Photoshop Elements 3.0. Global changes can be applied to the photograph whilst it is still in 16-bit mode, the file can then be converted to 8 bits/channel and the local alterations applied. This is the process that the professionals have been using for years and now Elements gives you the power to follow suit.

Common high-bit misconceptions

1 Elements can't handle high-bit images. Not true. The previous version of the program couldn't handle high-bit pictures but Elements 3.0 now uses a reduced feature set with 16-bit images. And even with this limitation there are enough features available to ensure quality enhancement of your images.

2 My camera can only capture in 8-bit mode so high bit doesn't concern me. At your peril. A 16-bit capture mode on your camera would be the ultimate, but failing that, convert your standard camera images to 16-bit before making major global changes. Though not as advantageous as a full 16-bit image your edits will be smoother and less posterized.

3 High-bit images are too big for me to handle and store. Yes high-bit images are twice the file size of 8-bit and this does slow down machines with limited resources, but if this is a concern put up with the inconvenience of a slow machine whilst you make tonal and color changes then convert to a speedier 8-bit file for local changes.

4 I can't use my favorite tools and features in high-bit mode so I don't use high-bit images at all. You are loosing quality in your images needlessly. Perform your global edits in 16-bit mode and then convert to 8-bit for the application of your favorite low-bit techniques.

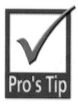

Ensure quality capture and enhancement with 16 bit and RAW files

1 Capture all images in the highest color depth possible. This will help to ensure the best possible detail, tone and color in your pictures.

2 If you have a camera that can capture RAW files then ensure that this feature is activated as well. As it provides the best quality files to work with.

Professional tonal control

The Brightness/Contrast feature that we looked at in the last chapter is a great way to start to change the tones in your images, but as your skill and confidence increase you might find that you want a little more control. Adobe included the Histogram feature and the Levels function from Photoshop in Elements for precisely this reason.

Editor: Window > Histogram

Version 1.0/2.0: Image > Histogram

The first step in taking charge of your pixels is to become aware of where they are situated in your image and how they are distributed between black and white points. The Histogram palette displays a graph of all the pixels in your image. The left-hand side represents the black values, the right the white end of the spectrum. As we already know, in a 24-bit image there are a total of 256 levels of tone possible from black to white – each of these values is represented on the graph. The number of pixels in the image with a particular brightness or tone value is displayed on the graph by height. See Figure 5.7.

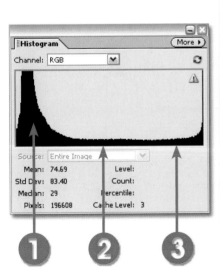

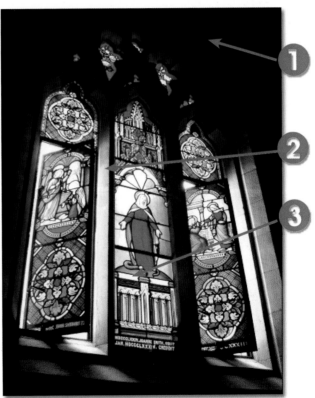

Figure 5.7 *The Histogram provides graph-based information about the spread of pixel tones within your image so that you can see the number of pixels grouped in the shadows (1), midtones (2) and highlights (3) areas.*

Book resources at: **www.guide2elements.com**

ADVANCED TECHNIQUES

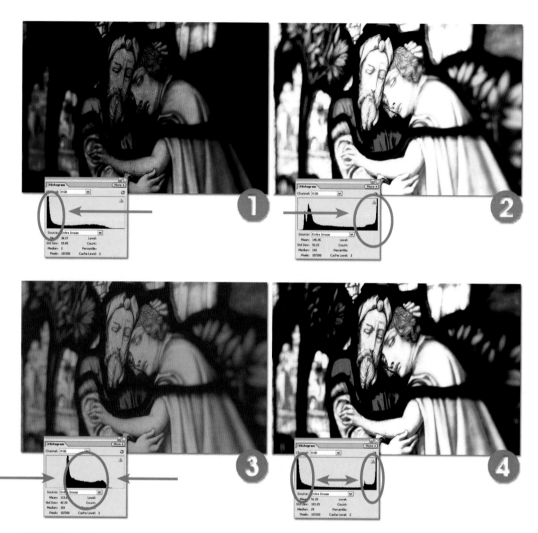

Figure 5.8 *With practice you can diagnose the problems with your photos and predict the way that your picture looks by the shape of the graph in the Histogram palette and the Levels feature. (1) The pixels are bunched to the left end of the graph for underexposed images and (2) to the right end for overexposed ones. (3) Pixels are bunched together in the middle of the graph for flat images. (4) The pixels are spread right out to the left and right edges for contrasty pictures.*

Knowing your images

After a little time viewing the histograms of your images, you will begin to see a pattern in the way that certain styles of photographs are represented. Overexposed pictures will display a large grouping of pixels to the right end of the graph, whereas underexposure will be represented by most pixels bunched to the left. Flat images or those taken on an overcast day will show all pixels grouped around the middle tones and contrasty pictures will display many pixels at the pure white and black ends of the spectrum. See Figure 5.8.

Previously, we have fixed these tonal problems by applying one of the automatic correction features, such as Auto Contrast or Auto Levels, found in Elements or by using a simple slider control such as Brightness/Contrast. All of these tools remap the pixels so that they sit more evenly across the whole of the tonal range of the picture. Viewing the histogram of a corrected picture will show you how the pixels have been redistributed. See Figure 5.9.

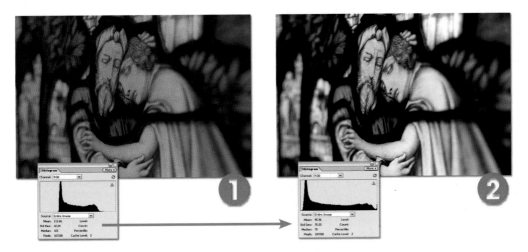

Figure 5.9 *The Auto Levels or Auto Contrast feature redistributes pixels in the graph between the black and white points. (1) Before Auto Levels. (2) After Auto Levels.*

Editor: Enhance > Adjust Lighting > Levels

Version 2.0: Enhance > Adjust Brightness/Contrast > Levels
Version 1.0: Enhance > Brightness/Contrast > Levels

If you want to take more control of the process than is possible with the auto solutions, open the Levels dialog. Looking very similar to the Histogram, this feature allows you to interact directly with the pixels in your image. As well as a graph, the dialog contains two slider bars. The one directly beneath the graph has three triangle controls for black, midtones and white, and represents the input values of the picture. The slider at the bottom of the box shows output settings, and contains black and white controls only. See Figure 5.10.

To adjust the pixels, drag the input shadow (left end) and highlight (right end) controls until they meet the first set of pixels at either end of the graph. When you click OK, the pixels in the original image are redistributed using the new white and black points. Altering the midtone control will change the brightness of the middle values of the image, and moving the output black and white points will flatten, or decrease, the contrast. Clicking the Auto button is like selecting Enhance > Auto Levels from the menu bar.

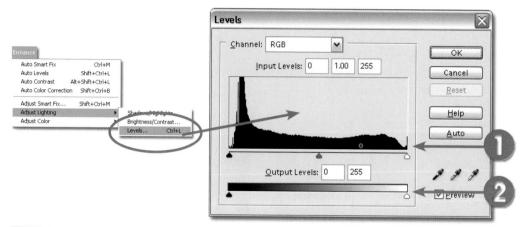

Figure 5.10 *The Levels control allows you to interactively control the spread of pixels within your image.*
(1) Input values. (2) Output values.

Adjusting tones with Levels

Use the following guide to help you make tonal adjustments for your images using levels:

1 *To increase contrast* – Move the input black and white controls to meet the first group of pixels.

2 *To decrease contrast* – Move the output black and white points towards the center of the slider.

3 *To make middle values darker* – Move the input midtone control to the right.

4 *To make middle values lighter* – Move the input midtone control to the left.

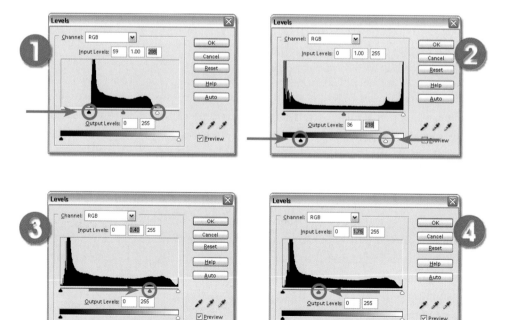

1 Select Enhance > Adjust Lighting > Levels.

2 Change contrast and midtone values by adjusting input and output sliders.

3 Select OK to finish.

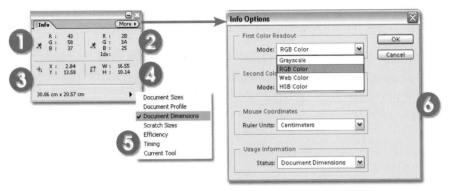

Figure 5.11 The Info dialog displays a readout of the precise values of a group of pixels. (1) First readout. (2) Second readout. (3) Sample position. (4) Selection marquee size. (5) Document information. (6) Info dialog options.

Pegging black and white points

On the right-hand side of the levels dialog is a set of three eyedropper buttons used for sampling the black, gray and white pixels in your image. Designed to give you ultimate control over the tones in your image, these tools are best used in conjunction with the Info palette (Window > Info). See Figure 5.11.

To use this technique, start by making sure that the Info palette is visible and then select the black point eyedropper from the levels dialog. Locate the darkest point in the picture by moving the dropper cursor over your image and watching the values in the Info palette. Your aim is to find the pixels with RGB values as close to 0 as possible. By clicking on the darkest area you will automatically set this point as black in your graph (and your picture). Next, select the white point eyedropper, locate the highest value and again click to set. With highlight and shadow values both pegged, all the values in the picture will be adjusted to suit. When sampling white areas, you should avoid specular highlights such as the shine from the surface of a metallic object, as these parts of the picture contain no printable details. See Figure 5.12.

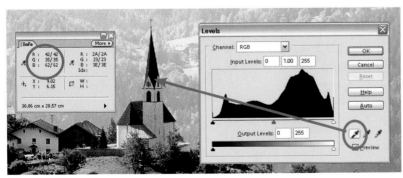

Figure 5.12 With the aid of the details in the Info dialog locate the darkest and lightest points in your picture and peg these with the black and white point eyedroppers from the Levels feature.

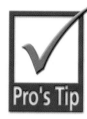

Color correction with the gray point eyedropper

The gray point eyedropper performs in a similar manner to the color cast command. With the tool selected, the user clicks on an area in the picture that should be a neutral gray. The color of the area is changed to neutral gray or equal amounts or red, green and blue, changing with it all the other pixels in the image. This tool is particularly useful for neutralizing color casts.

1 Select Window > Info.

2 Select Enhance > Adjust Lighting > Levels.

3 Peg highlights and shadow areas using the Levels' eyedropper tools and values in the Info palette.

4 Select OK to finish.

Make Levels changes in 16 bit

Levels changes can be performed and indeed should be performed when your photographs are in 16-bit mode. Adjusting your contrast and brightness here will give you much smoother gradation of tones and preserve more detail in your final picture.

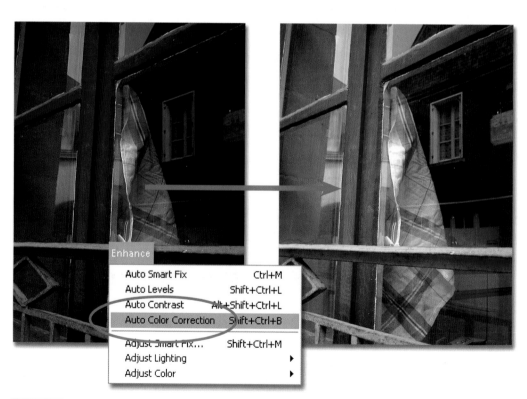

Figure 5.13 *The Auto Color Correction feature provides a one-click solution to most color cast problems.*

Advanced color control

In traditional imaging it is very difficult to manipulate the hues in an image. Thankfully, this is not the case in digital picture making. Fine control over color intensity and location is an integral part of the new technology. Apart from the Variations and Color Cast features that we looked at in the last chapter, Elements also contains the Hue/Saturation command and the Auto Color feature.

Editor: Enhance > Auto Color Correction

Version 2.0: Enhance > Auto Color Correction

This feature works in a similar way to Auto Levels and Auto Contrast in that it identifies the shadows, midtones and highlights in an image and uses these as a basis for image changes. The feature adjusts the contrast of the image by remapping the shadows and highlights to black and white, and neutralizes any color casts by balancing the red, green and blue values in the picture's midtones.

As with most auto functions, this tool works well for the majority of images. For most users this is a good place to start to enhance and correct images, but for those occasions where Auto Color Correction produces poor results then my suggestion is to undo the automatic changes and rework the picture using either the Variations or Color Cast features. See Figure 5.13.

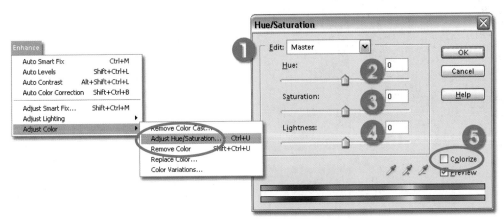

Figure 5.14 *The Hue/Saturation control provides control over the color within your image. (1) Target tones selected for adjustment. (2) Color slider. (3) Strength slider. (4) Lightness slider. (5) Colorize option.*

Editor: Enhance > Adjust Color > Hue/Saturation

Version 2.0: Enhance > Adjust Color > Hue/Saturation
Version 1.0: Enhance > Color > Hue/Saturation

To understand how this feature works you will need to think of the colors in your image in a slightly different way. Rather than using the three-color model (Red, Green, Blue) that we are familiar with, the Hue/Saturation control breaks the image into different components – Hue or color, Saturation or color strength, and Lightness (HSL). See Figure 5.14.

The dialog itself displays slider controls for each component, allowing the user to change each factor independently of the others. Moving the Hue control along the slider changes the dominant color of the image. From left to right, the hue's changes are represented in much the same way as colors in a rainbow. Alterations here will provide a variety of dramatic results, most of which are not realistic and should be used carefully. Moving the Saturation slider to the left gradually decreases the strength of the color until the image is converted to a grayscale. In contrast, adjusting the control to the right increases the purity of the hue and produces images that are vibrant and dramatic. The lightness slider changes the density of the image and works the same way as the Brightness slider in the Brightness/Contrast feature. You can use this feature to make slight adjustments when a color change darkens or lightens the midtones of the image but more critical brightness changes should be made with the Levels feature.

By selecting the Colorize option and then moving the Hue control, it is possible to simulate sepia or blue toned prints. The option converts a colored image to a monochrome made up of a single dominant color and black and white. See Figure 5.15.

1 Select Enhance > Adjust Color > Hue/Saturation.

2 Select Colorize option to make toned prints.

3 Change Hue, Saturation and Lightness by adjusting sliders.

4 Select OK to finish.

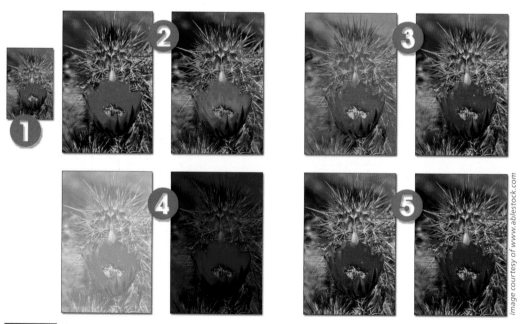

Image courtesy of www.ablestock.com

Figure 5.15 The Hue/Saturation feature provides you with the ability to change the color in your pictures in a variety of ways. (1) Original picture. (2) Moving the Hue slider changes the dominant colors in the image. (3) The Saturation slider controls the strength or purity of colors in the picture. (4) Movements of the Lightness slider control the brightness of the picture.(5) Selecting the Colorize option changes the image to a monochrome, containing tones made up of one main color, white and black. Moving the Hue slider with this option checked produces 'toned' photographs.

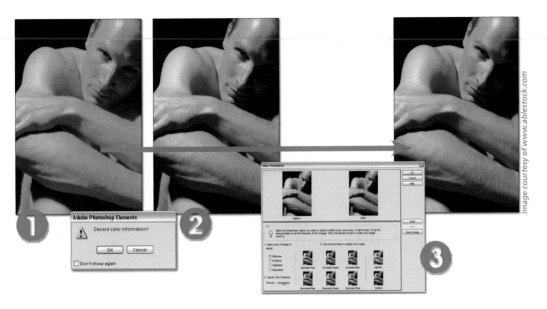

Image courtesy of www.ablestock.com

Figure 5.16 *The Variations control can also be used to tint your monochrome pictures. (1) Start by changing the color photo to grayscale (Image > Mode > Grayscale), (2) then switch the monochrome back into RGB color mode (Image > Mode > RGB Color). (3) Now open the Color Variations control (Enhance > Adjust Color > Color Variations) and click on the thumbnails to tint your picture.*

Editor: Enhance > Adjust Color > Color Variations

Version 2.0: Enhance > Adjust Color > Color Variations
Version 1.0: Enhance > Variations

The variations command that we looked at in the last chapter can also be used to convert full color images to tinted monochromes. First, change your color image to grayscale (Image > Mode > Grayscale), then change the grayscale picture back to RGB Color (Image > Mode > RGB Color). Your image will still appear to be a grayscale but now color can be added. Open the Variations command (Enhance > Adjust Color > Color Variations) and tone your picture by clicking on the appropriate thumbnails. For some users this method might be a little easier to use than the Hue/Saturation command, as the results and color alternatives are previewed and laid out clearly. See Figure 5.16.

1 Open color image.

2 Select Image > Mode > Grayscale to convert your image.

3 Select Image> Mode > RGB Color.

4 Select Enhance > Adjust Color > Color Variations.

5 Adjust strength of the color changes using the Color Intensity slider.

6 Pick the thumbnails to change image color.

7 Check progress by viewing the Before/After thumbnails.

8 Click OK to finish.

FEATURE SUMMARY

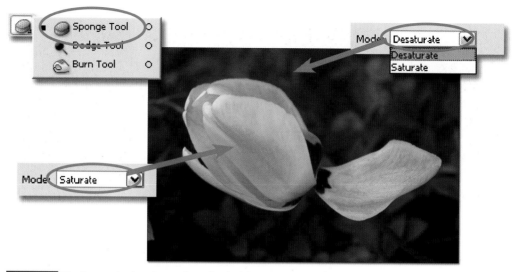

Figure 5.17 *The Sponge tool can be used to selectively increase or decrease the saturation of parts of the image. (1) Desaturate. (2) Saturate.*

Sponge

It is possible to draw a viewer's attention to a particular part of an image by increasing its saturation. The difference in color (contrast) makes the saturated part of the picture a new focal point. The effect can be increased greatly by desaturating (reducing the color strength) the areas around the focal point. The Sponge tool is designed to make such saturation changes to the color within your photos. It can be used to saturate or desaturate and, in grayscale mode, it will even decrease or increase contrast. As with most other tools, size and mode can be changed in the options bar. Changing the Flow settings in the bar alters the rate at which the image saturates or desaturates. See Figure 5.17.

1 Pick the Sponge tool from the toolbox.

2 Select brush size, type and flow rate from the options bar.

3 Select the mode to use – Saturate or Desaturate.

4 Drag over the image part to change.

Editor: Filter > Adjustments > Posterize

Version 2.0/1.0: Image > Adjustments > Posterize

The Posterize feature reduces the number of colors within an image. This produces a graphic design type illustration with areas of flat color from photographic originals. This type of image has very little graduation of tone; instead, it relies on the strength of the colors and shapes that make up the image for effect. The user inputs the number of tones for the images and Elements proceeds to reduce the total palette to the selected few. See Figure 5.18.

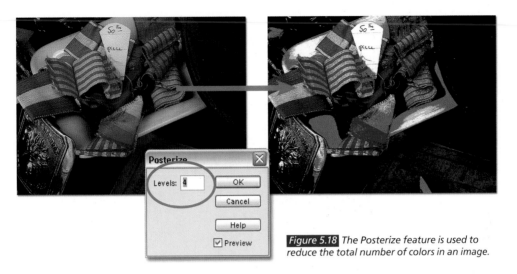

Figure 5.18 The Posterize feature is used to reduce the total number of colors in an image.

FEATURE SUMMARY
1 Select Filter > Adjustments > Posterize.
2 Input the number of levels required.
3 Select OK to finish.

Editor: Filter > Adjustments > Invert

Version 2.0/1.0: Image > Adjustments > Invert

The Invert command produces a negative version of your image. The feature literally swaps the values of each of the image tones. When used on a grayscale image the results are similar to a black and white negative. However, this is not true for a color picture as the inverted picture will not contain the typical orange 'mask' found in color negatives. See Figure 5.19.

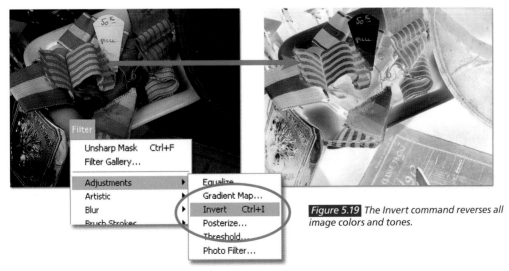

Figure 5.19 The Invert command reverses all image colors and tones.

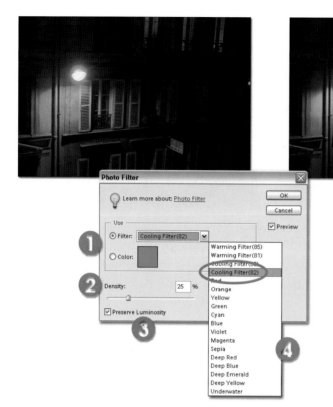

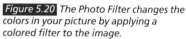

Figure 5.20 The Photo Filter changes the colors in your picture by applying a colored filter to the image.
(1) Filters to select from or use the color swatch to make your own.
(2) Adjust the strength of the filter with the density slider.
(3) Click the Preserve Luminosity option to ensure that the overall brightness of the picture doesn't change.
(4) Preset filter list.

Editor: Filter > Adjustments > Photo Filter

The Photo Filter is a new addition to the feature line-up in Elements, first appearing in the CS version of Photoshop. The tool applies a colored filter to your picture and simulates the effects that traditional photographers could achieve by screwing a colored piece of glass, or gel, to the front of their camera lenses. The change in color that this technique produces can be used for visual effect, such as making a cloudy day appear more sunny (by applying a warm-up filter) or to help correct color cast problems like those displayed in the example. See Figure 5.20. Here a Cooling Filter(82) is applied to the warm image to help eliminate the yellow cast.

Also included in the feature dialog are areas for you to select the exact color of the filter applied, a density slider that controls the strength of the filter and the Preserve Luminosity checkbox that ensures that overall tone of your picture doesn't darken or lighten with your filter changes.

1 Select the Filter > Adjustments > Photo Filter.

2 Ensure that the Preview and Preserve Luminosity options are selected.

3 Pick the filter from the drop-down list or double-click the color swatch to pick the color more precisely.

4 Adjust the density of the filter to suit the image. Click OK to apply.

FEATURE SUMMARY

Book resources at: **www.guide2elements.com**

High quality sharpening techniques

Sometimes, during the image capture process, the picture loses some of the subject's original clarity. This can be especially true if you are scanning small prints or negatives at high resolutions. To help restore some of this lost clarity, it is a good idea to get into the habit of applying sharpening to images straight after capture (although ensure that your digital camera has not already done this as an automatic feature). Elements provides a variety of filters, as well as a specialized tool just for sharpening. We have already looked at the Auto Sharpen option that is available in the Auto Fix dialog of the Photo Browser but here we will examine the other sharpening features Elements has to offer.

I should say from the outset that although these features will improve the appearance of sharpness in an image, it is not possible to use these tools to 'focus' a picture that is blurry. In short, sharpening won't fix problems that arise from poor camera technique; the only solution for this is ensuring that images are focused to start with. That said, let's get sharpening.

Editor: Filter > Sharpen > Sharpen and Sharpen More
Version 2.0/1.0: Filter > Sharpen > Sharpen or Sharpen More

Most digital sharpening techniques are based on increasing the contrast between adjacent pixels in the image. When viewed from a distance, this change makes the picture appear sharper. These two filters are designed to apply basic sharpening to the whole of the image and the only difference between the two is that Sharpen More increases the strength of the sharpening effect. See Figure 5.21.

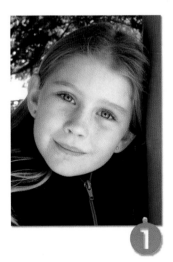 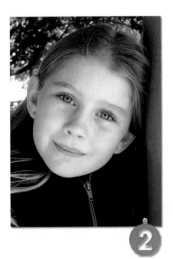 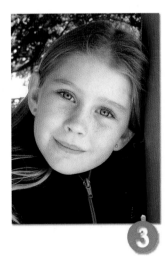

Figure 5.21 *The two basic sharpening filters provide automatic sharpening of all the pixels in your photographs. 1) No Sharpening. (2) The Sharpen filter applied. (3) The Sharpen More filter applied.*

Book resources at: **www.guide2elements.com**

ADVANCED TECHNIQUES

Editor: Filter > Sharpen > Sharpen Edges

Version 2.0/1.0: Filter > Sharpen > Sharpen Edges

One of the problems with sharpening is that sometimes the effect is detrimental to the image, causing areas of subtle color or tonal change to become coarse and pixelated. These problems are most noticeable in image parts such as skin tones and smoothly graded skies. To help solve this problem, Adobe included another filter in Elements, Sharpen Edges, which concentrates the sharpening effects on the edges of objects only. Use this filter when you want to stop the effect being applied to smooth image parts. See Figure 5.22.

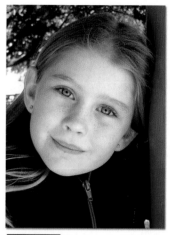

Figure 5.22 The Sharpen Edges filter restricts the effect to the edges of image parts only.

1 Select Filter > Sharpen > Sharpen or Sharpen More for standard sharpening.

2 Select Filter > Sharpen > Sharpen Edges to isolate the sharpening effects to the edges in the image.

Editor: Filter > Sharpen > Unsharp Mask

Version 2.0/1.0: Filter > Sharpen > Unsharp Mask

This feature is based on an old photographic technique for sharpening images that used a slightly blurry mask to increase edge clarity. The digital version offers the user control over the sharpening process via three sliders – Amount, Radius and Threshold. By careful manipulation of the settings of each control the sharpness of images destined for print or screen can be improved. Beware though, too much sharpening is very noticeable and produces problems in the image, such as edge halos, that are very difficult to correct later. See Figure 5.23.

Before using the Unsharp Mask filter, make sure that you are viewing your image at 100%. If you intend to print the sharpened image, make test prints at different settings before deciding on the final values for each control. Repeat this exercise for any pictures where you want the best quality, as the settings for one file might not give the optimum results for another picture that has a slightly higher or lower resolution.

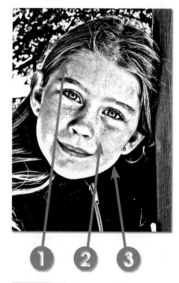

Figure 5.23 Overuse of the Unsharp Mask filter can lead to irreversible problems.
(1) Too much contrast.
(2) Coarse skin tones.
(3) Halos.

The Unsharp Mask controls

The *Amount* slider controls the strength of the sharpening effect. Values of 50–100% are suitable for low-resolution pictures, whereas settings between 150% and 200% can be used on images with a higher resolution. See Figure 5.24.

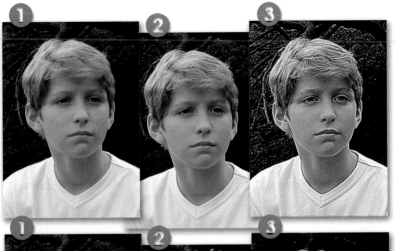

Figure 5.24
The Amount slider controls the strength of the sharpening effect.
(1) Amount = 50%.
(2) Amount = 150%.
(3) Amount = 500%.

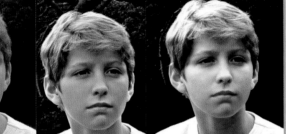
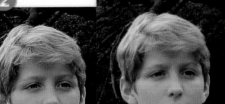
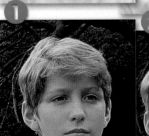

Figure 5.25
The Radius slider determines the number of edge pixels that are sharpened.
(1) Radius = 1.0 pixels.
(2) Radius = 20 pixels.
(3) Radius = 250 pixels.

Figure 5.26
The Threshold slider controls the point at which the effect is applied.
(1) Threshold = 0 levels.
(2) Threshold = 8 levels.
(3) Threshold = 100 levels.

The *Radius* slider value determines the number of pixels around the edge that is effected by the sharpening. A low value only sharpens edge pixels. Typically, values between 1 and 2 are used for high-resolution images, settings of 1 or less for screen images. See Figure 5.25.

The *Threshold* slider is used to determine how different the pixels must be before they are considered an edge and therefore sharpened. A value of 0 will sharpen all the pixels in an image, whereas a setting of 10 will only apply the effect to those areas that are different by at least 10 levels or more

Book resources at: **www.guide2elements.com**

ADVANCED TECHNIQUES

from their surrounding pixels. To ensure that no sharpening occurs in sky or skin tone areas, set this value to 8 or more. See Figure 5.26.

FEATURE SUMMARY

1 Select Filter > Sharpen > Unsharp Mask.

2 Adjust Amount slider to control strength of filter.

3 Adjust Radius slider to control the number of pixels surrounding an edge that is included in the effect.

4 Adjust Threshold slider to control what pixels are considered edge and therefore sharpened.

Elements' sharpening tools

In addition to using a filter to sharpen your image, it is also possible to make changes to specific areas of the picture using one of the two sharpening tools available. The Blur and Sharpen tools are located in the Elements toolbox. See Figure 5.27.

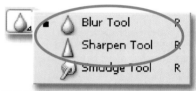

Figure 5.27 *The Blur and Sharpen tools can be used to apply sharpening to specific areas within an image.*

The size of the area they change is based on the current brush size. The intensity of the effect is controlled by the Strength value found in the options bar. As with the airbrush tool, the longer you keep the mouse button down the more pronounced the effect will be. These features are particularly useful when you want to change only small parts of an image rather than the whole picture. See Figure 5.28.

FEATURE SUMMARY

1 Select the Blur or Sharpen tool from the toolbox.

2 Adjust the size and style of the tool with the Brush palette in the options bar.

3 Change the intensity of the effect by altering the Strength setting.

4 Blur or sharpen areas of the image by clicking and dragging the tool over the picture surface.

5 Increase the change in any one area by holding the mouse button down.

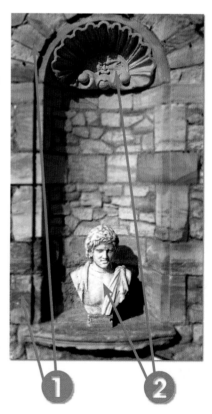

Figure 5.28 *The Sharpen/Blur tools can be used to direct the eye of the viewer by making some areas of an image more prominent than others. (1) Blurred area. (2) Sharpened area.*

Retouching techniques

Used for more than just enhancing existing details, these techniques are designed to rid images of visual information, like dust and scratches, which can distract from the main picture.

Editor: Filter > Noise > Dust & Scratches

Version 2.0/1.0: Filter > Noise > Dust & Scratches

It seems that no matter how careful I am, my scanned images always contain a few dust marks. The Dust & Scratches filter in Elements helps to eliminate these annoying spots by blending or blurring the surrounding pixels to cover the defect. The settings you choose for this filter are critical if you are to maintain image sharpness whilst removing small marks. Too much filtering and your image will appear blurred, too little and the marks will remain. See Figure 5.29.

To find settings that provide a good balance, first try adjusting the threshold setting to zero. Next, use the preview box in the Filter dialog to highlight a mark that you want to remove. Use the zoom controls to enlarge the view of the defect. Now drag the Radius slider to the right. Find, and set, the lowest radius value where the mark is removed. Next, increase the threshold value gradually until the texture of the image is restored and the defect is still removed. See Figure 5.30.

1 Select Filter > Noise > Dust & Scratches.

2 Move preview area to highlight a mark to be removed.

3 Zoom the preview to enlarge the view of the mark.

4 Ensure that the threshold value is set to zero.

5 Adjust Radius slider until the mark disappears.

6 Adjust threshold until texture returns and mark is still not visible.

7 Click OK to finish.

FEATURE SUMMARY

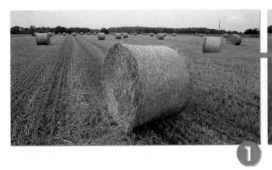 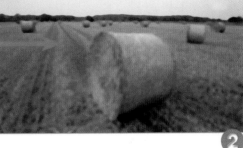

Figure 5.29 *Too much Dust & Scratches filtering can destroy image detail and make the picture fuzzy. (1) Original picture. (2) Photo after too much dust and scratches filtration.*

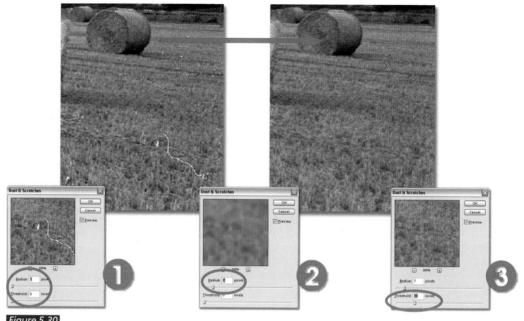

Figure 5.30
Follow the three-step process to ensure that you choose the optimal settings for the Dust & Scratches filter. (1) Set both sliders to minimum (all the way to the left). Preview the dust mark area. (2) Adjust the Radius slider until the mark disappears. (3) Raise the Threshold slider to regain texture in the non-marked area of the image.

Clone Stamp

In some instances the values needed for the Dust & Scratches filter to erase or disguise picture faults are so high that it makes the whole image too blurry for use. In these cases it is better to use a tool that works with the problem area specifically rather than the whole picture surface.

The Clone Stamp tool samples an area of the image and then paints with the texture, color and tone of this copy onto another part of the picture. This process makes it a great tool to use for removing scratches or repairing tears or creases in a photograph. Backgrounds can be sampled and then painted over dust or scratch marks, and whole areas of a picture can be rebuilt or reconstructed using the information contained in other parts of the image. See Figure 5.31.

Using the Clone Stamp tool is a two-part process. The first step is to select the area that you are going to use as a sample by Alt-clicking (Windows) or Option-clicking (Macintosh) the area. See Figure 5.32. Now move the cursor to where you want to paint and click and drag to start the process. See Figure 5.33.

The size and style of the sampled area are based on the current brush and the opacity setting controls the transparency of the painted section.

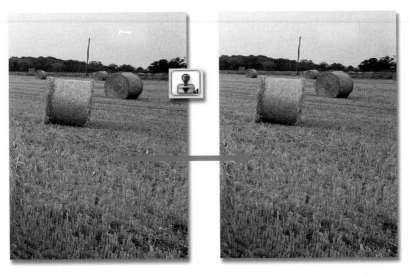

Figure 5.31 *The Clone Stamp tool is perfect for retouching the marks that the Dust & Scratches filter cannot erase.*

1 Pick the Clone Stamp tool from the toolbox.

2 Adjust the brush size via the brush palette in the options bar.

3 Set the opacity for the painted area.

4 Position the mouse cursor on a part of the image you want to sample and Alt-click (Windows) or Option-click (Macintosh) to set.

5 Move the tool to the area of the image you want to use the sample to cover and click-drag to paint.

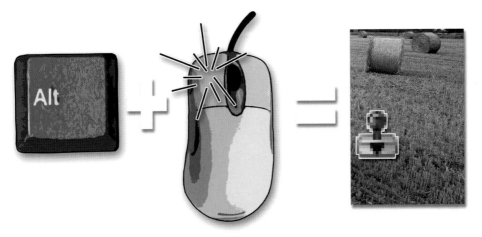

Figure 5.32 *Alt-click (Windows) or Option-click (Macintosh) to mark the area to be sampled.*

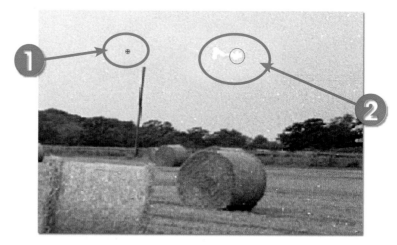

Figure 5.33 *Move the cursor over the mark and click to paint over with the sampled texture. (1) Sample point. (2) Retouching area.*

Spot Healing Brush

In recognition of just how tricky it can be to get seamless dust removal with the Clone Stamp tool, Adobe decided to include the Spot Healing Brush in Elements 3.0. After selecting the tool you adjust the size of the brush tip using the options in the tool's option bar and then click on the dust spots and small marks in your pictures. The Spot Healing Brush uses the texture that surrounds the mark as a guide to how the program should 'paint over' the area. In this way, Elements tries to match color, texture and tone whilst eliminating the dust mark. The results are terrific and this tool should be the one that you reach for first when there is a piece of dust or a hair mark to remove from your photographs. See Figure 5.34.

FEATURE SUMMARY
1 Locate the areas to be repaired.
2 Adjust the brush size to suit the size of the mark.
3 Click on the spot to repair.

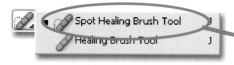

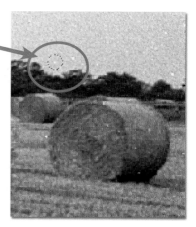

Figure 5.34 *The Spot Healing Brush tool is designed for quick, accurate repair of dust and hair marks. To use simply select the tool, adjust the size of the brush tip to suit the dust mark and then paint it out.*

Healing Brush tool

The Clone Stamp tool is good but the best way to remove unwanted detail from your pictures is with the amazing new Healing Brush tool. Designed to work in a similar way to the Clone tool, the user selects the area (Alt-click) to be sampled before painting and then proceeds to drag the brush

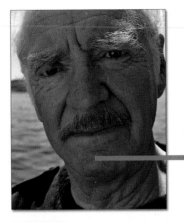

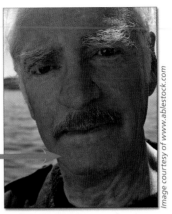

Image courtesy of www.ablestock.com

Figure 5.35 *The new Healing Brush tool works wonders for removing unwanted details. It even can provide a little digital plastic surgery when required.*

tip over the area to be repaired. The tool achieves such great results by merging background and source area details as you paint. Just as with the Clone Stamp tool the size and edge hardness of the current brush determines the characteristics of the Healing Brush tool tip.

One of the best ways to demonstrate the shear power of the Healing Brush is to remove the wrinkles from an aged face. Though I'm not sure of the ethics of such an action it is a request that is often put to me. In the example, the deep crevices of the fisherman's face have been easily removed with the tool. The texture, color and tone of the face remain even after the 'healing' work is completed because the tool merges the new areas with the detail of the picture beneath. See Figure 5.35.

FEATURE SUMMARY

1 The first step is to locate the areas of the image that need to be retouched.

2 Hold down the Alt key (Opt key – Mac) and click on the area that will be used as a sample for the brush. Notice that the cursor changes to cross hairs to indicate the sample area.

3 Move the cursor to the area to heal and click and drag the mouse to 'paint' over the problem picture part. After you release the mouse button Elements merges the newly painted section with the image beneath. See Figure 5.36.

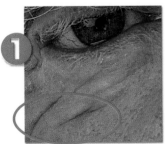
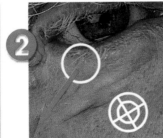
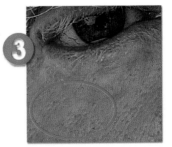

Figure 5.36 *(1) Locate the areas to be healed. (2) Alt-click the source that you will use in the repairs. (3) Drag the brush tip over the area to be repaired.*

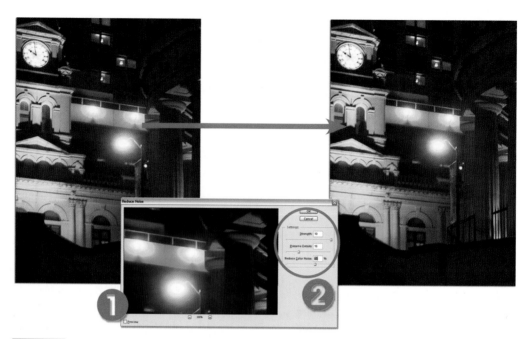

Figure 5.37 *The new Reduce Noise filter is great for making pictures taken when your camera is set on a high ISO value, less noisy. (1) Preview. (2) Noise reduction controls.*

Editor: Filter > Noise > Reduce Noise

Many new digital cameras have a variety of ISO settings to choose from. When shooting in sunny, or bright conditions you generally use values of 100 or 200 giving sharp and noise-free results, but when you select a higher value such as 1600 for use at night, or in low light, the resultant pictures can become very noisy. Many camera manufacturers included Noise Reduction features as part of the camera functions but sometimes the length of time the camera takes to process the file means that it is almost impossible to take a series of night-time pictures rapidly. If this is your requirement then you are stuck with grainy photographs because you have had to shoot with the Noise Reduction feature turned off.

With just this sort of problem in mind, the Adobe engineers included a new Noise Reduction filter (Filter > Noise > Reduce Noise) in Elements 3.0. The feature includes a preview window, a Strength slider, a Preserve Details control and a Reduce Color Noise slider. As with the Dust and Scratches filter you need to be careful when using this filter to ensure that you balance removing noise whilst also retaining detail.

The best way to guarantee this is to set your strength setting first ensuring that you check the results in highlights, midtone and shadow areas. Next gradually increase the preserve details value until you reach the point where the level of noise that is being reintroduced into the picture is noticeable and then back off the control slightly (make the setting a lower number). For photographs with a high level of color noise (random speckles of color in an area that should be a smooth flat tone) you will need to adjust this slider at the same time as you are playing with the Strength control.

FEATURE SUMMARY

1 Open the noisy image and select the Filter > Noise > Reduce Noise filter.

2 Drag the Preserve Details slider to the left and then gradually move the Strength slider to the right until the noise is at an acceptable level.

3 Now slowly move the Preserve Details slider to the right until there is an acceptable balance between detail and noise in your picture.

Adding texture to an image

At first, the idea of making a smooth, evenly graduated image more textured seems to be at odds with the general direction that digital technology has been heading over the last few years. Research scientists and technicians have spent much time and money ensuring that the current crop of cameras, scanners and printers is able to capture and produce images so that they are in effect texture- or grainless. The aim has been to disguise the origins of the final print so that the pixels cannot be seen.

For me to introduce to you at this stage a few techniques that intentionally add noticeable texture to your image may seem a little strange, but despite the intentions of the manufacturers, many digital image makers do like the atmosphere and mood that a 'grainy' picture conveys. See Figure 5.38. All the techniques use filters to alter the look of the image. Filter changes are permanent, so it is always a good idea to keep a copy of the unaltered original file on your hard drive, just in case.

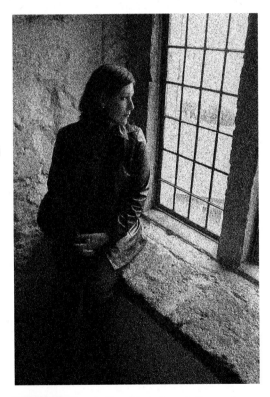

Figure 5.38 Despite the all techniques in the previous section which were designed to reduce the marks in our pictures there are many photographers who like texture and who regularly use other techniques to intentionally put back desirable textures into their photographs.

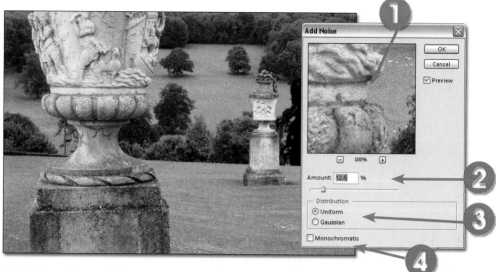

Figure 5.39 *Use the Add Noise filter for basic texture additions. (1) Preview thumbnail. (2) Filter strength. (3) Noise type. (4) Monochromatic checkbox.*

Editor: Filter > Noise > Add Noise

Version 2.0/1.0: Filter > Noise > Add Noise

The Add Noise filter is one of four options contained under the Noise heading in the Filter menu. Using this feature adds extra contrasting pixels to your image to simulate the effect of high-speed film. See Figure 5.39. When the filter is selected, you are presented with a dialog that contains several choices. A small zoomable thumbnail window is provided so that you can check the appearance of the filter settings on your image. There is also the option to preview the results on the greater image by ticking the Preview box. The strength of the effect is controlled by the Amount slider and the type of noise can be switched from Uniform, a more even effect, to Gaussian, for a speckled appearance. The Monochromatic option adds pixels that contrast in tone only and not color to the image. See Figure 5.40.

1 Select the Add Noise filter from the Noise section of the Filter menu.

2 Adjust thumbnail preview to a view of 100% and tick the Preview option.

3 Select Uniform for an even distribution of new pixels across the image, or pick Gaussian for a more speckled effect.

4 Tick the Monochromatic option to restrict the effect to changes in the tone of pixels rather than color.

5 Adjust the Amount slider to control the strength of the filter, checking the results in both the thumbnail and full image previews.

6 Click OK to finish.

FEATURE SUMMARY

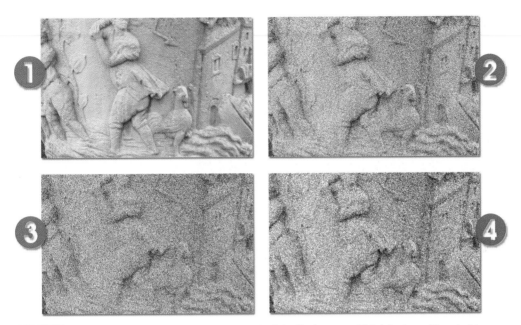

Figure 5.40 *The Add Noise filter settings control the look of the final texture. (1) Original non-filtered picture. (2) Uniform Distribution selected. (3) Gaussian Distribution selected. (4) Uniform Distribution and Monochrome settings selected.*

Editor: Filter > Texture > Grain

Version 2.0/1.0: Filter > Texture > Grain

Found under the Texture option in the Filter menu, the Grain filter, at first glance, appears to offer the same style of texture changes as the Add Noise feature, but the extra controls in the dialog give the user the chance to add a range of different texture types to their images. See Figure 5.41.

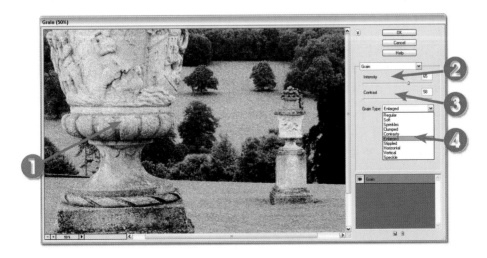

Figure 5.41 *The Grain filter provides a little more control over the type of texture that is added to your images. (1) Preview thumbnail. (2) Filter strength. (3) Effect contrast. (4) Grain style.*

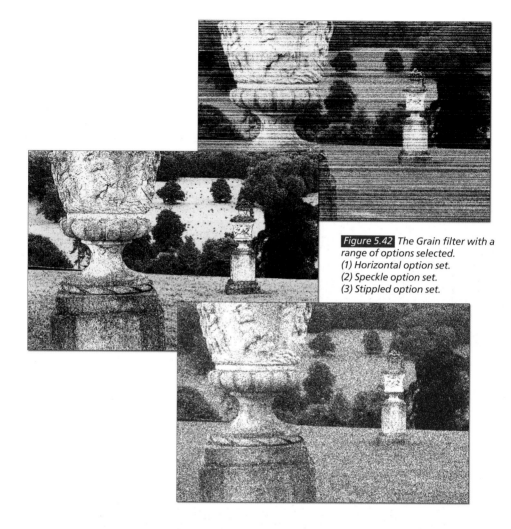

Figure 5.42 The Grain filter with a range of options selected.
(1) Horizontal option set.
(2) Speckle option set.
(3) Stippled option set.

The dialog provides a thumbnail preview of filter changes. The Intensity slider controls the strength of the effect and the Contrast control alters the overall appearance of the filtered image. The Grain Type menu provides 10 different choices of the style of texture that will be added to the image. By manipulating these three settings, it is possible to create some quite different and stunning texture effects. See Figure 5.42.

1 Select the Grain filter from the Texture section of the Filter menu.

2 Adjust thumbnail preview to a view of 100%.

3 Select Grain Type from the menu.

4 Adjust the Intensity slider to control the strength of the filter, checking the results in the thumbnail preview.

5 Alter the Contrast slider to change the overall appearance of the image.

6 Click OK to finish.

FEATURE SUMMARY

Editor: Filter > Texture > Texturizer

Version 2.0/1.0: Filter > Texture > Texturizer

The Texturizer filter provides a slightly different approach to the process of adding textures to images. With this feature much more of the original image detail is maintained. The picture is changed to give the appearance that the photo has been printed onto the surface of the texture. The Scaling and Relief sliders control the strength and visual dominance of the texture, whilst the Light Direction menu alters the highlight and shadow areas. See Figure 5.43. Different surface types are available from the Texture drop-down menu. See Figure 5.44. The feature also contains the option to add your own files and have these used as the texture that is applied by the filter to the image.

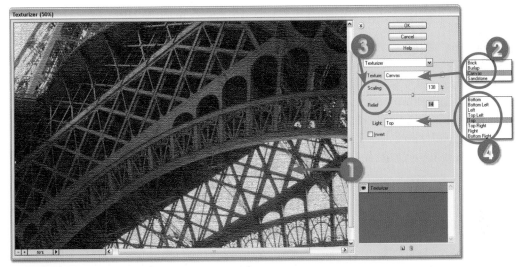

Figure 5.43 *The Texturizer filter changes the image so that it appears to have been printed onto a textured surface. (1) Preview thumbnail. (2) Texture type. (3) Texture settings. (4) Light direction.*

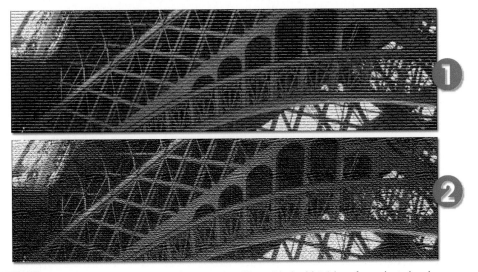

Figure 5.44 *The example is textured using the Texturizer filter with the (1) Brick surface selected and (2) Burlap surface selected.*

ADVANCED TECHNIQUES

1 Select the Texturizer filter from the Texture section of the Filter menu.

2 Adjust thumbnail preview to a view of 100%.

3 Select Texture type from the drop-down menu.

4 Move the Scaling slider to change the size of the texture.

5 Adjust the Relief slider to control the dominance of the filter.

6 Select a Light Direction to adjust the highlights and shadow areas of the texture.

7 Tick the Invert box to switch the texture position from 'hills' to 'valleys' or reverse the texture's light and dark tones.

8 Click OK to finish.

Making your own textures

Being able to make your own texture files is the real bonus of the Texturizer filter. This ability gives the user the chance to extend the available surface options by adding customized Elements files that have been designed, or captured, especially for the purpose. Any Elements or Photoshop file (.PSD) can be loaded as a new texture via the Load Texture option in the side-arrow menu, top right of the Texturizer dialog. Simply locate the file using the browsing window and then adjust the Scaling, Relief and Lighting controls as you would for any of the built-in surface options.

1 Shoot, scan or design a texture image and save as an Elements or Photoshop file (.PSD). See Figure 5.45.

2 Select the Texturizer filter from the Texture options of the Filters menu.

3 Pick the Load Texture item from the drop-down list in the Texture menu. See Figure 5.46.

4 Browse folders and files to locate texture file.

5 Click file name and then open to select.

6 Once back at the Texturizer dialog, treat like any other surface option. See Figure 5.47.

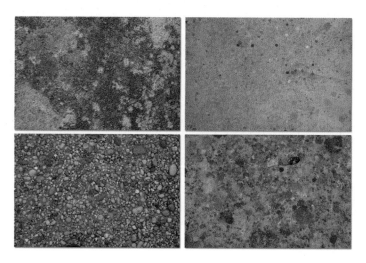

Figure 5.45 Shoot your own texture photos and save the images as an Elements or PSD file.

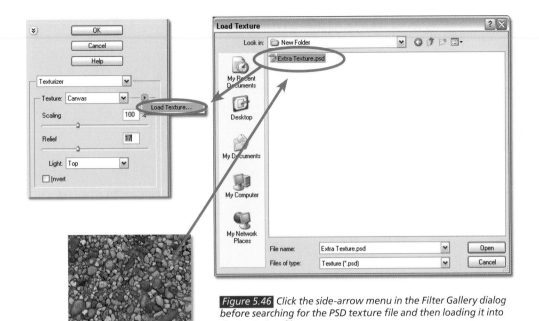

Figure 5.46 Click the side-arrow menu in the Filter Gallery dialog before searching for the PSD texture file and then loading it into the texturizer filter.

Figure 5.47 Apply the new texture to your image.

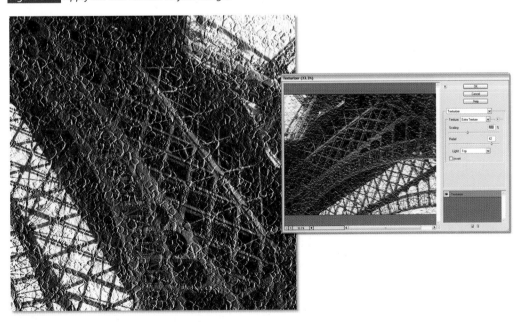

Changing the size of your images

As we have seen in earlier chapters, the size of a digital image is measured in pixel dimensions. These dimensions are determined at the time of capture or creation. Occasionally, it is necessary to alter the size of your digital photograph to suit different output requirements. For instance, if you want to display an image that was captured in high resolution on a website, you will need to reduce the pixel dimensions of the file to suit.

Grouped under the Resize option of the Image menu, Elements provides a couple of sizing features which can be used to alter the dimensions of your picture. PROCEED WITH CAUTION. Increasing or decreasing the dimensions of your images directly affects the quality of your files, so my suggestion is that until you are completely at home with these controls always make a backup file of your original picture before starting to resize.

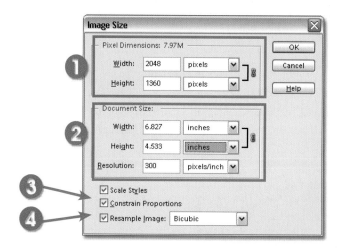

Figure 5.48 The Image Size dialog controls the dimensions and resolution of your pictures. (1) Pixel Dimensions section. (2) Document Size section. (3) Constrain Proportions checkbox. (4) Resample checkbox and drop-down menu.

Editor: Image > Resize > Image Size

Version 2.0/1.0: Image > Resize > Image Size

The Image Size dialog provides several options for manipulating the pixels in your photograph. At first glance the settings displayed here may seem a little confusing, but if you can make the distinction between the Pixel Dimensions of the image (shown in the topmost section of the dialog) and the Document Size (shown in the middle), it will be easier to understand. See Figure 5.48.

Pixel Dimensions represent the true digital size of the file.

Document Size is the physical dimensions of the file represented in inches (or centimeters) based on using a specific number of pixels per inch (resolution or dpi).

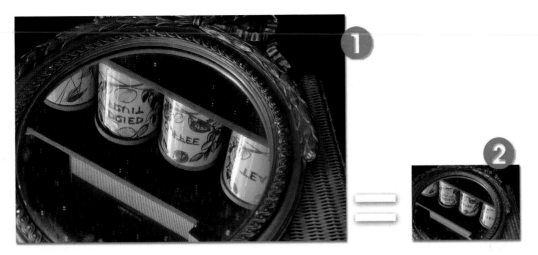

Figure 5.49 *The example image contains 1800 × 1200 pixels and can be output to a print that is 6 inches × 4 inches or 1.8 inches × 1.2 inches, depending on how the pixels are spread (resolution).*
(1) 6 × 4 inches @ 300 dpi = 1800 × 1200 pixels. (2) 1.8 × 1.2 inches @ 1000 dpi = 1800 × 1200 pixels.

Non-detrimental size changes

A file with the same pixel dimensions can have several different document sizes based on altering the spread of the pixels when the picture is printed (or displayed on screen). In this way you can adjust a high-resolution file to print the size of a postage stamp, postcard or a poster by only changing the dpi or resolution. This type of resizing has no detrimental quality effects on your pictures as the original pixel dimensions remain unchanged. See Figure 5.49.

To change resolution, open the Image Size dialog and uncheck the Resample Image option. Next, change either the resolution, width or height settings to suit your output. See Figure 5.50.

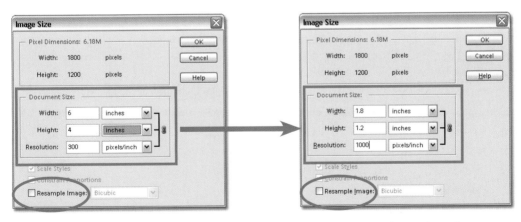

Figure 5.50 *Non-detrimental size changes, or the changes that don't lose picture quality, can be made to your image if the Resample Image option is always left unchecked.*

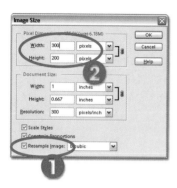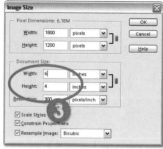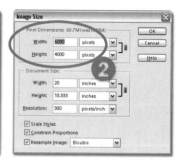

Figure 5.51 *With the Resample Image option selected, it is possible to increase and decrease the total number of pixels in your image. (1) Resample Image option ticked. (2) New pixels' dimensions. (3) New document size.*

Upsizing and downsizing

This said, in some circumstances it is necessary to increase or decrease the number of pixels in an image. Both these actions will produce results that have less quality than if the pictures were scanned or photographed at precisely the desired size at the time of capture. If you are confronted with a situation where you are unable to recapture your pictures, then Elements can increase or decrease the image's pixels' dimensions. Each of these steps requires the program to interpolate, or 'make up', the pixels that form the resized image. See Figure 5.51. To increase the pixels or upsize the image, tick the Resample Image checkbox and then increase the value of any of the dimension settings in the dialog. To decrease the pixels or downsize the image, decrease the value of the dimension settings.

Image Size dialog settings

To keep the ratio of width and height of the new image the same as the original, tick the Constrain Proportions checkbox.

Interpolation quality and speed are determined by the options in the drop-down menu next to the Resample Image checkbox. Bicubic is the best setting for photographic images.

FEATURE SUMMARY

1 Select Image Size from the Resize option under the Image menu.

2 Tick the Resample Image checkbox for changes to the pixels' dimensions of your image.

3 Uncheck the Resample Image option for changing image resolution.

4 Adjust the dimension settings to suit your output requirements.

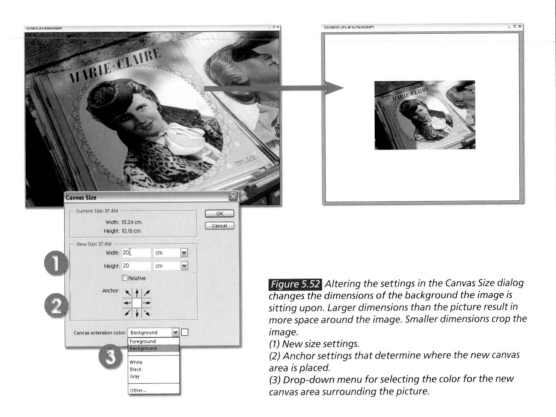

Figure 5.52 Altering the settings in the Canvas Size dialog changes the dimensions of the background the image is sitting upon. Larger dimensions than the picture result in more space around the image. Smaller dimensions crop the image.
(1) New size settings.
(2) Anchor settings that determine where the new canvas area is placed.
(3) Drop-down menu for selecting the color for the new canvas area surrounding the picture.

Editor: Image > Resize > Canvas Size

Version 2.0/1.0: Image > Resize > Canvas Size

Just to add a little more complexity to the picture size discussion, Elements also provides the ability to change the size of the canvas that your photograph is sitting upon. Alterations here result in no change to the size of the image, but rather are reflected in the visual space that the picture sits in.

This feature is particularly useful if you want to add several images together. Increasing the canvas size will mean that each of the extra pictures can be added to the newly created space around the original image.

To change the canvas size, select Canvas Size from the Resize selection of the Image menu and alter the settings in the New Size section of the dialog. You can control the location of the new space in relation to the original image by clicking one of the sections in the Anchor diagram. Leaving the default setting here will mean that the canvas change will be spread evenly around the image. See Figure 5.52.

FEATURE SUMMARY

1 Select Canvas Size from the Resize option under the Image menu.

2 Alter the values in the New Size section of the dialog.

3 Set the anchor point in the Anchor diagram.

4 Click OK to complete.

Pro's Tip

Increasing the canvas size with the Crop tool

Pros use the crop tool to quickly increase the size of the canvas that the picture sits in. First zoom out from the picture so that it sits smaller in the work space, then select the Crop tool and drag a marquee around the whole image. After releasing the mouse button, click on one of the side or corner handles and drag the crop marquee outwards until it is the size and shape of the new canvas. Double-click to complete the canvas resize. The new canvas will be the color of the current background color. See Figure 5.53.

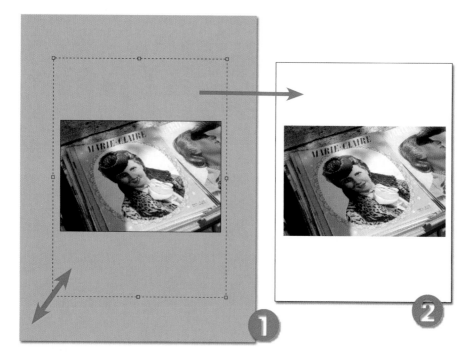

Figure 5.53 *The Crop tool can be used to increase the size of the canvas by dragging the crop marquee outside the dimensions of the picture. (1) Make the crop marquee larger than the picture. (2) Double-click inside the crop marquee to increase the canvas size.*

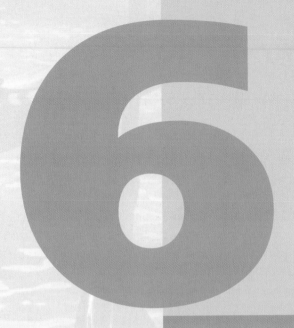

6

Using Selections and Layers

Selection basics

Modifying selections

Selections in action

Layers and their origins

Layers in action

For those users who are a little familiar with both selections and layers, it might seem a bit strange to group these features together, but to my mind they both deal with a similar idea – isolating specific sections of an image to make them easier to manipulate. They also represent two Elements features that are central to many advanced manipulation and enhancement techniques.

Selection basics

Until now, we have assumed that any changes being made to an image will be applied to the whole of the picture, but before too long it will become obvious that there are many imaging scenarios that would benefit from being able to restrict alterations to a specific part of a picture. For this reason, most image-editing packages contain features that allow the user to isolate small sections of an image that can then be altered independently of the rest of the picture.

When a selection is made, the edges of the isolated area are indicated by a flashing dotted line, which is sometimes referred to as the 'marching ants'. See Figure 6.1. When a selection is active, any changes made to the image will be restricted to the isolated area. See Figure 6.2. To resume full image-editing mode, the area has to be Deselected (Select > Deselect).

The selection features contained in Elements can be divided into two groups:

• *Drawing selection tools*, or those that are based on selecting pixels by drawing a line around the part of the image to be isolated.

• *Color selection tools*, or those features that distinguish between image parts based on the color or tone of the pixels.

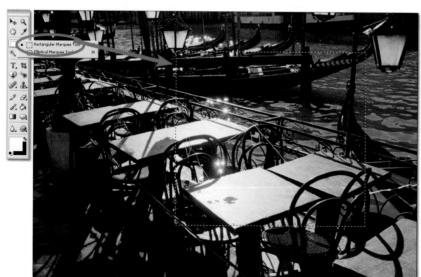

Figure 6.1 The edges of an active selection are indicated using a flashing dotted line or 'marching ants'.

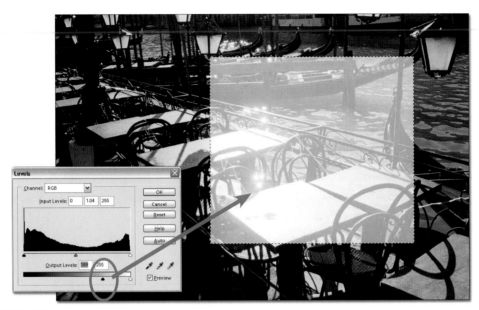

Figure 6.2 *Image alterations made when a selection is active are restricted to the area of the selection.*

Drawing selection tools (see Figures 6.3 and 6.4)

The new Selection Brush tool, along with the tools contained in the Marquee and Lasso tool sets, are used to draw around the pixels in an image.

Marquee tools

By clicking and dragging the Rectangular or Elliptical Marquees, it is possible to draw rectangle- and oval-shaped selections. Holding down the Shift key whilst using these tools will restrict the selection to square or circular shapes, whilst using the Alt (Windows) or Options (Mac) keys will draw the selections from their centers. The Marquee tools are great for isolating objects in your images that are regular in shape, but for less conventional shapes you will need to use one of the Lasso tools.

Lasso tools

The normal Lasso tool works like a pencil, allowing the user to draw freehand shapes for selections. In contrast, the Polygonal Lasso tool draws straight edge lines between mouse-click points. Either of these features can be used to outline and select irregular-shaped image parts. See Figure 6.5.

A third tool, the Magnetic Lasso, helps with the drawing process by aligning the outline with the edge of objects automatically. See Figure 6.6. It uses contrast in color and tone as a basis for determining the edge of an object. The accuracy of the 'magnetic' features of this tool is determined by three settings in the tool's options bar. See Figure 6.7. Edge Contrast is the value that a pixel has to differ from its neighbor to be considered an edge. Width is the number of pixels either side of the

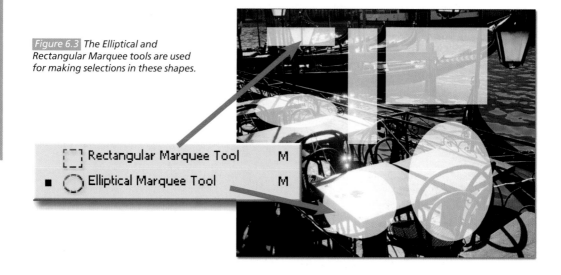

Figure 6.3 *The Elliptical and Rectangular Marquee tools are used for making selections in these shapes.*

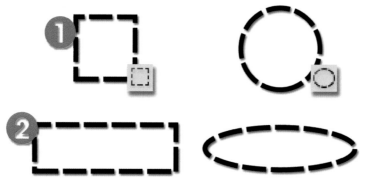

Figure 6.4 *Holding down the Shift key when using the Marquee tools will constrain the selection to either a square or a circle.*
(1) Constrained.
(2) Unconstrained.

pointer that are sampled in the edge determination process and Frequency is the distance between fastening points in the outline. For most tasks, the Magnetic Lasso is a quick way to obtain accurate selections, so it is good practice to try this tool first when you want to isolate specific image parts.

Selection Brush tool

Responding to photographers' demands for even more options for making selections, Adobe included the Selection Brush for the first time in version 2.0 of Elements. The tool lets you paint a selection onto your image. The size, shape and edge softness of the selection are based on the brush properties you currently have set. These can be altered in the brush presets pop-up palette located in the options bar. See Figure 6.8.

Image courtesy of www.ablestock.com

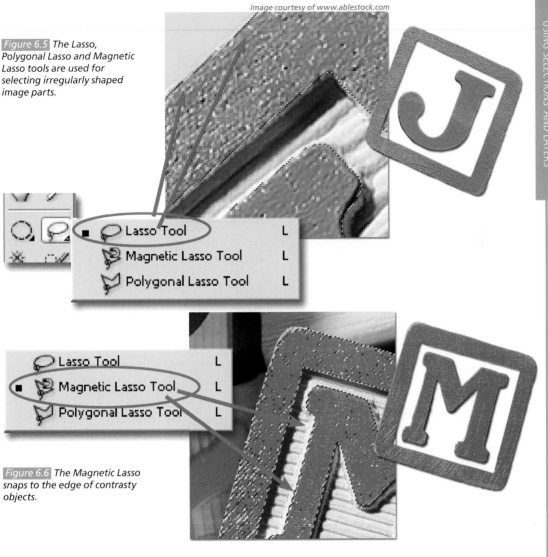

Figure 6.5 *The Lasso, Polygonal Lasso and Magnetic Lasso tools are used for selecting irregularly shaped image parts.*

Figure 6.6 *The Magnetic Lasso snaps to the edge of contrasty objects.*

Figure 6.7 *The settings in the Magnetic Lasso's options bar alter how the tool snaps to the outline of particular image parts.*

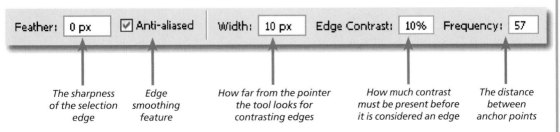

Feather: 0 px   ☑ Anti-aliased   Width: 10 px   Edge Contrast: 10%   Frequency: 57

The sharpness of the selection edge — *Edge smoothing feature* — *How far from the pointer the tool looks for contrasting edges* — *How much contrast must be present before it is considered an edge* — *The distance between anchor points*

The tool can be used in two modes – Selection and Mask.

• The *Selection mode* is used to paint over the area you wish to select. The Mask mode works by reverse painting in the areas you want to 'mask from the selection'.

• The *Mask mode* is particularly well suited for showing the soft or feathered edge selections made when painting with a soft-edged brush.

Holding down the Alt (Windows) or Option (Mac) keys whilst dragging the brush switches the tool from adding to the selection to taking away from the area. See Figure 6.9.

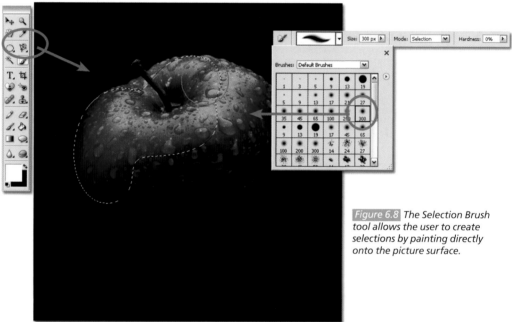

Figure 6.8 The Selection Brush tool allows the user to create selections by painting directly onto the picture surface.

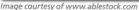

Image courtesy of www.ablestock.com

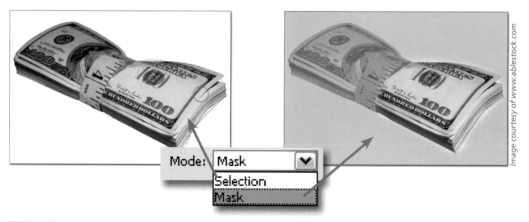

Figure 6.9 The Selection Brush can work in either Selection or Mask modes.

Drawing selection tool summaries

Rectangular and Elliptical Marquee tools

1 After selecting the tool, click and drag to draw a marquee on the image surface.

2 Hold down the Shift key whilst drawing to restrict the drawn shape to either a square or a circle.

3 Hold down the Alt (Windows) or Option (Mac) key to draw the shape from its center.

Lasso tool

1 After selecting the tool, click and drag to draw the selection area by freehand.

2 Release the mouse button to join the beginning and end points and close the outline.

Polygonal Lasso tool

1 After selecting the tool, click and release the mouse button to mark the first fastening point.

2 To draw a straight line, move the mouse and click again to mark the second point.

3 To draw a freehand line, hold down the Alt (Windows) or Option (Mac) key and click and drag the mouse.

4 To close the outline, either move the cursor over the first point and click or double-click.

Magnetic Lasso tool

1 After selecting the tool, click and release the mouse button to mark the first fastening point.

2 Trace the outline of the object with the mouse pointer. Extra fastening points will be added to the edge of the object automatically.

3 If the tool doesn't snap to the edge automatically, click the mouse button to add a fastening point manually.

4 Adjust settings in the options bar to vary the tool's magnetic function.

5 To close the outline, either double-click or drag the pointer over the first fastening point.

Selection Brush tool (from version 2.0 onwards)

1 After selecting the tool, adjust the settings in the options bar to vary the brush size, shape and hardness (edge softness).

2 To make a selection, change the mode to Selection and paint over the object with the mouse pointer.

3 To make a mask, change the mode to Mask and paint over the area outside the object with the mouse pointer.

4 Holding down the Alt (Windows) or Option (Mac) whilst painting will change the action from adding to the Selection/Mask to taking away from the Selection or Mask.

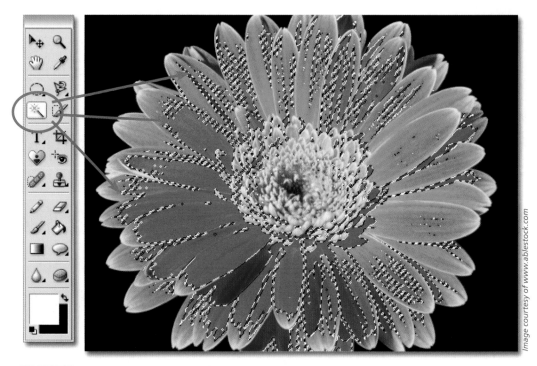

Image courtesy of www.ablestock.com

Figure 6.10 *The Magic Wand selects pixels of similar color and tone.*

Color selection tools

Unlike the Lasso and Marquee tools, the Magic Wand makes selections based on color and tone. See Figure 6.10. When the user clicks on an image with the Magic Wand tool, Elements searches the picture for pixels that have a similar color and tone. With large images this process can take a little time, but the end result is a selection of all similar pixels across the whole picture.

How identical a pixel has to be to the original to be included in the Magic Wand selection is determined by the Tolerance value in the options bar. See Figure 6.11. The higher the value here, the less alike the two pixels need to be, whereas a lower setting will require a more exact match before a pixel is added to the selection. Turning on the Contiguous option will only include the pixels that are similar and are adjacent to the original pixel in the selection. See Figure 6.12.

FEATURE SUMMARY
1 With the Magic Wand tool, active click onto the part of the image that you want to select.

2 Modify the Tolerance of the selection by altering this setting in the options bar.

3 Constrain the selection to adjacent pixels only, by checking the Contiguous option.

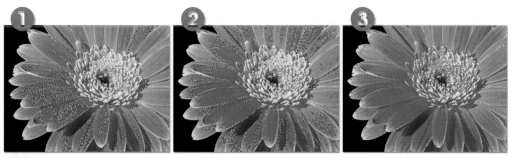

Figure 6.11 *The Tolerance setting determines how alike pixels need to be before they are included in the selection. (1) Tolerance setting 10. (2) Tolerance setting 50. (3) Tolerance setting 130.*

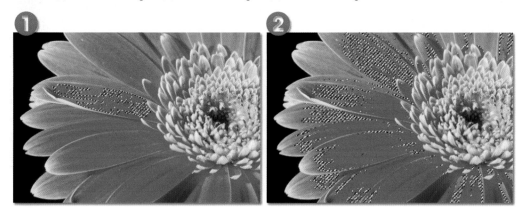

Figure 6.12 *The Contiguous option restricts the selection to those pixels adjacent to where the tool was first clicked on the image surface. (1) A selection made with the Contiguous option turned on. (2) A selection with the option turned off.*

Modifying selections

With some complex images, no one selection technique will be able to isolate all the pixels required; instead, a combination of tools is needed to make the final outline. To aid with this, Adobe has included several selection possibilities in the options bar of all tools. See Figure 6.13.

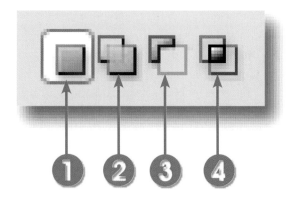

Figure 6.13 *The choices in the selection tools options bar determine how the new selection interacts with the existing one.*
(1) New selection.
(2) Add to selection.
(3) Subtract from selection.
(4) Intersect with selection.

With these options, it is possible to 'add to', or 'subtract from', an existing selection or even use the 'intersection' of two separate selections as the basis for a third. Simply choose a different selection option when using a new tool. For those users who prefer to use keyboard shortcuts, holding down the Shift key whilst using a selection tool will add to an existing outline, whereas using the Alt (Windows) or Option (Mac) keys will subtract. See Figures 6.14 and 6.15.

All of this may seem a little complex to start with, but it is important to persevere, as good selecting skills are critical for a lot of advanced editing techniques and besides, after some practice, making multi-tool complex selections will become second nature to you.

FEATURE SUMMARY

1 Add to a selection by either holding down the Shift key whilst using another selection tool or clicking the 'Add to selection' button in the options bar.

2 Subtract from a selection by either holding down the Alt (Windows) or Option (Mac) keys whilst using another selection tool or clicking the 'Subtract from selection' button in the options bar.

3 Use the intersection of a new and existing selection to form a third outline by clicking the 'Intersect with selection' button in the options bar before making a new selection.

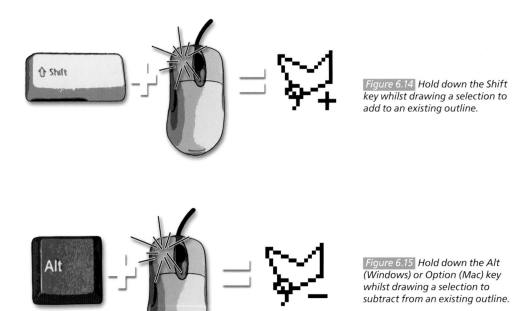

Figure 6.14 Hold down the Shift key whilst drawing a selection to add to an existing outline.

Figure 6.15 Hold down the Alt (Windows) or Option (Mac) key whilst drawing a selection to subtract from an existing outline.

Selections in action

Advanced dodging and burning

Previously, we have used the Dodge and Burn tools to adjust the tones in our images. Now, using carefully made selections, it is possible to darken, or lighten, whole areas of your pictures.

1 To start, use the Lasso or Selection Brush tool to select a portion of your image.

2 Next, open the Levels dialog (Enhance > Adjust Lighting > Levels).

3 Move the midtone input slider to the left to lighten the selected tones, or to the right to darken them. Notice that the levels changes have successfully dodged, or burned, the image. There is one problem with the results though; the changes are noticeable because of the sharp edge of the selection. A little modification is needed.

4 Undo (Edit > Undo) the levels adjustment and then, with the selection still active, apply a Feather (Select > Feather) to its edge. This command will soften the edge of the selection and make the change between areas that have been altered, and sections that have been left unchanged, more gradual. See Figures 6.16 and 6.17.

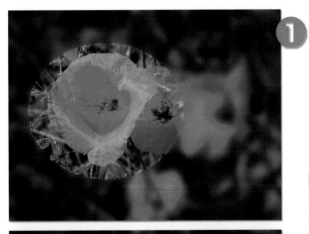

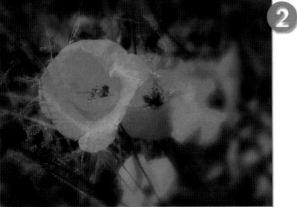

Figure 6.16 Changes made with a sharp-edged selection (1) are more obvious than when they are applied to a selection with a feathered edge (2).

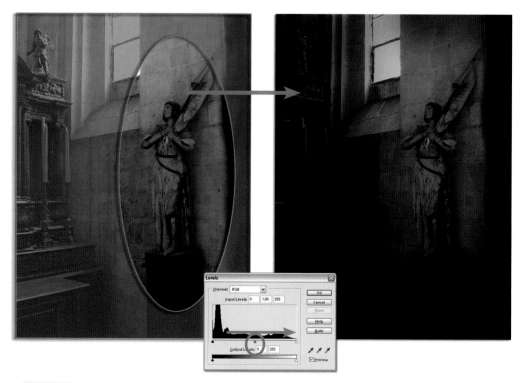

Figure 6.17 Using a feathered edge selection it is possible to easily lighten or darken whole areas of an image.

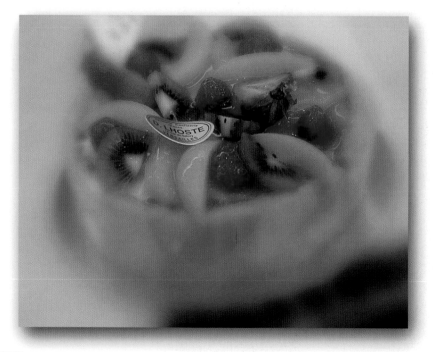

Figure 6.18 Shallow depth of field effects are the current picture fashion for food photographers.

Artificial depth of field

These days it is difficult to open the color magazine from a weekend paper without being confronted by a shallow depth of field picture. It seems that this photographic technique is very popular with food photographers in particular; the majority of the image is blurry, save for a single small and sharply focused portion. See Figures 6.18 and 6.19.

A similar effect can be created digitally using simple selection techniques.

FEATURE SUMMARY

1 Again, start the process by making a feathered selection of the part of your image that you want to remain sharp.

2 Next, invert (Select > Inverse) the selection so that the rest of the image is now isolated.

3 Using the Gaussian Blur filter (Filter > Blur > Gaussian Blur), change the sharpness of the selection until the desired effect is achieved.

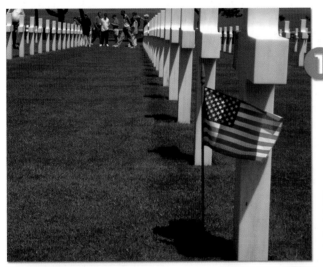

Figure 6.19 You can create a digital look-alike version of shallow depth of field effects by combining a feather selection and the Gaussian Blur filter. (1) Before depth of field technique. (2) After depth of field technique.

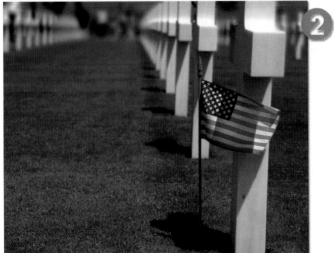

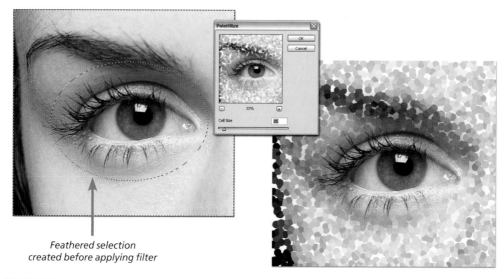

Feathered selection
created before applying filter

Figure 6.20 *The effects of filters can be restricted to specific areas of a picture by making a selection first and then applying the filter.*

Filtering a selection

In Chapter 4, we looked at some of the dramatic ways that we can change the look of an image using the filters that are supplied with Photoshop Elements. You can gain more control over the where and how the filters are applied to your pictures by combining their use with carefully created selections.

1 By selecting a portion of the picture first, it is possible to restrict the effects of a filter to this one section of the image.

2 Feathering the selection before applying the filter will help blend the changes into the rest of the image. See Figure 6.20.

Selective saturation changes

Color, as well as tone, texture and focus, can direct the viewer's eye within a picture. Burning and dodging and depth of field effects are designed to control the way that the audience sees an image and, more importantly, which parts of the picture become the points of focus. Using the selection tools, as well as the Hue/Saturation control, Elements provides a further option for helping to establish focal points within your pictures.

The result is a photograph where the viewer's eye is drawn to the saturated area of the image. Remember complete desaturation will result in a grayscale image. Making this degree of change to the inverted selection would produce a dramatic picture that is both black and white and color. See Figure 6.21.

FEATURE SUMMARY

1 Start by making a selection of the most visually important part of the picture.

2 Then, open the Hue/Saturation feature (Enhance > Adjust Color > Hue/Saturation) and increase the saturation of this part of the picture.

3 Next, invert (Select > Inverse) the selection so that the rest of the image is now selected and, using the Hue/Saturation control again, reduce the saturation.

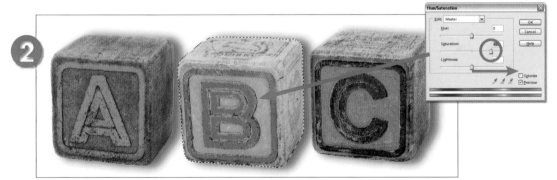

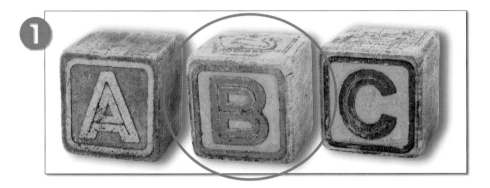

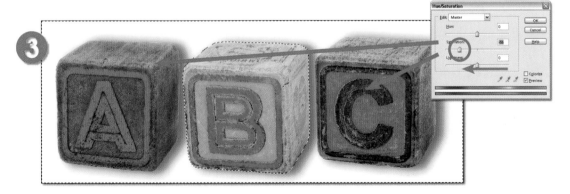

Figure 6.21 *Focal points can be created in an image by saturating a selection and desaturating the inverse selection. (1) Select the focal point. (2) With the selection active, saturate this portion of the picture. (3) Inverse the selection and desaturate the rest of the picture.*

Layers and their origins

The first image-editing programs used a flat file format. See Figure 6.22. All the information for the file was contained in a single plane and all changes made to the image were permanently and irreversibly stored in this file. It did not take users and software manufacturers long to realize that a more efficient and less frustrating way to work was to build an image from a series of picture parts each contained on its own layer.

The concept was not entirely new; the cell animation industry has used the idea for years. Each character and prop was painted onto a transparent plastic sheet, which was then layered together over a solid background. When seen from above, the components and the background appeared to be a single image.

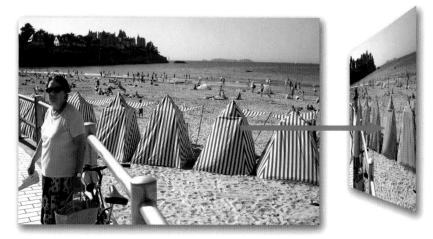

Figure 6.22 *A flat file contains all the image information in a single plane.*

Adobe in Photoshop and Photoshop Elements has based its layers system on this idea. See Figure 6.23. When an image is first created and opened in the editing package, it becomes the background by default. Any other images that are copied and pasted onto the image, or text that is added to the picture, become a layer that sits on top of this background. Just as with the animation version, the uppermost layer is viewed first and the other layers and background then show through the transparent areas of each other layer.

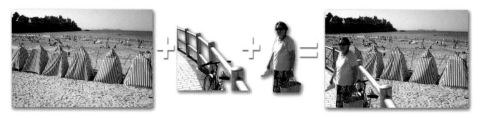

Figure 6.23 *Multilayered image files are used by most editing programs as a way to separate different picture components whilst keeping them available for editing and enhancement purposes.*

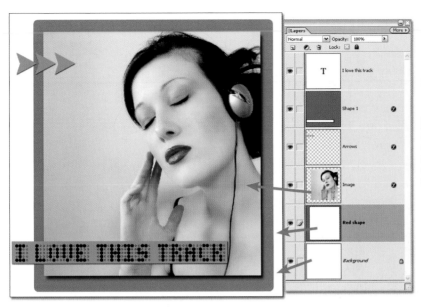

Figure 6.24 The Layers palette in Elements shows the content and position of each layer within the stack.

The Layers palette

Undoubtedly this whole idea might seem a little confusing to the new user, but the benefits of a system that allows picture parts to be moved and adjusted independently far outweigh the time it will take to understand the concept. To help visualize the setup, Elements contains a specialist Layers palette that shows each of the individual layers, their position in the layer stack and a small thumbnail of their contents. See Figure 6.24.

A transparent area is represented by a checkerboard gray and white pattern that surrounds any image parts that are smaller than the background. The eye, sitting to the left of the thumbnail, shows that the layer is visible. Clicking on this icon will make the eye disappear and visually remove the image part from the whole picture. Only one layer in the stack can be manipulated at a time and for this reason it is called the 'working layer'. See Figure 6.25. This layer will be colored differently than the others and will show a brush icon between the eye and the thumbnail. Clicking on a different layer in the area to the right of the thumbnail will make this layer the new working layer. See Figure 6.26.

When the full image is saved as an Elements file in PSD format, all the individual layers are maintained and can be manipulated individually when the picture is opened next. This is not true if the image is saved in other formats like standard TIFF or JPEG. Here the information contained in each layer is merged together at the time of saving to form one flat file.

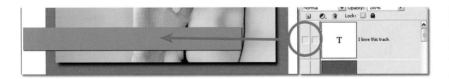

Figure 6.25 Clicking the 'eye' icon removes that layer from view in the image.

Layer types

Image layers

Several different types of layers can be added to an Elements image; of these the most simple, and probably obvious, is the image layer. When an image part is copied and pasted it automatically makes a new layer. This is true whether the picture part came from the original image or from another already opened. When this new layer is selected as the working layer it can be moved around the image surface using the Move tool. The contents can also be changed in size and shape using one of the four options found in the Transform menu (Image > Transform > Free Transform or Skew or Distort or Perspective). See Figure 6.27. These features allow you to manipulate the layer to fit the other components of the image.

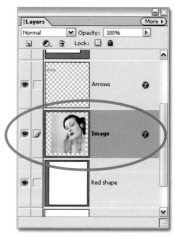

Figure 6.26 *The active or working layer is a different color to the others in the stack.*

The background layer is a special image layer. Its dimensions define the image size. It is also locked by default, meaning that it cannot be moved. You can restrict the movement of other key layers by clicking the Lock icon in the top part of the layers palette. Ticking the Transparency option located next to the Lock icon will not allow any changes made to the layer to impinge on the transparent area.

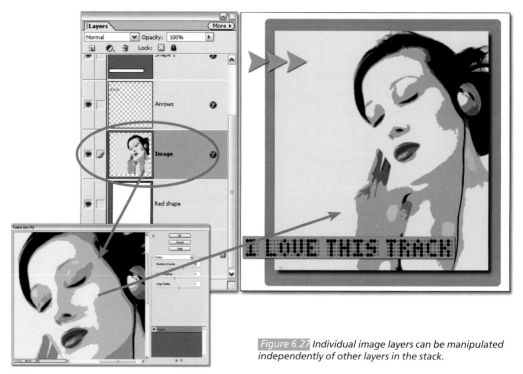

Figure 6.27 *Individual image layers can be manipulated independently of other layers in the stack.*

Type layers

Type layers do not show a thumbnail of their contents in the Layers palette. See Figure 6.28. A large 'T' is positioned in its place and the first few words of the text are used as the layer's name. Unlike other packages, Elements' type layers remain editable even after they have been saved, provided that the file has been saved in the PSD format.

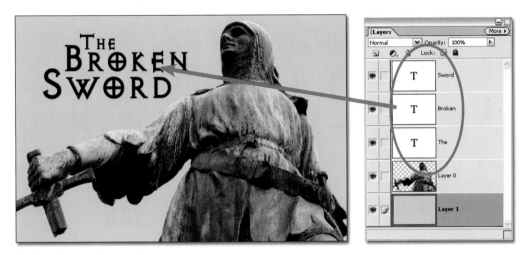

Figure 6.28 *Elements uses editable type layers for any text that is added to images.*

Adjustment layers

Adobe added adjustment layers to Photoshop as a way for users to change the look of images whilst retaining the integrity of the image file. Familiar image-change features, such as Levels and Hue/Saturation, are available as adjustment layers, and depending on where they are placed in the layer stack will alter either part, or all, of the image. See Figure 6.29.

Adjusting your images using these types of layers is a good way of ensuring that the basic picture is not changed in any way. The other advantage is that the settings in the adjustment layers can be edited and changed at a later date, even after the file has been saved. Users can access the original settings used to make the alteration by double-clicking the Dialog icon on the left-hand side of the adjustment layer.

Fill layers

Users can also apply a Solid Color, Gradient or Pattern to an image as a separate layer. These three selections are available as a separate item (Layer > New Fill Layer) under the Layer menu or grouped with the adjustment layer options via the quick button at the bottom of the Layers palette. See Figure 6.30.

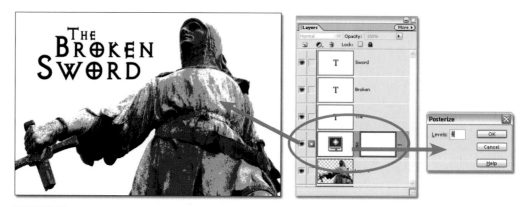

Figure 6.29 *Adjustment layers alter the look of all layers that are positioned beneath them in the stack, unless they are grouped with the layer beneath by holding the Option/Alt key down and clicking the dividing line between each in the Layers palette.*

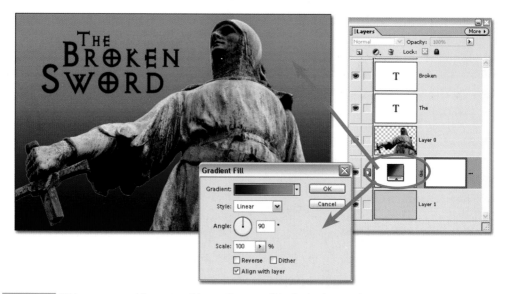

Figure 6.30 *Fill layers are a quick way to add a gradient or solid color background to an image.*

Layer transparency

Until this point we have assumed that the contents of each layer were solid. When it is placed on top, and in front, of the contents of another layer, it obscures the objects underneath completely. And for most imaging scenarios this is exactly the way that we would expect the layers to perform, but occasionally it is desirable to allow some of the detail, color and texture of what is beneath to show through. To achieve this effect, the 'transparency' of each layer can be interactively adjusted via the Opacity slider control in the top right-hand corner of the palette. See Figure 6.31. Keep in mind that making the selected layer less opaque will result in it being more transparent.

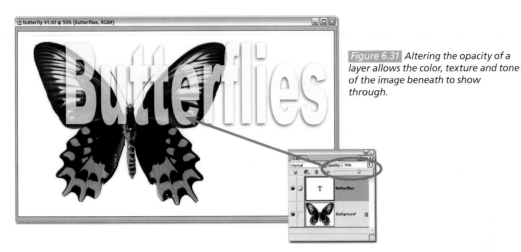

Layer blend modes

The layer blending modes extend the possibilities of how two layers interact. See Figures 6.32 and 6.33 . Twenty-two (up from 21 for version 2.0) different mode options are available in the drop-down menu to the left of the Opacity slider in the Layers palette. For ordinary use the mode is kept on the Normal selection, but a host of special effects can be achieved if a different method of interaction, or mode, is selected. The mode options are the same ones available for use with tools like the Paintbrush and Pencil, and some advanced editing or enhancement techniques are based on their use.

Experimenting with different modes will help you understand how they affect the combining of layers and will also help you to determine the best occasions to use this feature.

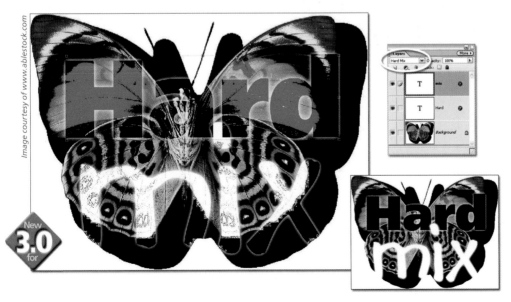

Image courtesy of www.ablestock.com

Figure 6.32 Version 3.0 adds one new blending mode, Hard Mix, to the 17 that were already available in version 1.0 of the program and the 21 from version 2.0.

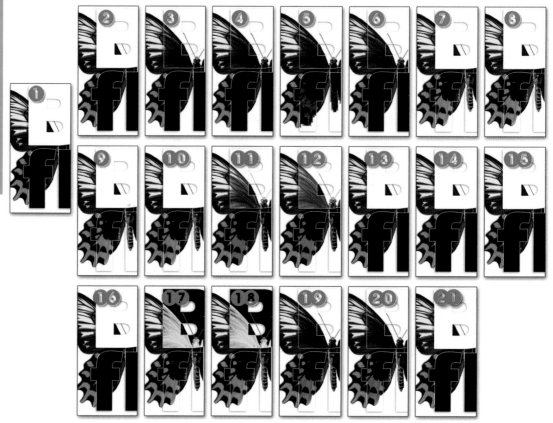

Figure 6.33 *Layer blending modes control the way that two separate layers interact. (1) Normal. (2) Dissolve. (3) Darken. (4) Multiply. (5) Color Burn. (6) Linear Burn. (7) Lighten. (8) Screen. (9) Color Dodge. (10) Linear Dodge. (11) Overlay. (12) Soft Light. (23) Hard Light. (14) Vivid Light. (15) Linear Light. (16) Pin Light. (17) Difference. (18) Exclusion. (19) Hue. (20) Saturation. (21) Luminosity.*

Layer Styles

Early on in the digital imaging revolution, users started to place visual effects like drop shadows or glowing edges on parts of their pictures. A large section of any class teaching earlier versions of Photoshop was designated to learning the many steps needed to create these effects. With the release of packages like Elements, these types of effects have become built-in features of the program. Now, it is possible to apply an effect like a 'drop shadow' to the contents of a layer with the click of a single button. See Figure 6.34.

Adobe has grouped all these layer effects under a single palette called Styles and Effects. As with many features in the program, a thumbnail version of each style provides a quick reference to the results of applying the effect. To add the style to a selected layer, simply click on the thumbnail.

Multiple styles can be applied to the one layer and the settings used to create the effect can be edited by double-clicking the 'f' icon on the selected layer in the palette. Remove a layer style by selecting Layer > Layer Style > Clear Layer Style whilst selecting the layer with the style applied.

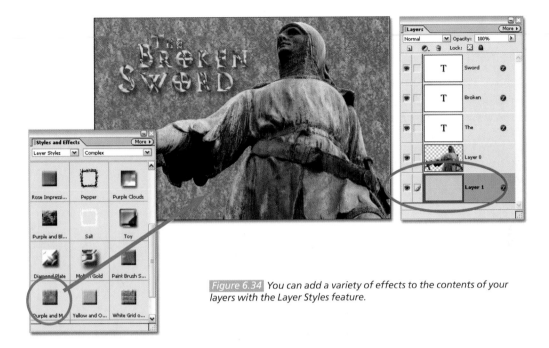

Figure 6.34 *You can add a variety of effects to the contents of your layers with the Layer Styles feature.*

Adding Elements' Layer Styles

If you spread your styles wings a little further there are many sites on the web that offer free downloadable styles that can be added to your library. Usually, the files are downloaded in a compressed form such as a zip. The file needs to be extracted and then saved to the adobe\photoshopelements\presets\styles folder before use. The next time you start Elements you will have a smorgasbord of new styles to apply to your images. See Figure 6.35.

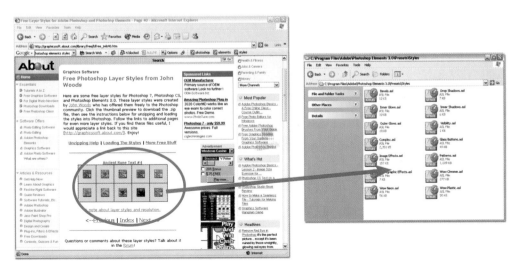

Figure 6.35 *Extending the library of styles you have available to you is as simple as downloading new examples from the net and installing them in the Elements Styles folder.*

Layers in action

Adding drop shadows

Adding a drop shadow edge to your image A simple drop shadow edge can make a picture look as though it is floating in front of the background. Producing this look for your own images is a process that contains a few steps that combine some layer and layer styles techniques.

1 First, change the image layer from being a locked background layer to an image layer by selecting the Layer > New > Layer From Background option.

2 Next, create a new layer (Layer > New > Layer) and drag it beneath the image layer.

3 Then, increase the canvas size (Image > Resize > Canvas Size) to 120% of the original in both height and width, and fill (Edit > Fill) the bottom layer with white.

4 Finally, select the image layer, open the Layer Styles palette, select the drop shadow options and click on the style thumbnail you wish to use. See Figure 6.36.

FEATURE SUMMARY

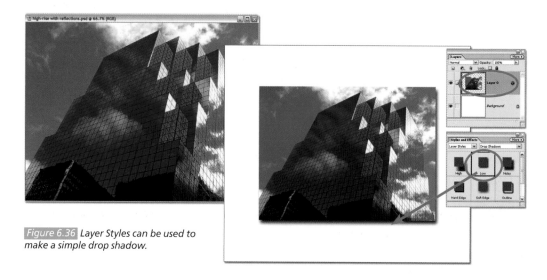

Figure 6.36 Layer Styles can be used to make a simple drop shadow.

Straightening the edges of buildings

It is a familiar problem. When shooting architecture from ground level with a wide angle lens, the parallel edges of buildings appear to converge. Using the Transform feature on the image layer, you can straighten the sides of affected buildings.

1 Create a new, bigger, white layer beneath your image layer using the first three steps of the technique above.

2 Next, target the image layer and select the Perspective feature from the Transform options of the Image menu (Image > Transform > Perspective).

FEATURE SUMMARY

3 Drag the handles at the corners of the image outwards to straighten the building's edges.

4 Double-click in the middle of the layer to apply the changes.

5 Use the Crop tool to trim the newly shaped image to size. See Figure 6.37.

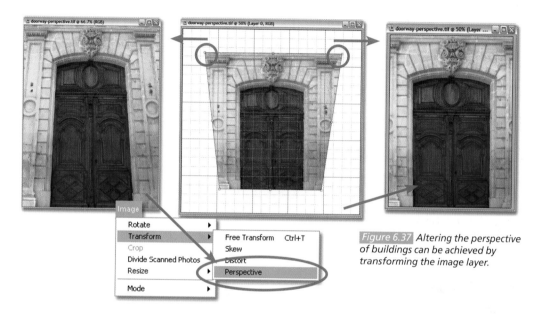

Figure 6.37 Altering the perspective of buildings can be achieved by transforming the image layer.

Creating a beach triptych

Bringing linked images together to help tell a story more fully is not a new idea. Photographers have been producing pictures in series since the Fox Talbot was in short trousers (well nearly). For the images to work well together they have to be good, strong pictures in their own right and they must also link with the other photographs in the group. The link (or theme) might be that the images were all taken at a single place, on the one day, feature the same person or have similar content. It is also important that characteristics like contrast, brightness and color are balanced across all images. See Figure 6.38.

Here we will use layers to help us create a single picture made up of three individual photographs taken on the same day at the beach. When three pictures are presented together in this fashion, the arrangement is sometimes called a triptych, a form favored by historical painters when creating their magnificent alter pieces. Although our humble montage will not be as grandiose as these pieces of art it will make use of the basic form of a main picture flanked by two smaller but related images.

1 Opening a suitable background picture. Lighten the whole image by selecting the Levels feature (Enhance > Adjust Lighting > Levels) and moving the black point output slider to the right.

Image courtesy of www.ablestock.com

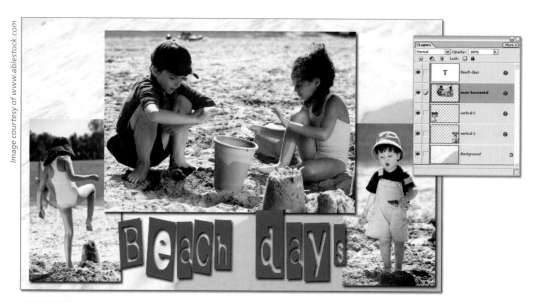

Figure 6.38 *Combining several photos together using basic layering skills can create interesting montage pictures.*

2 Open the photograph that is to be the centerpiece of the composition and click and drag it to the waiting background document. The picture will be stored on top of the background as a new layer.

3 Unless you are very lucky the main picture will not be exactly the right size and shape to suit your background. To trim the picture start by using the Rectangular Marquee to select the part of the picture you wish to keep. Next, check to see that the picture layer is selected and then invert the selection (Select > Inverse) so that the area to be trimmed is now selected, and press the Delete key.

4 Drag the two side pictures onto the background as well. Double-click the layer's label tags to change the name of each of the layers so that you don't get confused. To resize a picture select its layer and then choose the Scale feature (Image > Resize > Scale). Drag the corner handle, whilst holding down the Shift button (to ensure that the format stays the same), to resize the picture. Double-click inside the picture to apply the size changes.

5 With all the pictures now added, cropped and sized you can now select each layer and with the aid of the Move tool, position the pictures so that the composition is balanced. To move images behind or in front of others alter their order in the layer stack. Click and drag the layer higher to make the picture sit in front of other images. Now to add a little visual separation to each of the pictures we will give each a drop shadow. To do this click on the layer and then select the Low Drop Shadow option from the Layer Styles.

6 You can finish off the triptych by adding some text. To ensure that the font color suited the surrounding images the eyedropper tool was used to select a dark sand color from the main picture as Foreground color before setting the text. Next we selected the Horizontal Type tool, positioned the cursor on the document and chose the Earwig Factory font.

FEATURE SUMMARY

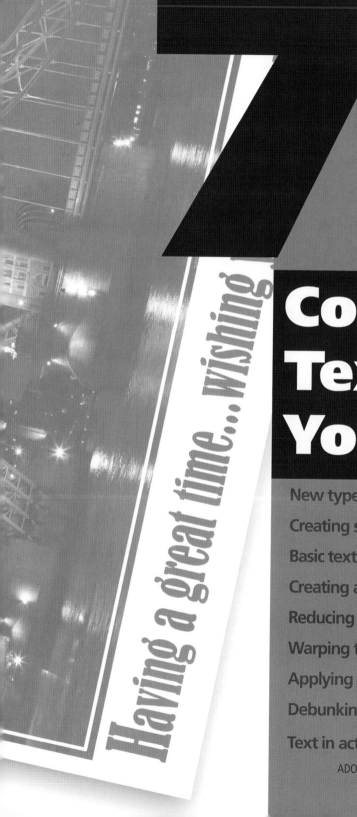

Having a great time.... Wishing

7

Combining Text with Your Images

New type features

Creating simple type

Basic text changes

Creating and using type masks

Reducing the 'jaggies'

Warping type

Applying styles to type layers

Debunking some type terms

Text in action

Digital imaging has blurred the boundaries between many traditional industries. No longer does the image maker's job stop the moment the illustration or photograph hits the art director's desk. With the increased abilities of software like Photoshop Elements has come the expectation that not only are you able to create the pictures needed for the job, but you will also be able to perform other functions like adding text. See Figure 7.1.

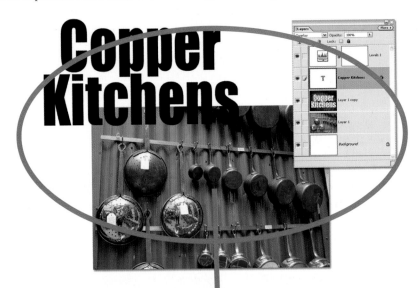

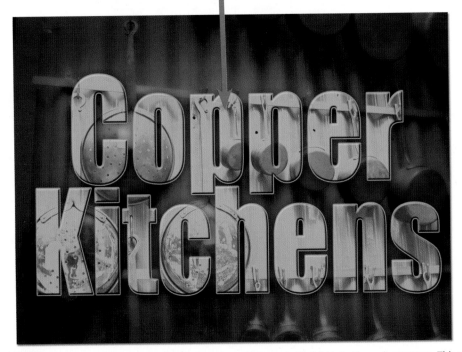

Figure 7.1 *Elements 3.0 has a range of sophisticated text features built right into the main program. This means that combining text and images in the one document has become a task that is easier to complete than ever before.*

Book resources at: **www.guide2elements.com**

Combining text and images is usually the job of a graphic designer or printer, but the simple text functions that are now included in most desktop imaging programs mean that more and more people are trying their hand at adding type to pictures. Elements provides the ability to input type directly onto the canvas rather than via a type dialog. This means that you can see and adjust your text to fit and suit the image beneath. Changes of size, shape and style can be made at any stage by selecting the existing text and applying the changes via the options bar. As the type is saved as a special type layer, it remains editable even when the file is closed, so long as it is saved and reopened in the Elements PSD format. See Figure 7.2.

New type features

Elements version 3.0 includes two new type features that are available directly from the tool's options bar.

Leading

The leading control adjusts the space between lines of text. In previous versions of the program Elements has determined the correct line spacing automatically. In version

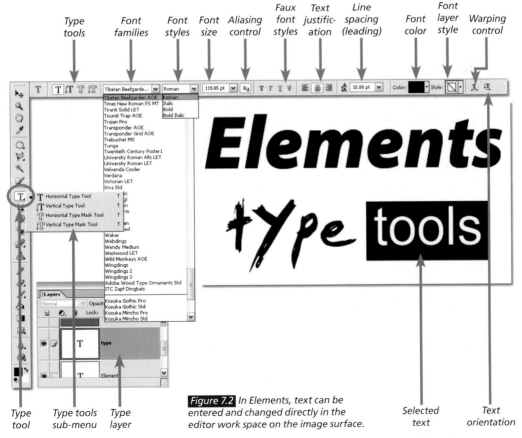

Figure 7.2 In Elements, text can be entered and changed directly in the editor work space on the image surface.

3.0 you have control over how close the letters on different lines are. As a starting point you should use the current font size as the leading value. To move the lines closer together use lower values. To move text lines further apart use a higher setting. To change the leading of an existing paragraph of text select all the lines and then alter the leading setting.

Font layer style

The second new feature is the Font Layer Style menu. Adding this feature to the type options bar means that you can now interactively add selected layer styles directly to your text without leaving the Type tool or navigating to the Layer menu or palette. To add a layer style to your text either select the style first and then add the text (complete with style) to the document or select a piece of existing type and then choose the style you wish to apply to it. Of course you can still add a style to your type layer later by selecting the option from the Styles and Effects palette.

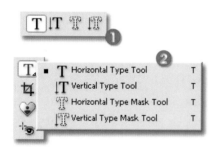

Figure 7.3 *Four text options are available via the (1) Type tool selection in the toolbox and the (2) buttons in the options bar.*

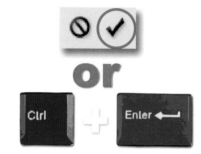

Figure 7.4 *Any text entered must be 'committed' to a type layer before other tools or menu choices can be used.*

Creating simple type

Two new Type tools were added to Elements in version 2.0 of the program over and above the two that were present in the initial release of the program. In version 3.0 you can select from Horizontal and Vertical Type tools, as well as Horizontal and Vertical Type Mask tools.

Of the standard Type tools (non-mask varieties), one is used for entering text that runs horizontally across the canvas and the other is for entering vertical type. See Figure 7.3. To place text onto your picture, select the Type tool from the toolbox. Next, click onto the canvas in the area where you want the text to appear. Do not be too concerned if the letters are not positioned exactly, as the layer and text can be moved later. Once you have finished entering text you need to commit the type to a layer. Until this is done you will be unable to access most other Elements functions. To exit the text editor, either click the 'tick' button in the options bar or press the Control + Enter keys in Windows or Command + Return for a Macintosh system. See Figure 7.4.

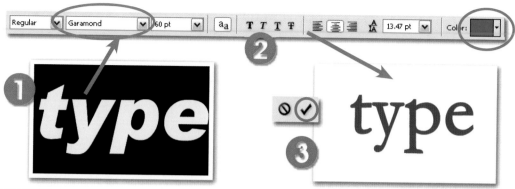

Figure 7.5 *The text options bar contains a number of settings for altering the style, font, color, aliasing, alignment and size of the type entered. To change the settings of your type, (1) select the text, (2) make the changes in the Type tool options bar and then (3) commit the changes by clicking the 'tick' icon in the bar.*

Figure 7.6 *Use the Move tool to arrange a type layer to move type whose layer has been selected.*

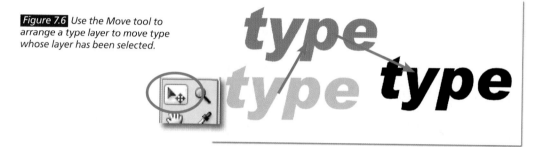

Basic text changes

All the usual text changes available to word processor users are contained in Elements. It is possible to alter the size, style, color and font of your type using the settings in the options bar. See Figure 7.5. You can either make the selections before you input your text or later by highlighting (clicking and dragging the mouse across the text) the portion of type that you want to change. In addition to these adjustments, you can also alter the justification or alignment of a line or paragraph of type.

After selecting the type to be aligned, click one of the justification buttons on the options bar. Your text will realign automatically on screen. After making a few changes, you may wish to alter the position of the text; simply click and drag outside of the type area to move it around. If you have already committed the changes to a text layer then select the Move tool from the toolbox, making sure that the text layer is selected, then click and drag to move the whole layer. See Figure 7.6.

Creating and using type masks

The Type Mask tools are used to provide precise masks or selections in the shape and size of the text you input. Rather than creating a new text layer containing solid colored text, the mask tools produce a selection outline. From this point on the text mask can be used as you would use any other selection. See Figure 7.7.

1 Choose the Type tool from the toolbox. To change between Type tools, click and hold on the tool to reveal the hidden options.

2 Click on the picture surface to position the start of the text.

3 Make changes to font type, size, style, justification and color by altering the settings in the options bar.

4 Enter your text using the keyboard or by pasting sections (Edit > Paste) from a copied word processing document.

5 For non-masked text, click and drag to move the text over the image background.

6 Commit entered text or changes to a type layer by clicking 'tick' in the options bar or by pressing Control + Enter (Windows) or Command + Return (Mac) keys.

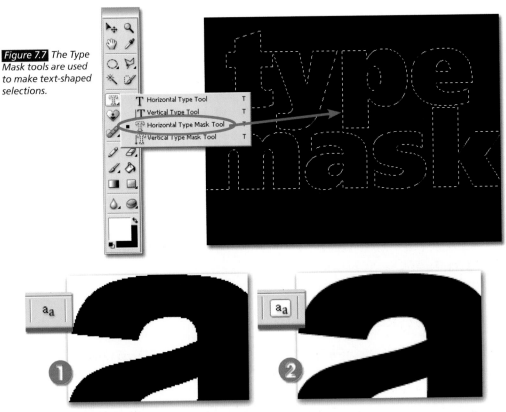

Figure 7.7 *The Type Mask tools are used to make text-shaped selections.*

Figure 7.8 *The anti-aliasing setting helps smooth out the edges of 'jagged' text. (1) Anti-aliased feature off. (2) Anti-aliased feature on.*

Reducing the 'jaggies'

One of the drawbacks of using a system that is based on pixels to draw sharp-edged letter shapes is that circles and curves are made up of a series of pixel steps. Anti-aliasing is a system where the effects of these 'jaggies' are made less noticeable by partially filling in the edge pixels. This technique produces smoother looking type overall and should be used in all print circumstances and web applications. See Figure 7.8. The only exception is where file size is critical, as anti-aliased web text creates larger files than the standard text equivalent. Anti-aliasing can be turned on and off by clicking the Anti-aliased button (versions 3.0/2.0) or checking the box (version 1.0) in the options bar.

1 Turn anti-aliasing on by clicking the Anti-aliased button (version 2.0) or checking the box (version 1.0) in the options bar, or by selecting Layer > Type > Anti-Alias On.

2 Turn anti-aliasing off by reclicking the button (version 2.0), unchecking the box (version 1.0) in the options bar or by selecting Layer > Type > Anti-Alias Off.

Warping type

One of the special features of the Elements type system is the 'Warping' feature. This tool forces text to distort to one of a range of shapes. An individual word, or even whole sentences, can be made to curve, bulge or even simulate the effect of a fish-eye lens. See Figure 7.9. The strength and style of the effect can be controlled by manipulating the bend and horizontal and vertical distortion sliders.

This feature is particularly useful when creating graphic headings for posters or web pages. See Figure 7.10.

1 Choose a completed type layer.

2 Select Layer > Type > Warp Text or pick the Type tool from the toolbox and click the Warp button in the options bar.

3 Choose the warp style from the drop-down menu.

4 Adjust the Bend, Horizontal Distortion and Vertical Distortion sliders.

5 Click OK to finish.

Applying styles to type layers

Elements' Layer Styles can be applied very effectively to type layers and provide a quick and easy way to enhance the look of your text. Everything from a simple drop shadow to complex surface and color treatments can be applied using this single click feature. See Figure 7.11. A collection of included styles can be found under the Layer Styles tab in the Palette Well or you can view the dialog by selecting the Show Layer Styles option from the Window menu. A variety of different style groups are available from the drop-down list and small example images of each style are provided as a preview of the effect. See Figure 7.12.

Additional styles can be downloaded from websites specializing in resources for Elements users. These should be installed into the Adobe\Photoshop Elements\Presets\Styles folder. The next time you start Elements, the new styles will appear in the Layer Styles palette.

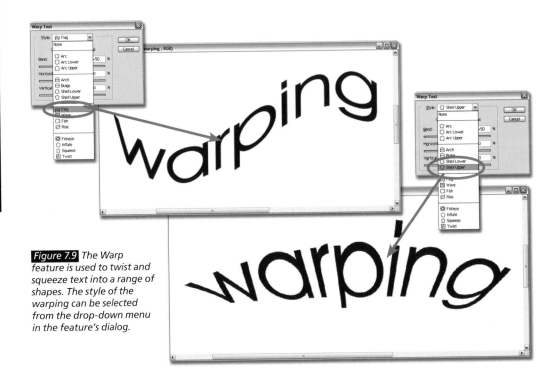

Figure 7.9 *The Warp feature is used to twist and squeeze text into a range of shapes. The style of the warping can be selected from the drop-down menu in the feature's dialog.*

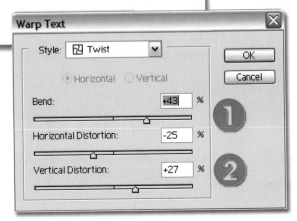

Figure 7.10 *The degree of (1) bend and (2) distortion of the text can be altered using the settings in the Warp text dialog.*

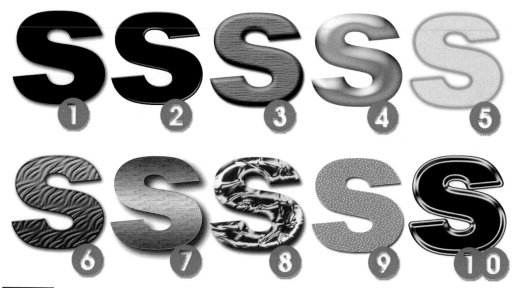

Figure 7.11 The look of text can be changed with a single click using Layer Styles. (1) Drop shadow. (2) Inner Ridge Bevel. (3) Wood Grain. (4) Pink Glass. (5) Purple Neon. (6) Waves. (7) Brushed Metal. (8) Molten Gold. (9) Cactus. (10) Chrome Fat.

To apply a style to a section of type, make sure that the text layer is currently active. Do this by checking that the layer is highlighted in the Layers palette. See Figure 7.13. Next, open and view the Layer Styles group you wish to use from the Layers and Effects palette. Click on the thumbnail of the style you want to apply to the text.

The changes will be immediately reflected in your image. See Figure 7.14. Multiple styles can be applied to a single layer and unwanted effects can be removed by using the Step Backward button (Undo) in the shortcuts bar or the Undo command (Edit > Undo Apply Style) or the Clear Style button (version 2.0) in the dialog.

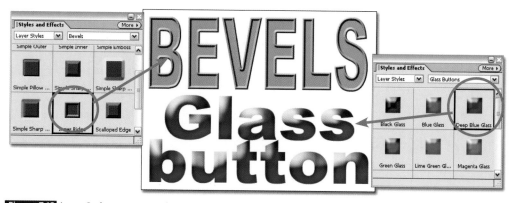

Figure 7.12 Layer Styles are grouped in menus around a common theme such as Drop Shadows, Bevels and Glass buttons. In version 3.0 of Elements Layer Styles are grouped with effects and filters in the Styles and Effects palette.

The settings of individual styles can be edited by double-clicking on the 'f' icon in the text layer and adjusting one or more of the style settings. See Figure 7.15.

FEATURE SUMMARY

1 Ensure that the text layer is selected.

2 View the Layer Styles palette by clicking its tab in the palette well or by selecting Show Layer Styles from the Window menu.

3 Choose the group and style to apply to your text from the drop-down list and thumbnails.

4 Edit style settings by double-clicking the 'f' symbol in the text layer.

5 Remove effects by selecting Edit > Undo Layer Styles.

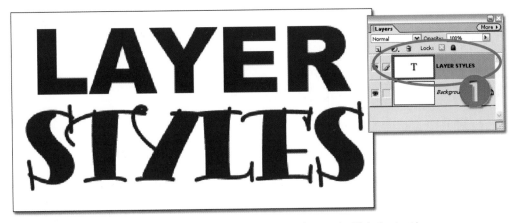

Figure 7.13 Make sure the type layer is selected before applying a layer style. (1) Active text layer.

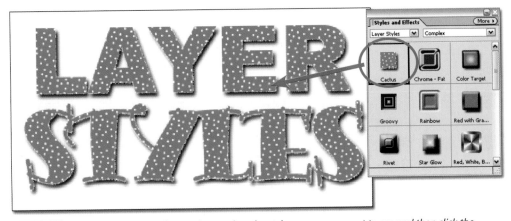

Figure 7.14 Open the Styles and Effects palette, select the styles group you want to use and then click the thumbnail of the style you want to apply.

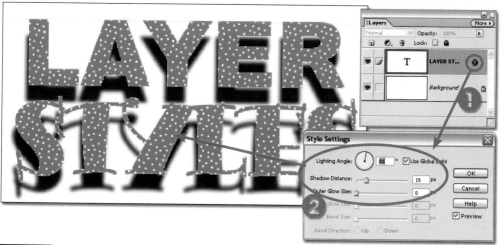

Figure 7.15 *(1) Double-click the 'f' at the left-hand side of the type layer to open the Style Settings dialog. (2) Use the controls in the dialog to the Layer Style settings.*

Debunking some type terms

Font size

The size of the text you place in your image files is measured as pixels, millimeters or points.

I find the pixel setting most useful when working with digital files, as it indicates to me the precise size of my text in relationship to the whole image. Millimeter and points values, on the other hand, vary depending on the resolution of the picture and the resolution of the output device. Some of you might be aware that 72 points approximately equals 1 inch, but this is only true if the picture's resolution is 72 dpi. At higher resolutions the pixels are packed more closely together and therefore the same 72 point type is smaller in size.

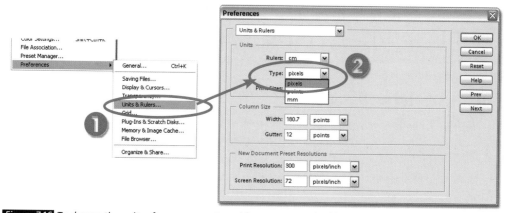

Figure 7.16 *To change the units of measurement used for type, go to the (1) Units & Rulers option in the Preferences menu and then (2) select the measure unit you want from the drop-down type menu.*

To change the unit of measurement used:

1 Windows or Mac OS 9.x users, select Edit > Preferences > Units & Rulers.

2 Mac OS X users, select Photoshop > Preferences > Units & Rulers.

3 Then alter the unit of measurement for Type. See Figure 7.16.

Font family and style

The font family is a term used to describe the way that the letter shapes look. Most readers would be familiar with the difference in appearance between Arial and Times Roman. These are two different families each containing different characteristics that determine the way that the letter shapes appear. The font style refers to the different versions of the same font family. Most fonts are available in regular, italic, bold and bold italic styles. See Figure 7.17.

You can download new fonts from specialist websites to add to your system. Some families are available free of charge, others can be purchased online. After downloading, the fonts should be installed into the fonts section of your system directory. Windows and Macintosh users will need to consult their operating system manuals to find the preferred method for installing new fonts on their computer.

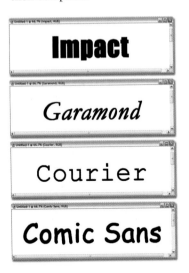

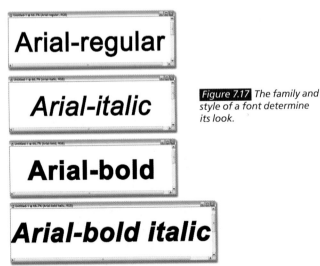

Figure 7.17 The family and style of a font determine its look.

Alignment and justification

These terms are often used interchangeably and refer to the way that a line or paragraph of text is positioned on the image. The left align, or left justify, feature will arrange all text to the left of the picture. When applied to a group of sentences, the left edge of the paragraph is organized into a straight vertical line whilst the right-hand edge remains uneven or ragged. Right align works in the opposite fashion, straightening the right-hand edge of the paragraph and leaving the left ragged. Selecting the center text option will align the paragraph around a central line and leave both left and right edges ragged. See Figure 7.18.

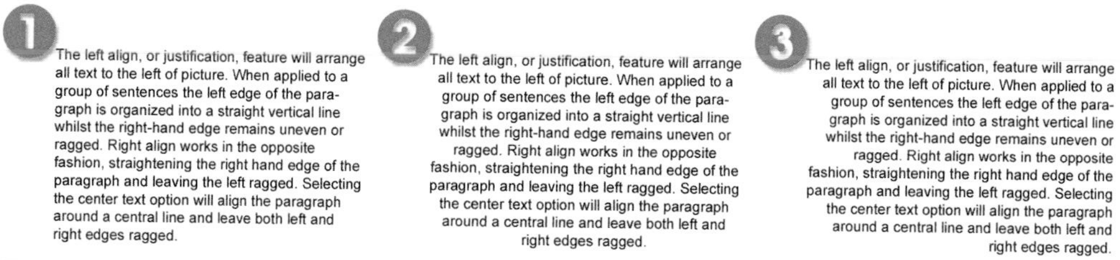

① The left align, or justification, feature will arrange all text to the left of picture. When applied to a group of sentences the left edge of the paragraph is organized into a straight vertical line whilst the right-hand edge remains uneven or ragged. Right align works in the opposite fashion, straightening the right hand edge of the paragraph and leaving the left ragged. Selecting the center text option will align the paragraph around a central line and leave both left and right edges ragged.

② The left align, or justification, feature will arrange all text to the left of picture. When applied to a group of sentences the left edge of the paragraph is organized into a straight vertical line whilst the right-hand edge remains uneven or ragged. Right align works in the opposite fashion, straightening the right hand edge of the paragraph and leaving the left ragged. Selecting the center text option will align the paragraph around a central line and leave both left and right edges ragged.

③ The left align, or justification, feature will arrange all text to the left of picture. When applied to a group of sentences the left edge of the paragraph is organized into a straight vertical line whilst the right-hand edge remains uneven or ragged. Right align works in the opposite fashion, straightening the right hand edge of the paragraph and leaving the left ragged. Selecting the center text option will align the paragraph around a central line and leave both left and right edges ragged.

Figure 7.18 *Type alignment controls how the text is arranged in the image. (1) Left align. (2) Center. (3) Right align.*

Leading

Originally referring to the small pieces of lead that were placed in between lines of metal type used in old printing processes, nowadays it is easier to think of the term referring to the space between lines of text. Unlike earlier versions of the program Elements 3.0 includes the ability to alter the leading of the type input in your documents. Start with a value equal to the font size you are using and increase or decrease from here according to your requirements. See Figure 7.19.

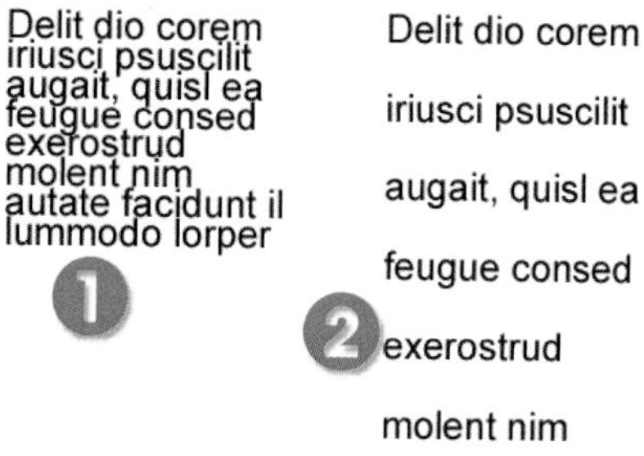

Delit dio corem iriusci psuscilit augait, quisl ea feugue consed exerostrud molent nim autate facidunt il lummodo lorper

①

Delit dio corem

iriusci psuscilit

augait, quisl ea

feugue consed

② exerostrud

molent nim

Figure 7.19 *Leading is the space between lines of text. 24 pixel type with (1) 18 pixel leading and (2) 48 pixel leading.*

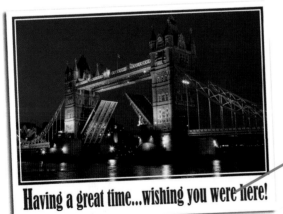

Having a great time...wishing you were here!

Figure 7.20 *Add some text and border to your favorite picture and then send it off to friends as a digital postcard.*

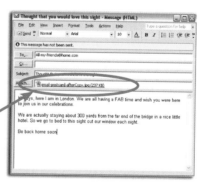

Text in action
Creating digital postcards

Add some true spice to your next email message by attaching a picture postcard featuring images of a recent party or sites from your latest holiday. Or why not combine your love of digital photography with the speed and convenience of email to produce the 21st century equivalent of the 'carte de visite' showcasing the latest family portrait? See Figure 7.20.

COMBINING TEXT WITH YOUR IMAGES

Sending your favorite pictures as email attachments is nothing new, but forget playing around with pixel dimensions, compression settings and special web file formats, Photoshop Elements is making the activity a simple affair.

Start with your candidate photograph open in the program, add some text and maybe a border and then click the Attach to E-mail button (nestled about midway along the shortcuts bar). Click to Auto convert the image to the right size, compression and format for web work and then Elements will automatically open a new email message with your picture attached. The only task left for you to do is to address the email, type in a suitable subject and add a few comments into the body of the email. Clicking the send button will 'post' your work of art and pithy words along to the lucky recipient. If you want a 'picture only' email then just add the address and a subject and send away.

1 Start by opening the picture to be used as the base image for the card. With white selected as the background color, choose the Crop tool and click and drag a rectangle around the whole of the image. Next grab the corner handles for the crop marquee and drag them outwards beyond the edges of the picture. Double-click inside the marquee to apply the crop. This creates a white border around your photograph.

2 Now select the rectangular selection tool and click and drag a marquee that is slightly smaller than the dimensions of the photograph. Move the selection by click-dragging the selection until it is positioned an even distance from the edges of the picture. Now edit stroke the selection with a thin white frame.

3 Use the Type tool and a fancy font to add a message to the bottom of the card in the white space created by the crop in step 1. To match the type color with the hues in the picture, use the eyedropper tool to select a suitable foreground color from the image before adding the text.

4 With the card picture now complete it is time for Photoshop Elements to do its magic. Click onto the Attach to E-mail button in the shortcuts bar. Select the Recipient from the contacts list.

5 Then select the size and quality of the picture attachment from the list of three in the dialog. Use the Optimize for Viewing On screen option for all email postcards.

6 Enter the message to include with your attachment and click OK. When the email program appears check that the picture, message, address and subject heading are all present before clicking send to 'post' your digital postcard.

FEATURE SUMMARY

More on the Attach to E-mail feature

Go to Chapter 10 for more details on how the Attach to E-mail feature works in Elements.

Book resources at: **www.guide2elements.com**

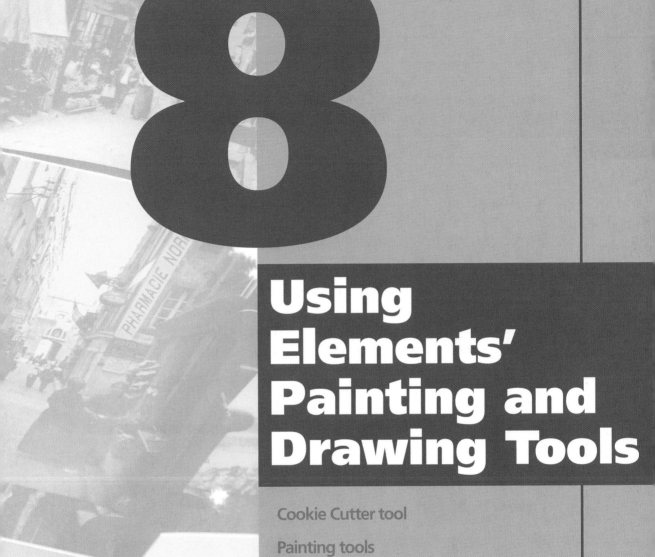

8

Using Elements' Painting and Drawing Tools

At some point during your imaging life you will need, or want, to create an image from scratch. Until now, we have concentrated on editing, adjusting and enhancing images that have been generated using either a camera or scanner; now we will look at how to use Elements' painting and drawing tools to create something entirely new.

Although the names are the same, the tools used by the traditional artists to paint and draw are quite different from their digital namesakes. The painting tools (the Paint Brush, Pencil, Eraser, Paint Bucket and Airbrush) in Elements are pixel based. That is, when they are dragged across the image they change the pixels to the color and texture selected for the tool. These tools are highly customizable and, in particular, the painting qualities of the Brush tool can be radically changed via the brush More Options palette.

The drawing tools (the Shape tools), in contrast, are vector or line based. The objects drawn with these tools are defined mathematically as a specific shape, color and size. They exist independently of the pixel grid that makes up your image. They produce sharp-edged graphics and are particularly good for creating logos and other flat colored artwork. See Figure 8.1.

Figure 8.1 *Drawing and painting tools are used to add non-photographed information to your images. (1) Drawing tools. (2) Painting tools.*

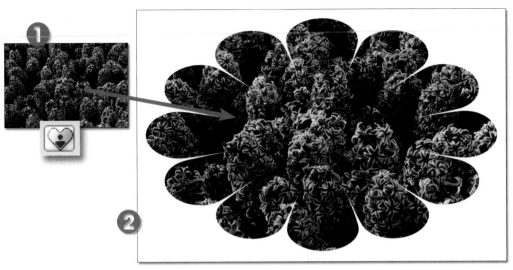

Figure 8.2 *The new Cookie Cutter tool functions much like a fancy cropping feature allowing users to remove the edges of their pictures in a range of graphic hard-edged shapes. Adding a feather value via the options bar softens the edge of the crop producing smoother transitions between the filled shape and the background.*

Cookie Cutter tool

Also included in this vector type (hard-edged) drawing tool group is the new Cookie Cutter tool. Though not strictly a drawing tool, the feature works in a very similar way to the Custom Shape tool as it too allows users to select and draw a range of predesigned shapes in the work space. It is after the drawing step that the two tools differ. The shape drawn with the Cookie Cutter is used to define the edges of the current image. In this way the feature functions as a fancy Crop tool providing a range of graphic designs that can be used to stampout the edges of your pictures. See Figure 8.2.

Paint tools

Paint Brush

The four main painting tools all apply color to an image in slightly different ways.

The Paint Brush lays down color in a similar fashion to a traditional brush. The size and shape of the brush can be selected from the list in the Brush Presets list (versions 3.0 and 2.0) or Brush palette (version 1.0) in the options bar. Changes to the brush characteristics can be made by altering the settings in the options bar and the More Options palette. See Figure 8.3.

In addition to changes to the size, painting mode and opacity of the brush, which are made via the options bar, you can also alter how the Paint Brush behaves. The new Brush Dynamics palette is used to creatively control your brush's characteristics.

The More Options palette

- **Spacing** determines the distance between paint dabs, with high values producing dotty effects.
- The **Fade** setting controls how quickly the paint color will fade to nothing. Low values fade more quickly than high ones.
- **Hue Jitter** controls the rate at which the brushes' color switches between foreground and background hues. High values cause quicker switches between the two colors.
- **Hardness** sets the size of the hard-edged center of the brush. Lower values produce soft brushes.
- The **Scatter** setting is used to control the way that strokes are bunched around the drawn line. A high value will cause the brush strokes to be more distant and less closely packed.
- **Angle** controls the inclination of an elliptical brush.
- The **Roundness** setting is used to determine the shape of the brush tip. A value of 100% will produce a circular brush, whereas a 0% setting results in a linear brush tip. See Figure 8.4.

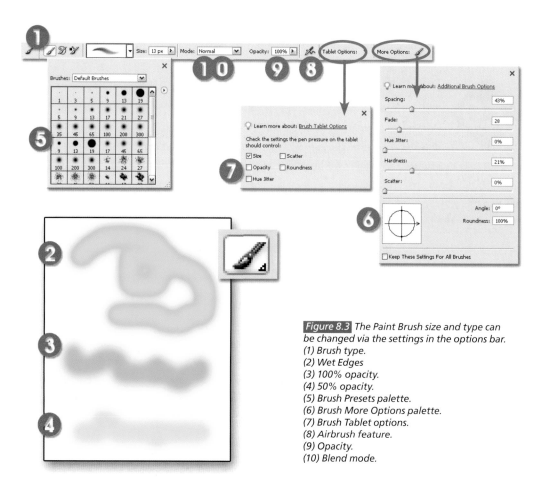

Figure 8.3 The Paint Brush size and type can be changed via the settings in the options bar.
(1) Brush type.
(2) Wet Edges
(3) 100% opacity.
(4) 50% opacity.
(5) Brush Presets palette.
(6) Brush More Options palette.
(7) Brush Tablet options.
(8) Airbrush feature.
(9) Opacity.
(10) Blend mode.

Version 1.0 users have a more limited set of brush controls accessed by clicking the thumbnail of the currently selected brush, in addition to pressing the More Options button. Completely new brushes can be added to the palette, in either version of the program, by selecting the side arrow in the Brush palette and choosing the New Brush option.

For the truly creative among us, extra custom-built brush sets are available for download and installation from websites specializing in Elements resources.

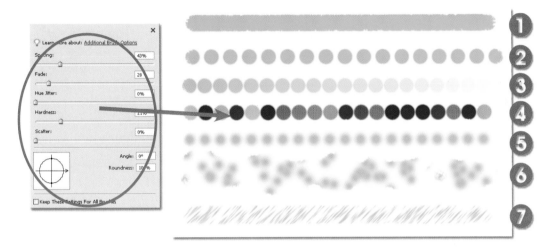

Figure 8.4 *The Elements brush engine provides a range of Brush Dynamics settings that allow users to completely control the behavior and characteristics of their brushes. (1) Normal. (2) Spacing increased. (3) Fade introduced. (4) Hue Jitter increased. (5) Hardness decreased. (6) Scatter increased. (7) Angle = 45°, Roundness = 0%.*

Airbrush

The Airbrush tool, located on the options bar of the Brush tool, sprays the paint color over the surface of the image. Although the size and style of the spray are determined by the selected brush (in the options bar), the edge of the area painted with this tool is a lot softer than the equivalent paint brush. Holding the mouse button down in one spot will build up the color in much the same way as paint from a spray can. See Figure 8.5.

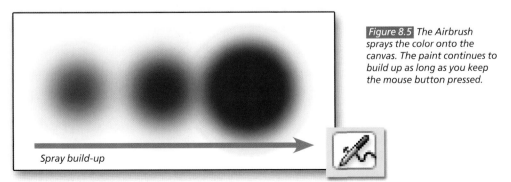

Figure 8.5 *The Airbrush sprays the color onto the canvas. The paint continues to build up as long as you keep the mouse button pressed.*

Spray build-up

Pencil

The Pencil differs from the other tools we have looked at so far in that it paints freehand lines. The thickness of these lines is dependent on the selected brush size. By clicking and dragging the mouse, the user can create freeform lines just as if you were using a pencil and a piece of paper. Using the tool in conjunction with the Shift key means that you can draw straight lines by clicking at the beginning and end points.

Don't confuse the Pencil with the line version of the Shape tool. The Pencil draws with pixels; the line tool defines a beginning and end point to a mathematical pixel-free line that is drawn only at the time that it is printed. See Figure 8.6.

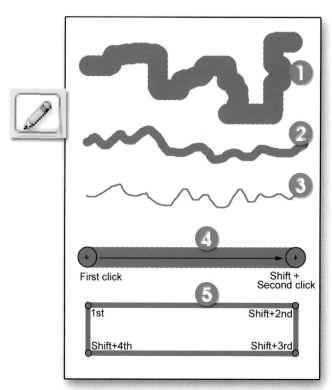

Figure 8.6 *The Pencil tool draws hard-edged lines.*
(1) 70 pixel pencil.
(2) 30 pixel pencil.
(3) 8 pixel pencil.
(4) To draw a straight line click to start the line and hold down the Shift key and click the mouse button a second time to mark the end of the line.
(5) The shift + click technique is used to draw a rectangle.

Paint Bucket

The Paint Bucket, though not usually considered a painting tool, is considered here because its main role is to apply color to areas of the image. The best way to describe how it functions is to imagine a Magic Wand tool that selected areas based on their color and then filled these selections with the foreground tint. In this way, the Paint Bucket selects and fills in a one-step action. See Figure 8.7.

Just like the Magic Wand, the Paint Bucket makes its selection based on the Tolerance value in the options bar. Higher Tolerance values mean pixels with greater difference in tone and color will be marked for color changes by the tool. The Anti-aliased, Contiguous and Use All Layers settings also work in the same was as they do for the Magic Wand.

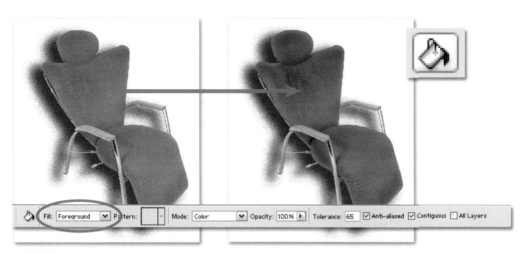

Figure 8.7 *The Paint Bucket tool selects and fills an area in the image based on pixel colors.*

In addition to applying color to selected areas, the Paint Bucket can also fill the area with a pattern. See Figure 8.8. Several default patterns are supplied with Elements or, if you are feeling adventurous, you can create your own using the following steps.

1 Select an area of an image using the Rectangular Marquee.

2 With the selection still active, select Define Pattern from the Edit menu.

3 Enter a name in the new pattern dialog.

4 The new pattern is now available for use from the Pattern palette of the Paint Bucket tool.

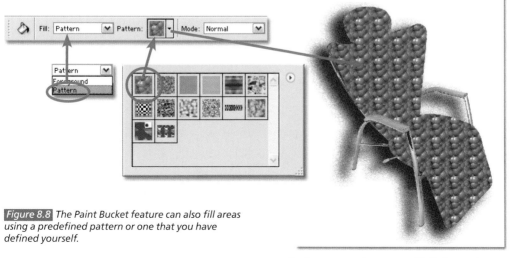

Figure 8.8 *The Paint Bucket feature can also fill areas using a predefined pattern or one that you have defined yourself.*

Choosing my paint colors

The color of the paint for all tools is based on the foreground color selected in the toolbox. To change this hue you can double-click the swatch and select another color from the palette or you can use the eyedropper to sample a color already existing in your image. See Figure 8.9.

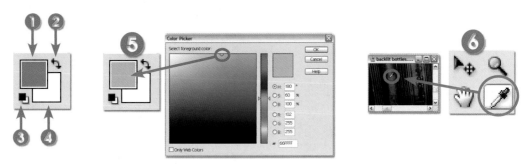

Figure 8.9 *All brushes paint with the color that is selected in the foreground/background swatches. (1) Foreground color. (2) Switch colors. (3) Default colors. (4) Background color. (5) Changing color using the Color Picker. (6) Changing color using the eyedropper to sample a new hue from a picture.*

Painting tools summary

1 Pick foreground color (painting color).

2 Select the painting tool from the toolbox.

3 Click the down arrow next to the sample brush in the options bar to select brush type.

4 Adjust brush opacity.

5 Adjust other options for a particular tool.

6 Drag brush over image surface to paint.

The Impressionist Brush tool

In addition to these standard painting options, Elements has a specialist Impressionist Brush tool that allows you to repaint existing images with a series of stylized strokes. By adjusting the special paint style, area, size and tolerance options, you can create a variety of painterly effects on your images. See Figure 8.10.

1 Pick Impressionist Brush from the toolbox (hidden under the Brush tool in Version 3.0).

2 Select brush size, mode and opacity from the options bar.

3 Set the style, area and tolerance values from the More Options palette.

4 Drag the brush over the image surface to paint.

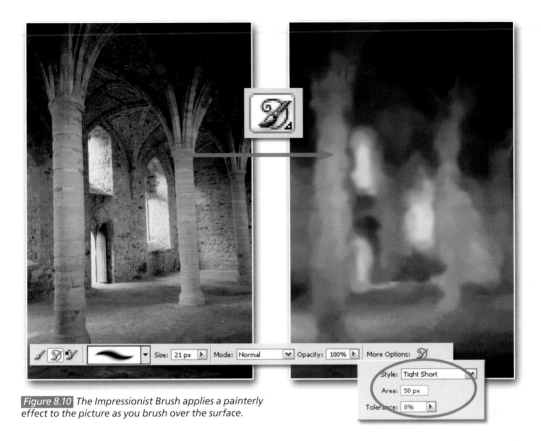

Figure 8.10 The Impressionist Brush applies a painterly
effect to the picture as you brush over the surface.

Color Replacement tool

The Color Replacement tool locates and replaces a specific color in an image with one of your
choosing. In this way it works a little like a more sophisticated version of the Red Eye Removal tool
in that you can choose both the color to be replaced as well as its substitute hue. See Figure 8.11.

1 Pick Color Replacement tool from the toolbox (hidden under the Brush tool in Version 3.0).

2 Select brush size and set mode to Hue, Sampling to Background Swatch and Limits to
Discontiguous in the options bar.

3 Using the eyedropper tool select the color from the picture that you want to replace as the
foreground color swatch.

4 Switch fore and background swatches.

5 Double-click on the foreground swatch and select a replacement color.

6 Click and drag the Color Replacement brush over the image surface to substitute the colors.

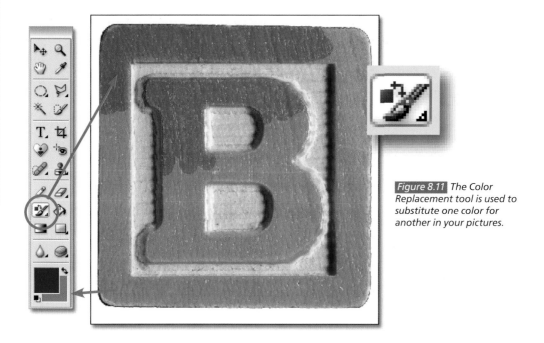

Figure 8.11 The Color Replacement tool is used to substitute one color for another in your pictures.

Erasing

The Eraser tool changes image pixels as it is dragged over them. If you are working on a background layer then the pixels are erased or changed to the background color. In contrast, erasing a normal layer will convert the pixels to transparent, which will let the image show through from beneath. See Figure 8.12.

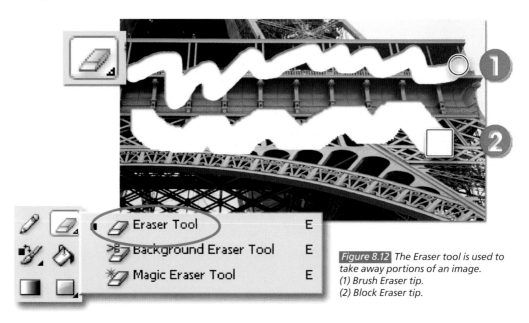

Figure 8.12 The Eraser tool is used to take away portions of an image.
(1) Brush Eraser tip.
(2) Block Eraser tip.

As with the other painting tools, the size and style of the eraser is based on the selected brush. But unlike the others the eraser can take the form of a paint brush, pencil or block. Setting the opacity will govern the strength of the erasing action.

Apart from the straight Eraser tool, two other versions of this tool are available – the Background Eraser and the Magic Eraser. These extra options are found hidden under the Eraser icon in the toolbox.

The *Background Eraser* is used to delete pixels around the edge of an object. This tool is very useful for extracting objects from their backgrounds. The tool pointer is made of two parts – a circle and a cross hair. The circle size is based on the brush diameter.

To use the tool, the cross hair is positioned and dragged across the area to be erased, whilst at the same time the circle's edge overlaps the edge of the object to be kept. The success of this tool is largely based on the contrast between the edge of the object and the background. The greater the contrast, the more effective the tool. Again, a Tolerance slider is used to control how different pixels need to be in order to be erased. See Figure 8.13.

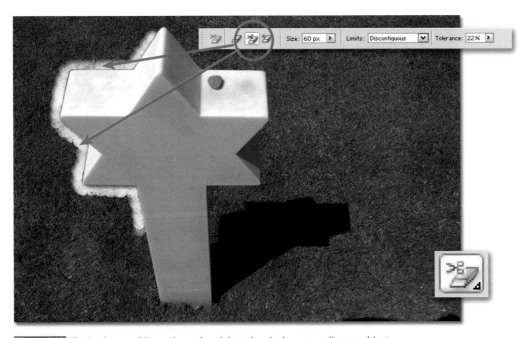

Figure 8.13 *The Background Eraser is used to delete the pixels surrounding an object.*

The *Magic Eraser* uses the selection features of the Magic Wand to select similarly colored pixels to erase. This tool works well if the area of the image you want to erase is all the same color and contrasts in tone or color with the rest of the image. See Figure 8.14.

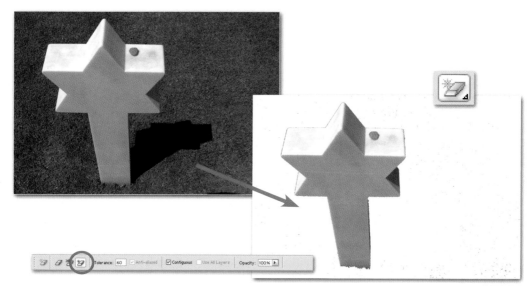

Figure 8.14 The Magic Eraser selects and erases pixels of similar color and tone.

FEATURE SUMMARY

1 Pick the Eraser tool type from the toolbox.

2 For the Eraser tool – select a brush size and style and choose the form that the tool will take.

3 For Magic Eraser and Background Eraser – set Tolerance and Contiguous values.

4 Drag over or click on the image to erase.

Better with a tablet

Many professionals prefer to work with a stylus and tablet when working with complex drawing tasks. The extra options provided by the pressure sensitivity of the stylus along with the familiar 'pencil and paper' feeling make using this approach more intuitive and often faster than using a mouse. When a stylus and tablet is installed on your machine you will be able to access the extra pen or stylus options available through the program. See Figure 8.15.

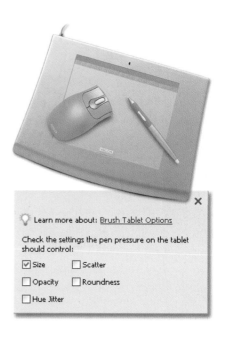

Figure 8.15 Elements contains support for pressure-sensitive devices such as Wacom Stylus and Tablets. Elements enables the user to link specific settings to the pressure setting of the stylus.

Painting tools in action

Creating rough-edged picture borders

Sometimes you might find that a clean hard-edged print border is not a look that suits your image. Instead, you may want to create a more unpredictable or broken edge to your photograph. Using the characteristics of some of the brushes supplied with Elements, it is possible to create a rough-edged shape that can be used as a border for a digital photograph.

Follow the steps below to make your first rough-edged print:

1 Start the process by opening an image that you want to apply the border effect to.

2 Determine the size of the picture in pixels using the Image > Resize > Image Size dialog. Create a new document (File > New) the same size or a little bigger than the photograph.

3 Set default foreground and background colors (black on white). Select the Brush tool and select a rough brush type from the many thumbnails in the Brush Presets.

4 Paint a large black area on the new document, leaving the edges white and clear of color.

5 Switch to the photograph document and select (Select > All) and copy (Edit > Copy) the whole image to memory.

6 Switch back to the drawn picture and paste (Edit > Paste) the photograph as a new layer on top of the drawn layer.

7 Change the blending mode of the photograph layer to screen to reveal the picture inside the roughly drawn outline. See Figure 8.16.

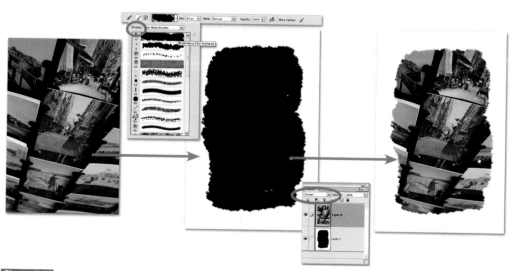

Figure 8.16 Create a rough-edged print by combining some drawing steps with a simple cut and paste technique.

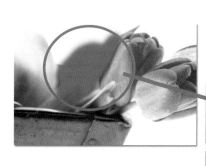

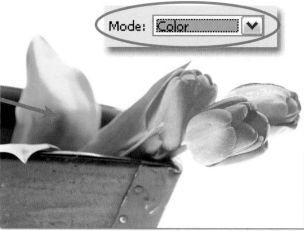

Figure 8.17 *Use the Brush tool in Color mode to add realistic tints to your black and white photographs.*

Hand coloring black and white photos

In this technique, we will use the Elements Brush tool to apply a color tint to a photograph. But to ensure that the detail from the image shows through the coloring we must modify the way the hue is added. By switching the Brush mode (this is similar to the Layers Blend mode options) from its Normal setting to a specialized Color setting the paint starts to act more like traditional water color paint. When the hue is applied the detail is changed in proportion to the tone beneath. Dark areas are changed to a deep version of the selected color and lighter areas are delicately tinted. See Figure 8.17.

1 With your image open in Elements check to see what color mode the picture is stored in. Do this by selecting Image > Mode and then locate which setting the tick is next to. For most black and white photographs the picture will be in Grayscale mode. If this is the case change it to RGB Color (Image > Mode > RGB Color).

2 You will not notice any difference in the picture as a result of its mode change but now the image is capable of holding colors (not just grays). Now double-click on the foreground swatch in the toolbox and select a color appropriate for your picture. Here I chose a dark green for the leaves.

3 Now select the Paintbrush tool from the toolbox and adjust its size and edge softness using the settings in the options bar. Start to paint onto the surface of the picture. You will notice straight away that the paint is covering the detail of the picture beneath. This is because the brush is still in Normal mode. Use Ctrl + Z to undo your painting.

4 In order for the brush to just color the picture (keeping the details from beneath) the tool must be in the Color mode. To make the change click on the Mode drop-down menu in the options bar and select the Color option towards the bottom of the list.

5 With the Color mode now selected start to apply the color again. Immediately you will notice the difference. The brush is now substituting the color for the gray tones in the picture and it is doing so proportionately – dark grey = dark green, light grey = light green.

6 Once the leaves and stems have been colored, select new colors for the flowers and finally
the bucket. The amount and areas of the picture that you choose to color is up to you. Some
photographs look great with only one colored section and the rest black and white.

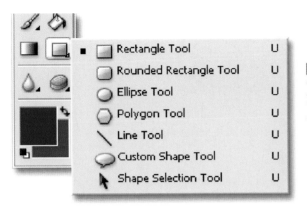

Figure 8.18 Only one Shape tool is shown
in the toolbox, but others can be viewed
by clicking and holding the mouse over
the small triangle in the bottom right
corner of the button.

Drawing tools

With the Shape tool it is possible to draw lines, rectangles, polygons and ellipses, as well as creating
your own custom shapes. After selecting the tool and picking the fill color, you can draw the shape
by clicking and dragging the mouse. Although only one Shape tool is visible in the toolbox at any
time, you can select a different option by clicking and holding the mouse button down over the tool
icon and then selecting the new tool from the list as it appears. See Figures 8.18 and 8.19.

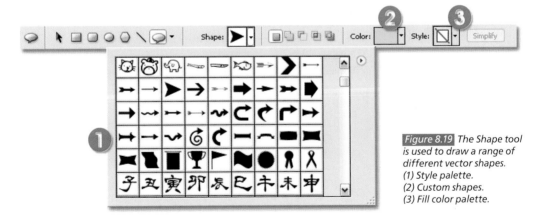

Figure 8.19 The Shape tool
is used to draw a range of
different vector shapes.
(1) Style palette.
(2) Custom shapes.
(3) Fill color palette.

A new shape layer is opened automatically when you select a tool and draw a new shape. In the
Layers palette you will notice that the shape is made up of two parts – the 'Fill' and the 'Path'.
Double-clicking the Fill icon will give you the opportunity to change the color. Double-clicking the
Path icon will allow you to edit the shape's name. See Figure 8.20.

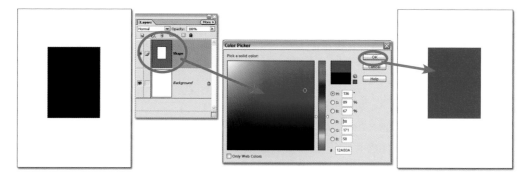

Figure 8.20 The fill color of a shape can be changed by double-clicking the shape in the shape's layer (version 2.0) or the color icon (version 1.0).

When you create multiple shapes on a single layer you have the opportunity to decide how overlapping areas interact. Two or more different shapes can be added to form a third and the intersection of shapes can be added or subtracted from the image. At first the Shape tool can seem a little confusing, but with practice you will be able to build up complex images by gradually adding and subtracting shapes. See Figure 8.21.

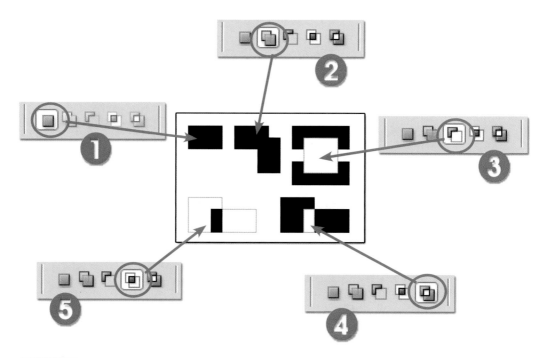

Figure 8.21 The way that successively drawn custom shapes interact can be customized via buttons on the options bar. (1) Single new shape. (2) Add shape to existing shape. (3) Subtract shape from existing shapes. (4) Subtract overlapping areas of existing shapes. (5) Use the intersection of the areas as a new shape.

1 Pick the Shape tool you require from the toolbox. Click and hold down the mouse button to reveal hidden options.

2 For a new shape pick the Create New Shape Layer option. For adding to an existing shape layer, select the layer and select the shape area option that suits your needs. You can pick from Add, Subtract, Intersect and Exclude.

3 Click on the color swatch to specify the fill color for the shape.

4 Click and drag on the image surface to draw the shape.

Even more shapes

Elements 3.0 comes supplied with a vast range of shapes. New shape sets can be added to those already visible as thumbnails by clicking the side arrow button in the Custom Shape Picker palette. If you can't find a favorite here then why not try some of the extra shape sets that can be downloaded from specialist Elements resources websites.

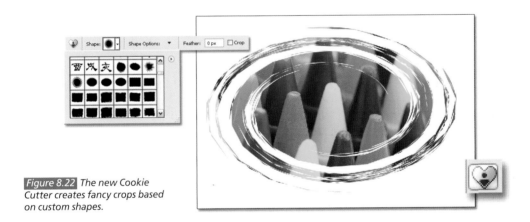

Figure 8.22 The new Cookie Cutter creates fancy crops based on custom shapes.

Cookie Cutter tool

The new Cookie Cutter tool is a two-step feature that crops your pictures in the shape of one of many 'cookie' designs that Elements is shipped with. The new feature is a great way to add interesting edge effects to your pictures. See Figure 8.22.

1 Open an image to crop and select the Cookie Cutter tool from the toolbox.

2 Click the Shape button in the options bar to reveal the pop-up menu of cookie shapes. Select the shape to use.

3 To soften the edge of cookie cutter crop, add a Feather value in the options bar.

4 Click and drag the tool over the surface of the picture. Let the mouse button go and click and drag the edge handles to adjust the size of the cookie shape to suit the picture.

5 Double-click inside the cookie shape or click the 'Tick' icon in the options bar to apply the crop.

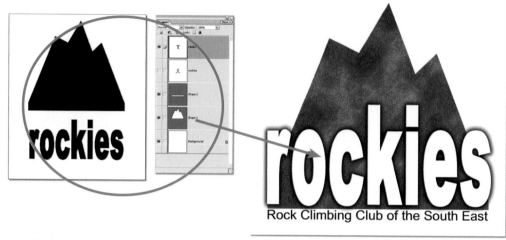

Figure 8.23 *Use the Shape and Type tools together with the Styles palette to create great logos.*

Drawing tools in action

Making a shape-based logo

The Custom Shape tool can be used alongside Elements' type and style features to create eye-catching logos.

Create a simple logo using the steps below:

1 Select the type family/style and custom shape that will form the base of the logo.

2 Make shape and type layers.

3 Apply Effects and Layer Styles features to the type and shape. See Figure 8.23.

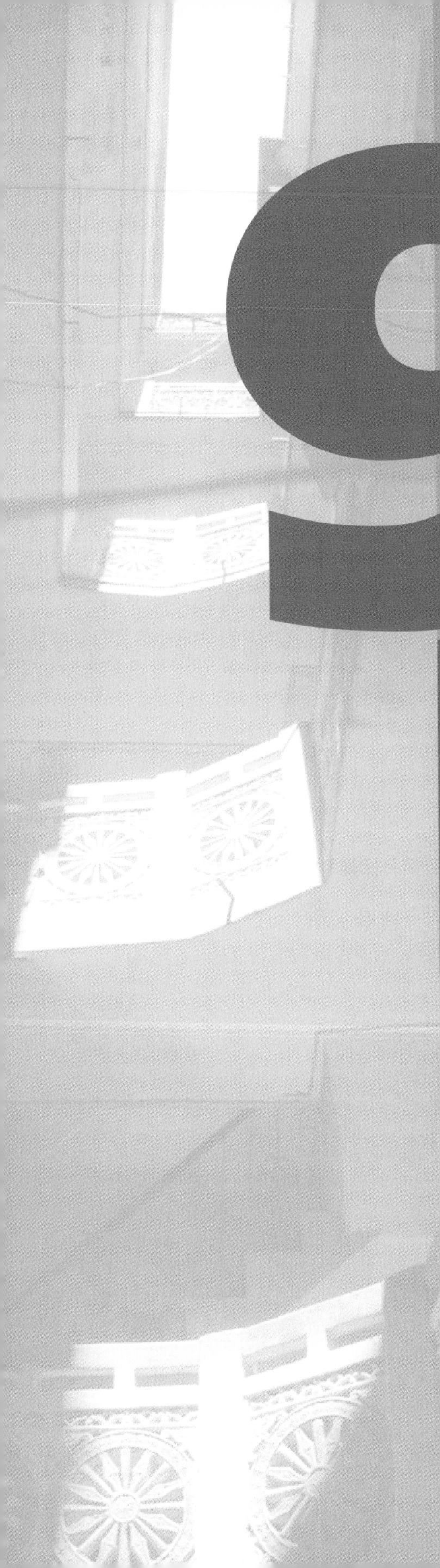

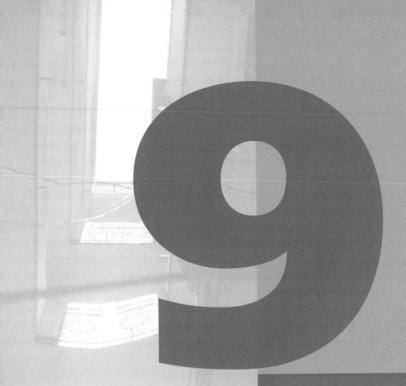

9

Creating Great Panoramas

Taking Photomerge images

Editor: File > New > Photomerge Panorama

Photomerge from the Photo Browser

Photomerge in action

Fixing panorama problems

Top tips from panoramic professionals

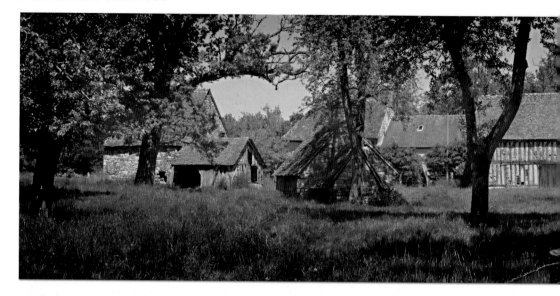

anoramic images have always been a very inspiring aspect of photography. Until now, making these types of pictures has been restricted to a small set of lucky individuals who are fortunate enough to own the specialized cameras needed to capture the wide images. With the onset of the latest image-editing packages, software manufacturers have now started to include features that allow users with standard cameras to create wonderful wide-angle vistas digitally. See Figure 9.1.

These extra pieces of software are sometimes referred to as stitching programs, as their actual function is to combine a series of photographs into a single picture. The edge details of each successive image are matched and blended so that the join is not detectable. See Figure 9.2.

Once all the photographs have been combined, the result is a picture that shows a scene of any angle of anything up to a full 360°. See Figure 9.3.

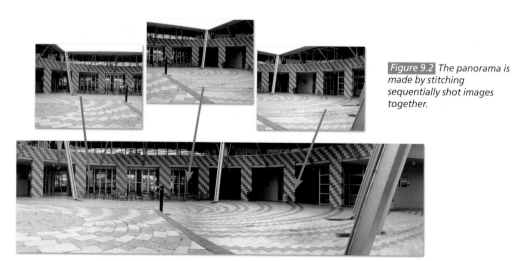

Figure 9.2 *The panorama is made by stitching sequentially shot images together.*

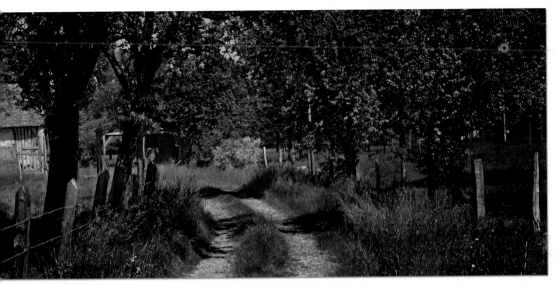

Figure 9.1 Many digital editing packages like Elements now include stitching packages that allow you to make dramatic panoramas from standard camera images.

Photomerge (Editor: File > New > Create Photomerge Panorama) is included free within Elements and is Adobe's version of the stitching technology. The version of Photomerge that was supplied with Elements 2.0 was updated to include enhanced support for larger file sizes and better fine-tuning controls. Photomerge version 3.0 sees a continuing of this evolution with better edge matching results and the ability to produce the composition as separate source picture layers.

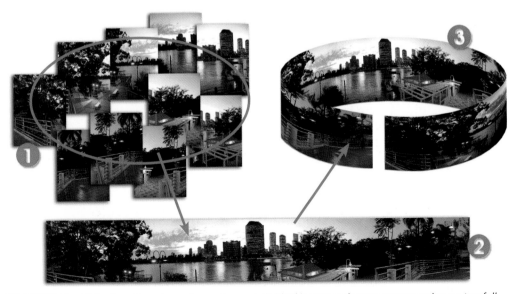

Figure 9.3 The stitched result can be made up of many individual images and can encompass a view up to a full 360°. (1) Individual source photos. (2) Stitched panorama. (3) 360° spinning panorama.

Taking Photomerge images

Although the Photomerge feature is designed to simplify and solve many of the problems associated with image stitching, a great deal of your own success will be based on how your source images are taken in the first place. A little care and planning at the shooting stage can ensure a successful panorama with little or no 'touch-up' work later. Use the following guidelines to help capture those vistas.

Image overlap

Photomerge works by identifying common edge elements in sequential images and using these as a basis for blending the two pictures together. When you are making your source photographs, ensure that they overlap by a minimum of 15% and a maximum of 40%. See Figure 9.4.

These settings give the program enough information to ensure accurate stitching. I find that if I locate a feature about one-third of the way in from the right-hand side of the viewfinder (or display screen) in one shot and then position the same detail one-third from the left in the next shot, I end up with sufficient overlap for Elements to process the picture. Overlapping images by more than 50% may seem like a good idea, but this can cause the image blending process to be less effective.

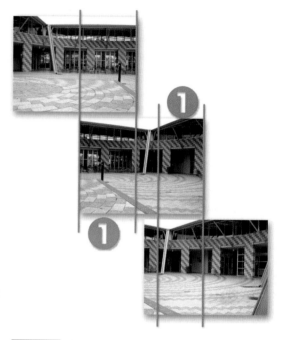

Figure 9.4 *It is important to overlap source images by between 30% and 70%. (1) Overlap between successive photographs.*

Keep the camera level

Although Photomerge is designed to adjust images that are slightly rotated, it is far better to ensure that all source images are level to start with. The easiest way to achieve this is by photographing your scene with your camera connected to a level tripod with a rotating head. If you are out shooting and don't have a tripod handy, try to locate a feature in the scene that remains horizontal in all shots and use this as a guide to keep your camera level when photographing your image sequence. See Figure 9.5.

Maintain focal length

Sometimes it is tempting to zoom in to capture a closer view of important details when you are in the middle of shooting a panorama sequence. Doing so will change the focal length of the lens and will make it very difficult or impossible to stitch this picture with all the others from the scene. Check what is the optimum focal length for the vista before starting to photograph and once you start to shoot don't touch the zoom control. See Figure 9.6.

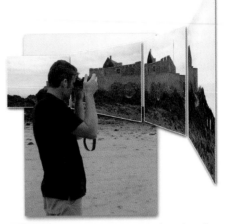

Figure 9.5 *Keep the camera level when shooting your scene.*

Pivot around the lens

Photomerge uses sophisticated perspective calculations to help reconstruct the scene you photographed. Changing your position, even by a few inches, will alter the perspective of all the images taken from that point on. Even the way that you hold and rotate the camera can alter the picture's vanishing point. To get the best results always try to pivot the camera around the axis (nodal point) of its lens; this will ensure that all the images in your sequence will have a similar perspective.

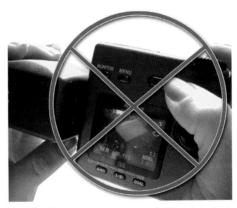

Figure 9.6 *Don't change focal length in the middle of a shooting sequence.*

Special panoramic heads designed to position the lens above the center of the tripod are available for this purpose. These virtual reality (VR) heads offset the camera so the nodal point of the lens is directly over the pivot point of the camera. Models are available for specific cameras or you can purchase a multi-purpose design that can be adjusted to suit a range of film and digital bodies. Shooting with these heads is by far the best way to ensure that you images stitch well. See Figure 9.7. If you are capturing your scene with a hand-held camera, then try to rotate your body around the camera, not the other way around. See Figure 9.8.

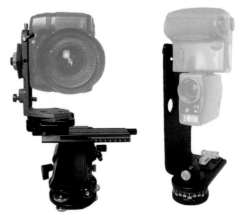

Figure 9.7 *A panoramic head for tripods is available for users who regularly shoot wide vistas. (Source: Kaidan and Manfrotto panoramic tripod heads).*

Book resources at: **www.guide2elements.com**

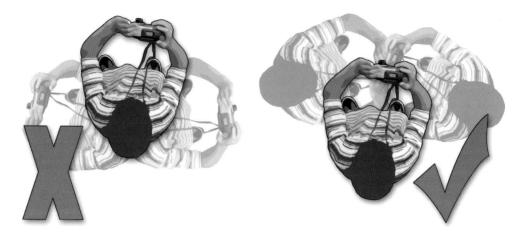

Figure 9.8 *If no tripod is available, pivot the camera around its lens, not around your body.*

Maximum image size no longer 2 megapixels

The original version of Photomerge found in Elements 1.0 was designed to stitch source images of 2 megapixels or less. Users with higher specification cameras using version 1.0 were able to interactively reduce the size of source images at the time of acquisition.

Thankfully the later versions of Photomerge can handle the higher resolution files produced by modern digital cameras with a minimum of fuss. However, keep in mind that you should only use images whose combined pixels dimensions suit your final product. There is no point, for instance, in stitching ten 5-megapixel source pictures if the final panorama will only be printed as an A4 or letter size photograph. The stitching process will take longer to process when working with the larger files than with ones suited to the small print size. It is better to set your camera to record a smaller file when shooting a panorama sequence that will be printed on small sheets of paper.

Maintain exposure

Modern cameras contain specialized metering systems designed to obtain the best exposure for a range of lighting conditions. Each time the camera is aimed at a scene, a new calculation is made for the brightest and darkest areas of the view. This system, though very helpful for normal picture taking, can be problematic when shooting panoramas, as the exposure needs to be constant throughout the shooting sequence.

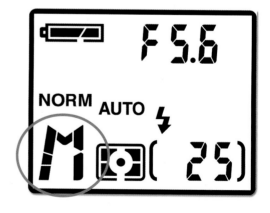

Figure 9.9 *Change the exposure system to manual to keep images consistent.*

Changing the exposure settings automatically for different image parts of the same scene will mean that key areas will appear as different tones in the stitched picture. See Figure 9.9. If possible, you should change your camera's metering system to manual for the period whilst you are capturing panoramic source images to ensure consistent exposures.

In shooting environments where there is a large range of brightness change from one part of the scene to the other, it is a good idea to shoot the source images for the scene twice using two different exposures – one set for the highlights and the other for the shadows. Before importing your images into Photomerge, you can combine the captured details from the two exposures and then stitch the evenly exposed result. See the Fixing panorama problems section at end of this chapter for an example of this technique.

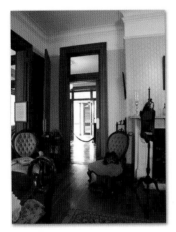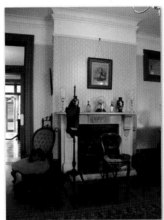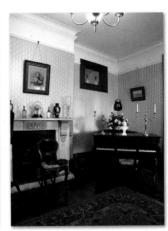

Figure 9.10 *Be careful of changes in color cast from frame to frame resulting from inconsistent white balance settings.*

Keep white balance consistent

A similar problem can occur with the auto white balance system contained in many digital cameras. This feature assesses not the amount of light entering the camera, but the color of the light, in order to automatically rid your images of color casts that result from mixed light sources in the scene. Leaving this feature set to auto can mean drastic color changes from one frame to the next as the camera attempts to produce the most neutral result. Switching to manual can produce results that are more consistent, but you must assess the scene carefully to ensure that you base your white balance settings on the most prominent light source in the scene. See Figure 9.10.

For instance, if you are photographing a wedding and two-thirds of the source shots are lit by sunlight, then this would probably be the best setting to use. For the experimenters amongst us, the one-third of the panorama not lit by sunlight could be shot a second time using a white balance setting that suits and these images substituted before stitching.

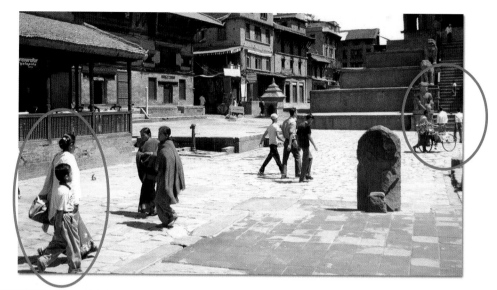

Figure 9.11 *Try to avoid placing moving objects at the edge of frames, as they will disappear or be ghosted when the images are stitched.*

Watch the edges

The edges of the image frame are the most critical part of the source picture. It is important to make sure that moving details such as cars, or pedestrians, are kept out of these areas. Objects that appear in the edge of one frame and not the next cause problems for the stitching program and may need to be removed or repaired later with other tools like the Clone Stamp. See Figure 9.11.

Editor: File > New > Photomerge Panorama

Version 2.0: File > Create Photomerge
Version 1.0: File > Photomerge

Now that we have successfully captured our source pictures let's set about stitching them together to form a panorama. When opening Photomerge you are presented with a simple dialog with Browse/Open and Remove options which prompt the user to nominate the picture files that will be used to make up the panorama. Suitable files are 'browsed' for and 'opened' into the Source Files section of the box. Any of the files listed here can be removed if incorrectly added by highlighting the file name and clicking the Remove button. See Figure 9.12. Version 1.0 users are presented with Image Reduction, Apply Perspective and Automatically Arrange choices at the very first screen and then are taken to the Add Files Type dialog.

Clicking OK exits the dialog and starts the initial opening and arranging steps in Photomerge. You will see the program load, match and stitch the image pieces together. If the pictures are stored in RAW or 16-bit form they will be converted to 8 bit during this part of the process as well. For the most part, Photomerge will be able to correctly identify overlapping sequential images and will place them side by side in the editing work space. In some instances, a few of the source files might not be able to be automatically placed and Elements will display a pop-up dialog telling you this has occurred. Don't be concerned about this as a little fine-tuning is needed even with the best panoramic projects and the pictures that haven't been placed can be manually moved into position in the main Photomerge work space. See Figure 9.13.

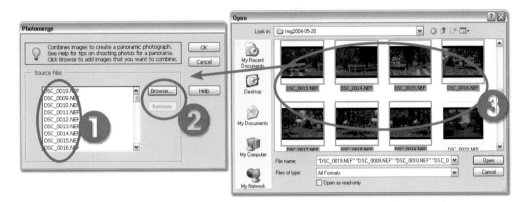

Figure 9.12 *Pick the files you want to use for the stitching process using the Browse dialog box. (1) Selected source files. (2) Browse and Remove buttons. (3) Add files window.*

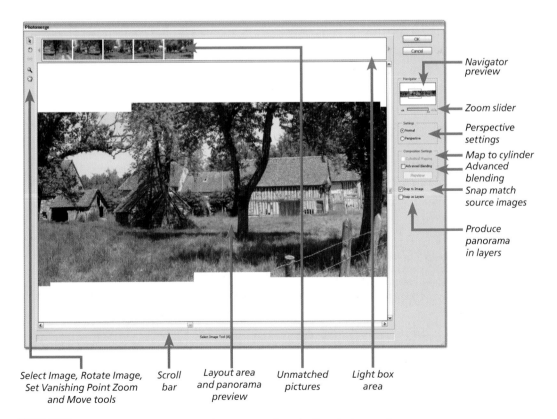

Select Image, Rotate Image,
Set Vanishing Point Zoom
and Move tools

Scroll
bar

Layout area
and panorama
preview

Unmatched
pictures

Light box
area

Navigator
preview

Zoom slider

Perspective
settings

Map to cylinder

Advanced
blending

Snap match
source images

Produce
panorama
in layers

Figure 9.13 *The main Photomerge dialog allows you to edit and adjust the layout of your panorama.*

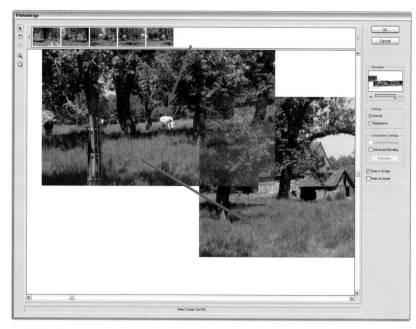

Figure 9.14 *You can move source images to and from the light box and layout areas by clicking and dragging them.*

Editing your panorama

Whilst in the Photomerge work space you can use the Select Image tool to move any of the individual parts of the panorama around the composition or from the layout to the light box area. Click and drag to move image parts. Holding down the Shift key will constrain movements to horizontal, vertical or 45° adjustments only. The Hand or Move View tool can be used in conjunction with the Navigator window to move your way around the picture. For finer control use the Rotate Image tool to make adjustments to the orientation of selected image parts. See Figure 9.14.

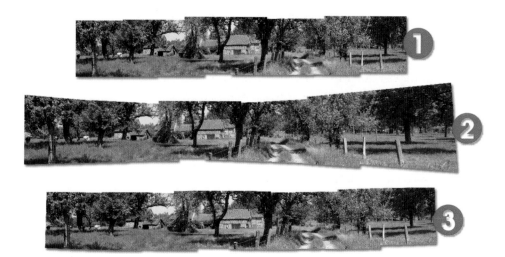

Figure 9.15 *The Cylindrical Mapping feature will help correct the 'bow tie' effect that can result from perspective adjustments. (1) Panorama with normal setting. (2) Perspective setting applied. (3) Cylindrical Mapping and Advanced Blending applied to perspective corrected panorama.*

The 'Use Perspective' option, together with the Set Vanishing Point tool, manipulate the perspective of your panorama and its various parts. Keep in mind when using the perspective tools that the first image that is positioned in the Composition area is the base image (light green border), which determines the perspective of all other image parts (red border). To change the base image, click on another image part with the Set Vanishing Point tool. To correct some of the 'bow tie'-like distortion that can occur when using these tools, check the Cylindrical Mapping option in the Composition area of the dialog. See Figure 9.15. The Advanced Blending feature, also available here, can be used to help minimize color inconsistencies or exposure differences between sequential images. It is not possible to use the perspective correction tools for images with an angle of view greater than 120°, so make sure that these options are turned off.

After making the final adjustments, the panorama can be completed by clicking the OK button in the Photomerge dialog box. This action creates a stitched file that no longer contains the individual images.

1   Select Photomerge Panorama from the File > New menu to start a new panorama.

2   Click the Browse button in the dialog box.

3   Search through the thumbnails of your files to locate the pictures for your panorama.

4   Click the Open button to add files to the Source Files section of the dialog.

5   *Version 1.0 only* – set the Image Size Reduction amount to reduce source file sizes. If you are using images greater than 2 megapixels, then a setting of 50% or more should be used.

6   *Version 1.0 only* – to get Elements to lay out the selected images check the 'Attempt to Automatically Arrange Source Images' box for manual layout control; leave the box unchecked.

7   *Version 1.0 only* – if you are using the 'Automatic Arrange' option then you can also choose to apply perspective correction across the whole of the composition. Do not use this feature if the panorama covers an angle of view greater than 120°.

8   Select OK to open the Photomerge main workspace. Edit the layout of your source images.

9   To change the view of the images use the Move View tool or change the scale and the position of the whole composition with the Navigator.

10 Images can be dragged to and from the light box to the work area with the Select Image tool.

11 With the Snap to Image function turned on, Photomerge will match like details of different images when they are dragged over each other.

12 Ticking the Use Perspective box will instruct Elements to use the first image placed into the layout area as the base for the composition of the whole panorama. Images placed into the composition later will be adjusted to fit the perspective of the base picture.

13 The Cylindrical Mapping option adjusts a perspective corrected image so that it is more rectangular in shape.

14 The Advanced Blending option will try to smooth out uneven exposure or tonal difference between stitched pictures.

15 The effects of Cylindrical Mapping as well as Advanced Blending can be viewed by clicking the Preview button.

16 The final panorama file is produced by clicking the OK button.

17 To produce the panorama document where the source images are kept as separate layers click the Keep as layers checkbox.

Photomerge from the Photo Browser

Photo Browser: File > New > Photomerge Panorama in Editor

In version 3.0 of Elements for Windows, the Photomerge feature can be accessed from the Photo Browser or Organizer work space as well as from within the Standard editor window. This means that you can locate and multi-select a series of source files using the Photo Browser before selecting the File > New > Photomerge Panorama in Editor menu option. This action will then open the Standard editor work space and then automatically add the selected pictures to the Photomerge add files dialog. At this point you can remove any of the files listed or add more pictures to the group. Once you click OK then Photomerge proceeds as normal. See Figure 9.16.

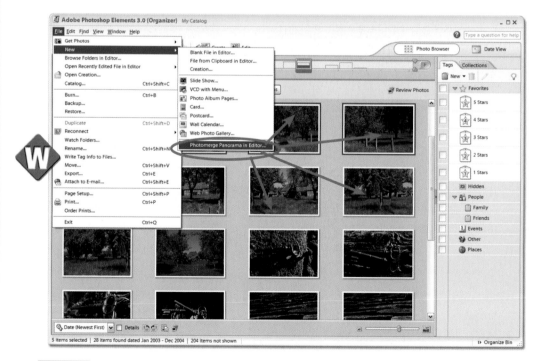

Figure 9.16 For Windows users Photomerge can be accessed from the Photo Browser or Organizer work space as well as from inside the Standard editor.

Macintosh File Browser: Automate > Photomerge

To accommodate Macintosh users, similar multi-select functionality is possible directly from the upgraded File Browser in the editor work space. To select a sequence of photos that will make up a panorama, select the initial source photo and then, whilst holding down the Shift key, click on the last photo in the series. Now to pass these multi-selected files to the Photomerge feature, choose Automate > Photomerge from inside the browser. Automatically the Photomerge feature opens and bypasses the add files dialog. The images you selected are arranged and a preview of their stitched appearance is displayed in the main Photomerge work space. See Figure 9.17.

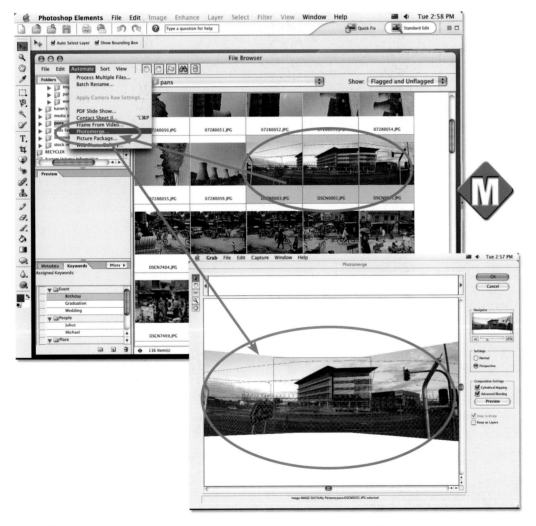

Figure 9.17 For Macintosh users Photomerge can be accessed from the upgraded File Browser in the editor work space.

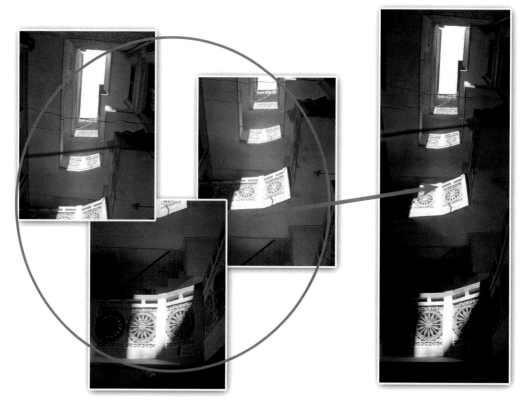

Figure 9.18 *Photomerge can be used for vertical stitching tasks as well as wide-angle vistas.*

Photomerge in action

Vertical stitches

For most of the time you will probably use Photomerge to make horizontal panoramas of wide vistas, but occasionally you may come across a situation where you can make use of the stitching technology to create vertical panoramas rather than horizontal ones.

When capturing the vertical source images, be sure to follow the same guidelines used for standard panoramas – check exposure, focus, white balance, focal length and shooting position. See Figure 9.18.

Document stitches

Don't restrict yourself to using the Photomerge technology for creating architectural or landscape images; the tool can also come in handy when you are trying to scan a document that is larger than your scanner bed. Take the situation of recreating a digital version of an old wall map.

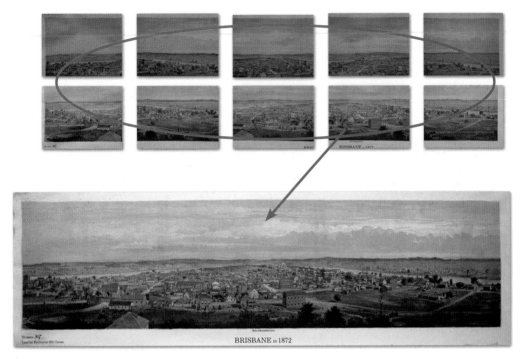

Figure 9.19 *Document stitching allows you to scan a large document in sections and then 'glue' it all back together again.*

The size of the document means that it will need to be captured in a series of section scans. The resultant files can then be stitched together to recreate a highly detailed digital version of the original document. See Figure 9.19.

Making panoramas that spin

When you produce a panorama that covers the full 360° of a scene, you not only have an image that can be used to make a wide vista print, but you also have the basic building block needed for creating an Apple QuickTime Virtual Reality (VR) movie. QuickTime allows the viewer to stand in the middle of the action and spin the image around themselves. It is like you are actually there.

Creating a QuickTime VR movie from your finished file is as simple as saving the stitched image as a Macintosh PICT file and then converting it to QuickTime format using Apple's free Make Panorama tool. The resulting file can be watched with any QuickTime player and has the added bonus of being able to be uploaded to the web and viewed online.

Windows users can make similar spinning panoramas using a small, economical utility called Pano2exe. The program converts JPEG output from Photomerge to a self-contained EXE or program file, which is a single easily distributable file that contains the image itself as well as a built-in viewer. See Figures 9.20 and 9.21.

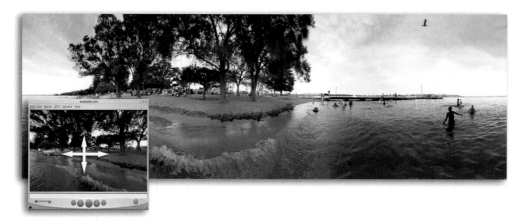

Figure 9.20 *Example panoramic flat file picture converted to a QuickTime VR movie using Apple's free Make Panorama tool available from http://developer.apple.com/quicktime/ quicktimeintro/tools/. Image courtesy of Geoff Jagoe of Mastery Media. www.mastery.com.au.*

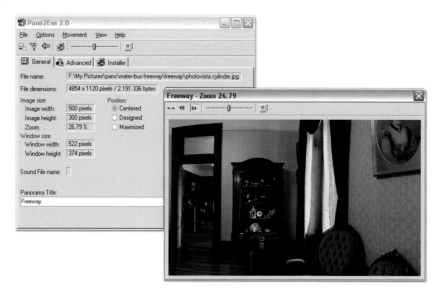

Figure 9.21 *The Pano2exe utility provides a convenient and economical way to convert your Photomerge vistas to distributable navigable panoramas. See www.change7.com for details.*

Fixing panorama problems

No matter how sophisticated the stitching technology, Photomerge included, there are often some small problems in the final picture where the blending process has not produced perfect results. Some of these defects can be corrected by re-editing the panorama itself: arranging, rotating and manually moving the problem source images to create a better blend. But there are also occasions where the stitching process is not at fault.

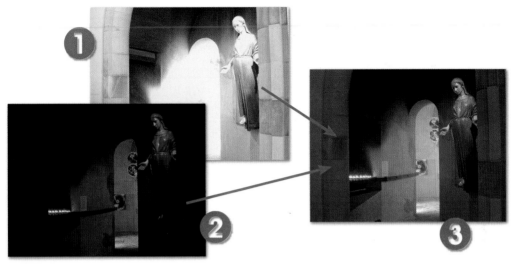

Figure 9.22 *Tricky exposure situations can be solved by shooting twice – make one image so that the exposure is adjusted for shadows and one for highlights – and then combine the details of both shots to produce the frame that contains both shadows and highlights that will be used for stitching. (1) Shadow details captured. (2) Highlight details captured. (3) Combined photograph with both highlights and shadows.*

The causes of these problems usually fall into one of two groups – subjects moving or changing at the edges of overlapping frames and differences in lighting and/or color between sequential images.

Solution 1 – Time your shooting sequence to accommodate moving objects in the frame. Wait till the objects are in the middle of the frame or are not in the frame at all before pushing the button.

Solution 2 – Shoot a single frame featuring the moving object so that, after stitching, the object can be cut and pasted into position over the top of the completed panorama.

Solution 3 – Shoot two complete sequences of source images, one with the camera's exposure system to suit the highlights of the scene and one with the settings adjusted for the shadows. Try adjusting your camera to 2 stops under the camera setting for the highlight picture and 2 stops over for the image in which the shadows are captured. Before stitching, combine the individual images into a single document. Arrange the layers so that the darkest picture is on top. Change the Blend mode of the dark layer Multiply and open the Levels feature. Drag the black point output slider to the center of the dialog to add the highlight detail to the midtone and shadow areas of the layer beneath. Save the combined image and then use the correctly exposed and detailed picture as one of the source images used for creating the panorama. See Figures 9.22 and 9.23.

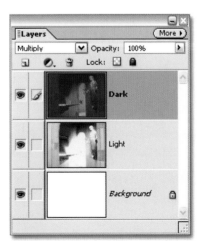

Figure 9.23 *Combine the two images to form a composite with details in highlights and shadows.*

Top tips from panoramic professionals

1 Panoramas are first and foremost a photographic exercise. Composition, lighting and point of view are all critical, although they have to be dealt with differently to traditional photography.

2 Adobe Photoshop Elements is your friend. The editing and enhancement tools found here can help fix those tiny image areas where Photomerge hasn't quite made the perfect stitch.

3 For web panoramas, use a source file with lots of pixels and compress heavily with Elements' Save for web jpeg feature. This often gives better results than a small number of pixels with light compression.

4 Pay attention to the level of your camera (or VR head), as level shots are much easier to stitch together.

5 If the lighting is difficult or there are moving items in the scene, shoot twice as many frames (usually by going around twice) with bracketing if appropriate. 'Panos are often taken with fixed values for exposure'.

From Geoff Jagoe of Mastery Media

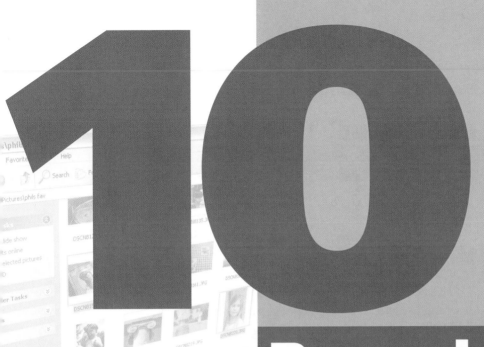

10

Preparing Images for the Web or Email

Images and the Net

Web compression formats side by side

Making your own web gallery

Sending images as email attachments

Making simple web animations with Elements

Creating your own slide shows

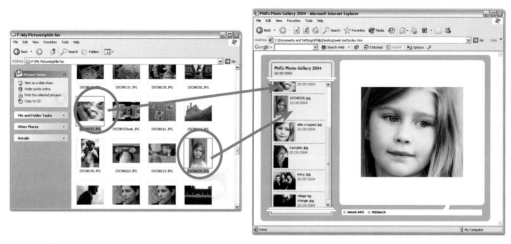

Figure 10.1 *In the web age it is critical that users are able to output their images in a format that is suitable for Net use quickly and easily.*

Since the first edition of this book, the World Wide Web has become an even greater part of our daily lives, and as I mentioned then, it is no longer sufficient to concentrate solely on the process of making great prints from digital files, as knowing how to output your pictures so that they are suitable for the web is not just a nice idea, it is now an essential part of the image-making process. In fact, there is a growing band of professional photographers whose work never becomes a print and only ever exists on our screens. Therefore, over the next few pages we will look at the skills you need to become a web-savvy image maker. See Figure 10.1.

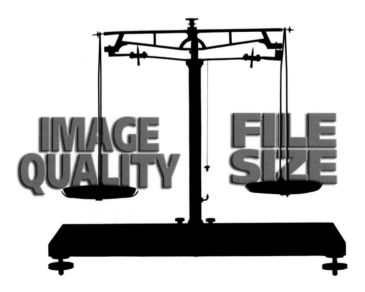

Figure 10.2 *Preparing any content for web use is concerned with balancing quality and file size. This is especially true when placing your pictures on the Internet. Too much quality will mean that your photos will take a long time to display, too little and they will download quickly but be of poor quality.*

Images and the Net

As most people access the web through a modem and telephone line the size of the images used for web work is critical. The larger the picture file, the slower it will download to your machine. So preparing your files for Net use is about balancing picture quality and file size. To help with this, two image file formats, JPEG and GIF, were developed to include a compression system that shrinks file sizes to a point where they can be used on a website or attached to emails. See Figure 10.2. The problem with both file formats is that small file size comes at a cost of image quality.

GIF

With the GIF or Graphics Interchange Format, it is only possible to save a picture with a maximum of 256 colors. As most photographic pictures are captured and manipulated in 24-bit (16.7 million colors), this limitation means that GIF images appear posterized and coarse compared with their full color originals. This isn't always the case, but because of the color restrictions this format is mainly used for logos and headings on web pages and not photographic imagery. GIF is also used for simple animations, as it has the ability to flick through a series of images stored in the one file. See Figure 10.3.

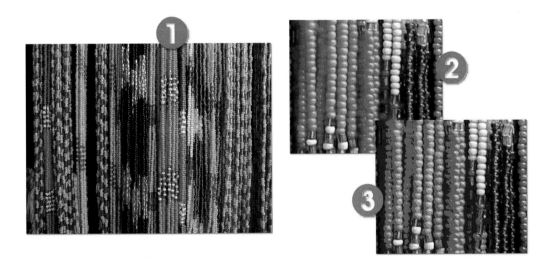

Figure 10.3 *The compression technology built into the GIF format makes files smaller by reducing the number of colors in your pictures to a maximum of 256 (8-bit). This means that GIF images are small and fast to display but the lack of colors makes them unsuitable for use with photographs. (1) Original 3.53 Mb picture containing 16.7 million colors. (2) Detail of original. (3) Detail of the same file converted to GIF format so that it is 0.43 Mb in size and contains 32 colors only.*

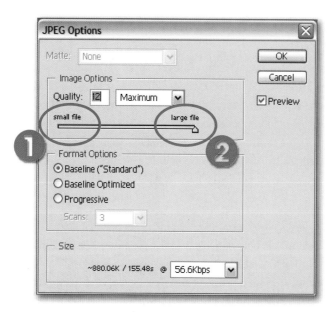

Figure 10.4 *The compression level in the JPEG format is selectable via the quality slider in the JPEG dialog. Moving the slider to the left (1) creates a small low quality file, moving it to the right (2) produces a better quality image but with a bigger file size.*

JPEG

In contrast, the JPEG format was developed specifically for still images. It is capable of producing very small files in full 24-bit color. When saving in this format it is possible to select the level of quality, or the amount of compression, that will be used with a particular image. See Figure 10.4.

In more recent years, two new formats, PNG (Portable Network Graphics) and JPEG 2000, have been developed that build upon the file format technology of JPEG and GIF. At present, these file types are not used widely but as time passes they are gaining more popularity.

JPEG 2000

JPEG 2000 (JPX or JP2) uses wavelet compression technology to produce smaller and sharper files than traditional JPEG. The downside to the new technology is that to make use of the files created in the JPEG 2000 file format online users need to install a plug-in into their web viewers. Native (i.e. built-in) browser support for the new standard will undoubtedly happen, but until then Elements users can freely exchange JP2 files with each other as support for the format is built right into the software.

PNG

PNG24 is a format that contains a lossless compression algorithm, the ability to save in 24-bit color mode and a feature that allows variable transparency (as opposed to GIF's on and off transparency choice). File sizes are typically reduced by 5–25% when saved in the PNG format. Greater space savings can be made by selecting the PNG8 version of the format, which allows the user to select the number of colors (up to 256) to include in the picture. Reducing the size of the color set results in smaller files and works in a similar way to the GIF. Most browsers and image-editing programs support the PNG format natively, so no extra viewer plug-in is necessary.

Though both these options offer great space savings, at present most web authors prefer to work with JPEG.

Elements versions 3.0 and 2.0 support saving your pictures to the newest version of the JPEG format – JPEG 2000. Access the format's own preview dialog via the Save As option in the File menu.

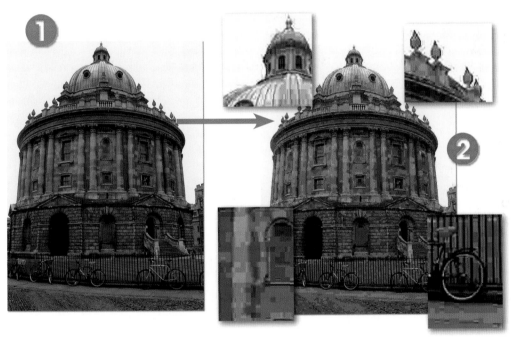

Figure 10.5 *Too much JPEG compression introduces artifacts or visual errors into your pictures. (1) Original uncompressed picture. (2) Overcompressed version of the photo showing extensive artifacts.*

Getting the balance right
All versions: File > Save for Web
All versions: File > Save As > JPEG 2000

Both JPEG formats, as well as GIF and PNG8, make small files by using 'lossy' compression algorithms. This means that image quality and information are lost as part of the compression process. In simple terms, you are degrading the picture to produce a smaller file. Too much JPEG compression, in particular, and the errors or 'artifacts' that result from the quality loss become obvious. See Figure 10.5.

So how much compression is too much? Well, Elements includes a special 'Save for Web' feature that previews how the image will appear before and after the compression has been applied. See Figure

10.6. Start the feature by selecting the Save for Web option from the File menu of either the Standard or Quick Fix editor work spaces. You are presented with a dialog that shows side-by-side 'before' and 'after' versions of your picture. The settings used to compress the image can be changed in the top right-hand corner of the screen. Each time a value is altered, the image is recompressed using the new settings and the results redisplayed.

JPEG, GIF and PNG can all be selected and previewed in the Save for Web feature. To preview JPEG 2000 compressed images use the Save As option in the File menu and select JPEG 2000 as the file type. This step will open the preview dialog specifically designed for this format. See Figure 10.7.

By carefully checking the preview of the compressed image (at 100% magnification) and the file size readout at the bottom of the screen, it is possible to find a point where both the file size and image quality are acceptable.

By clicking OK it is then possible to save a copy of the compressed file to your hard drive ready for attachment to an email or use in a web page.

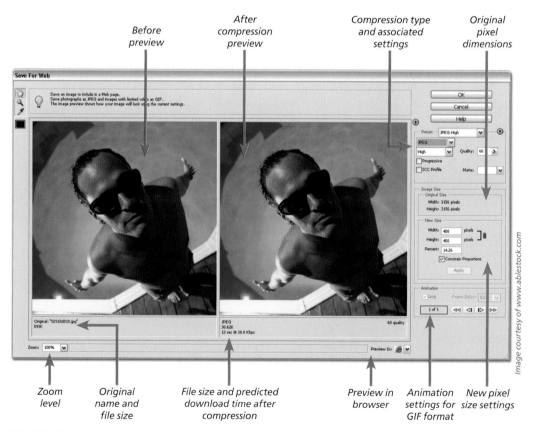

Figure 10.6 The Elements 'Save for Web' feature produces a side-by-side comparison of your image before and after compression. The Save for Web option is available from both the Standard and Quick Fix editor work spaces.

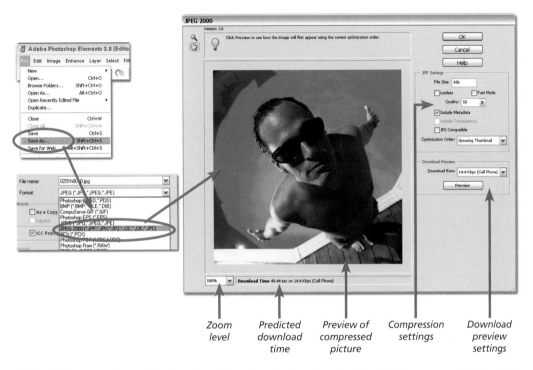

Zoom   Predicted   Preview of   Compression   Download
level   download   compressed   settings   preview
    time   picture   settings

Figure 10.7 *To start the JPEG 2000 preview dialog, select the Save As option from the File menu and pick the JPEG 2000 format.*

1 With an image already open in Elements, pick the Save for Web (Editor: File > Save for Web) or Save As (Editor: File > Save As > JPEG 2000) option.

2 Adjust the magnification of the images in the preview windows to at least 100% by using the Zoom tool or the Zoom drop-down menu.

3 Select the file format from the Settings area of the dialog.

4 Alter the image Quality for JPEG and JPEG 2000 or the number of Colors for GIF and PNG8.

5 Assess the compressed preview for artifacts and check the file size and estimated download times at the bottom of the dialog.

6 If the results are not satisfactory, then change the settings and recheck file size and image quality.

7 Click OK to save the compressed, web-ready file.

FEATURE SUMMARY

Web compression formats side by side

To give an indication of the abilities of each particular format, I optimized the same image and saved it in the five different web formats available in Elements 2.0. The differences in image quality and file sizes, as well as the best uses and features of each format, can be viewed in Table 10.1 and Figures 10.8 and 10.9.

File format	Compression settings	Best uses or format features					File size	Detail *
		Photo	Logo	Heading	Anim-ation	Trans-parency		
JPEG	Minimum	✓					791 Kb	1
	Maximum	✓					60 Kb	2
JPEG 2000	Minimum	✓					880 Kb	3
	Maximum	✓					49 Kb	4
PNG8	256 colors		✓	✓		✓	502 Kb	5
	16 colors		✓	✓		✓	216 Kb	6
PNG24	—	✓				✓	1358 Kb	7
GIF	256 colors		✓	✓	✓	✓	398 Kb	8
	16 colors		✓	✓	✓	✓	201 Kb	9

Table 10.1 Comparison of file formats suitable for web use. * See detail of the compression type and setting applied to the same photograph in Figure 10.9.

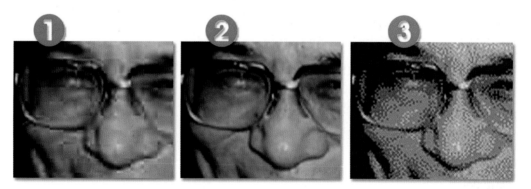

Figure 10.8 Details of compression comparisons. (1) JPEG maximum compression. (2) JPEG 2000 minimum compression. (3) PNG8 16 colors.

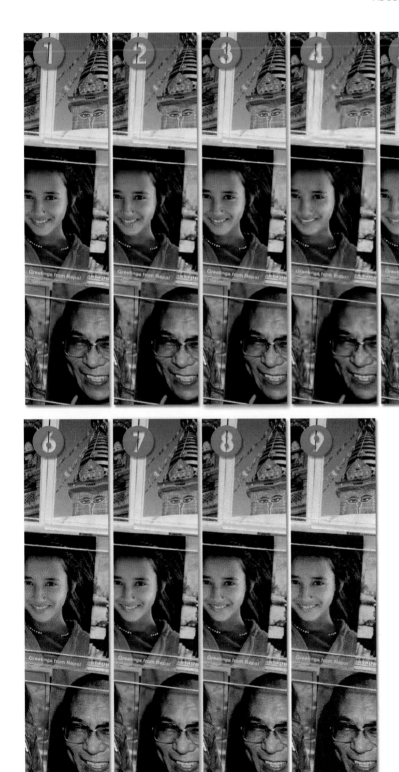

Figure 10.9 *Side-by-side comparisons of the image quality of a variety of web optimized file formats at different compression settings.*
(1) JPEG, minimum compression.
(2) JPEG, maximum compression.
(3) JPEG 2000, minimum compression.
(4) JPEG 2000, maximum compression.
(5) PNG8, 256 colors.
(6) PNG8, 16 colors.
(7) PNG24.
(8) GIF, 256 colors.
(9) GIF, 16 colors.

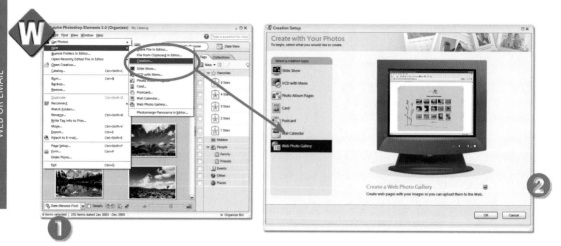

Figure 10.10 In the Windows version of Elements 3.0 the Web Photo Gallery feature is located in the new Photo Creations work space. You can also access the feature from either Editor by selecting File > New Creation which will then take you to the Photo Browser work space. (1) Photo Browser work space. (2) Photo Creations work space.

Making your own web gallery

Version 3.0: Photo Browser: File > New > Web Photo Gallery or select Editor: File > New Creation first
Version 2.0: File > Create Web Photo Gallery
Version 1.0: File > Automate > Web Photo Gallery

Never before in the history of the world has it been possible to exhibit your work so easily to so many people for such little cost. The web is providing artists, photographers and business people with a wonderful opportunity to be seen, but many consider making your own website a prospect too daunting to contemplate. Adobe has included in Elements an automated feature that takes a folder full of images and transforms them into a fully functioning website in a matter of a few minutes.

The Web Photo Gallery feature can be found under the File menu in versions 2.0 and 1.0 of the program but has been moved to the Photo Creations work space for version 3.0. See Figure 10.10. The main dialog contains sections where you can set the style of the website, the heading and colors used on the pages and the source and destination folders. A security option was added to the Elements 2.0 version of the feature. With this tool it is possible to add copyright and image text to the surface of the gallery pictures. This feature has been removed in version 3.0.

Multi-select pictures to include

New for version 3.0 is the ability for Windows users to multi-select pictures from the Photo Browser first before entering the feature rather than having to use all the pictures located in a single folder or directory as was the case in previous versions. In the same vein the revised Web Photo Gallery dialog contains a very useful Add/ Remove pictures section which displays a thumbnail list of those photos currently selected for inclusion in the website. In addition, the order that pictures appear in the web gallery can be changed by clicking and dragging thumbnails to new spots in the list.

Add or
Remove
photos to
the list

Change the
order that
pictures
display by
click-
dragging
to a new
position

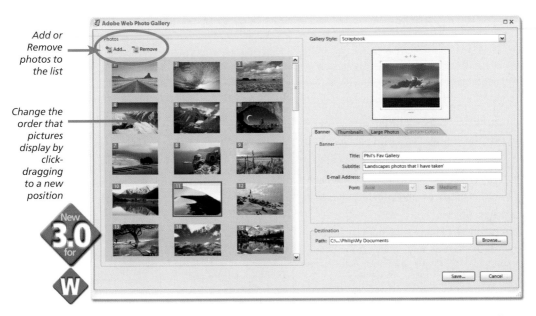

Figure 10.11 *The Windows version of the Web Photo Gallery dialog features Add and Remove buttons that allow users to make changes to the list of pictures to include in the site right from within the Web Photo Gallery dialog itself. Also the position of photos in the display sequence can be altered by moving thumbnails to a different place in the list.*

Version 3.0 users also have access to more template styles than the four initially provided in the first release of the program. See Figure 10.11.

The website produced is made up of a main or index page, a series of small versions of your pictures called thumbnails and a page for each image containing a larger gallery picture. You can navigate from one gallery page to another by clicking on the thumbnails. See Figure 10.12.

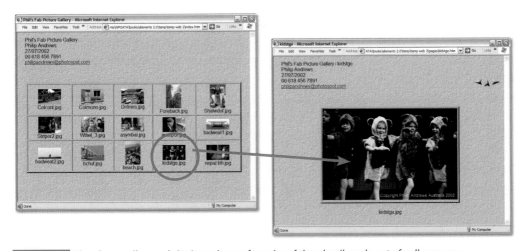

Figure 10.12 *The photo gallery website is made up of a series of thumbnails and a set of gallery pages.*

Built for speed

In the process of creating the site, all your images will be converted to JPEG files, so there are also options to alter the compression rate used for your pictures as well as their dimensions. Changing these two settings will modify the final size of the image files, and as we are already aware, file size is linked to the download speed of the site. So finding a good balance of file size and photo quality is the key to producing a series of pages that are easy to download and view. See Figure 10.13.

As there is no preview option in this Elements feature, it is worth making several different versions of the site containing images of varying sizes and compression rates. Each of the sites can then be tested for acceptable download speed and those that are deemed too slow can be deleted.

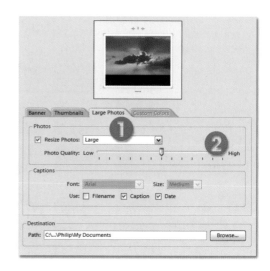

Figure 10.13 The image size and compression rate for each picture can be changed in the Large Photos section of the dialog.
(1) Photo quality or compression amount.
(2) Image size or final pixel dimensions.

Going live

With the site completed, the next step is to transfer all the files to some server space on the Net. Companies called ISPs, or Internet Service Providers, host the space. See Figure 10.14. The company that you are currently using for 'dial-up' connection to the Net will probably provide you 5–10 Mb of space as part of your access contract. As an alternative there are a range of hosting businesses worldwide that will store and display your gallery for free, as long as you allow them to place a small banner advertisement at the top of each of your pages. Whatever route you take, you will need to transfer your site's files from your home machine to the ISP's machine. This process is usually

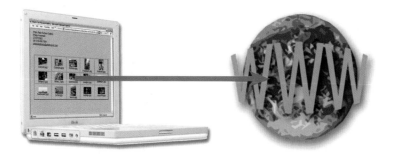

Figure 10.14 The completed website has to be transferred from your computer to a space on the Net hosted by an Internet Service Provider or ISP.

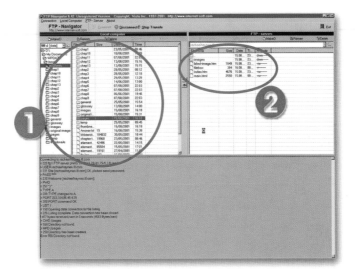

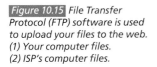

Figure 10.15 File Transfer
Protocol (FTP) software is used
to upload your files to the web.
(1) Your computer files.
(2) ISP's computer files.

handled by a small piece of software called an FTP or File Transfer Protocol program. Your service provider or hosting company will be able to guide you systematically through this process. See Figure 10.15.

When Elements created your site, the program made three folders or directories, titled 'images', 'thumbnails' and 'pages'. These were placed in your designated Destination folder along with one or two extra files (depending on the style you choose) – index.html and thumbnailFrame.html. Together, these are the core components of your website. See Figure 10.16.

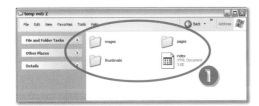

Figure 10.16 Elements stores your website and
its components in three folders and two extra
files on your hard drive. (1) Website
components.

Trouble-free web pages

To ensure that your site works without any problems, all of these components need to be uploaded to your ISP. You also shouldn't move, or rename, any of the folders, or their contents, as this will cause a problem when the pages are loaded into a web browser. See Figure 10.17. If you want to add extra images to your site, or change the ones you have, then it is easiest to make a completely new site to replace the old version.

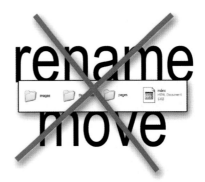

Figure 10.17 To ensure that your website works,
do not rename, or move, any of the files or folders
that hold the components for your site.

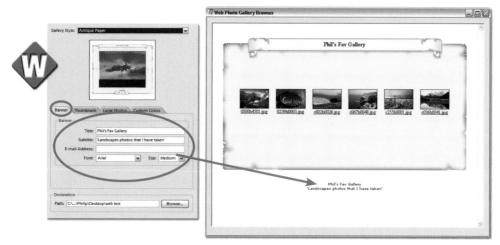

Figure 10.18 *The Banner section of the Web Photo Gallery dialog contains settings for the site's heading area.*

1 Select the pictures you want to include in the site from those thumbnails displayed in the browser. Hold down the CTRL key to multi-select individual files and the Shift key to select all the files in a list.

2 Select Photo Browser: File > New > Web Photo Gallery.

3 Choose the look that you want for your website from the options in the Gallery Style section of the dialog.

4 Under the Banner heading (tab) input the Title and subtitle for the gallery as well as your email address. Also select the font style and size to be used for the text included on the site. See Figure 10.18.

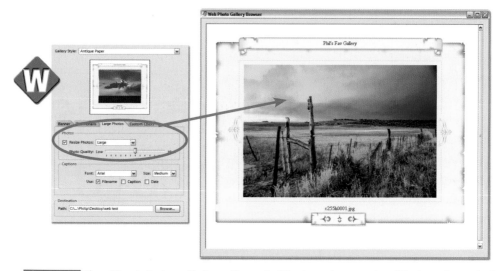

Figure 10.19 *The settings in the Large Photos section control the size and compression of the larger images in the site.*

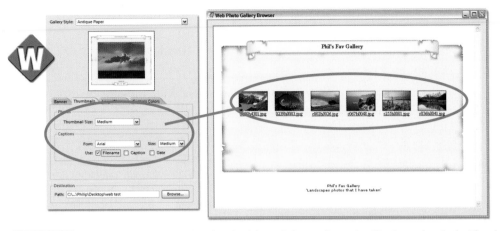

Figure 10.20 The settings used for the thumbnails of the website are determined by the options in the Thumbnails section of the dialog.

5 Select the destination folder that will be used to store the files and folders created during the process.

6 Rearrange, add or remove pictures from the thumbnail list.

7 Select the Large Photos tab and click the Resize option to get Elements to adjust the size of all pictures to suit the site. Choose the size your prefer from the drop-down menu. Adjust the Photo Quality or compression settings to suit your images and choose any captions that you want to be included. See Figure 10.19.

8 Select the Thumbnails tab, choose the size and the captions to include. If the web gallery style that you have selected allows it you can also select the font style and size. See Figure 10.20.

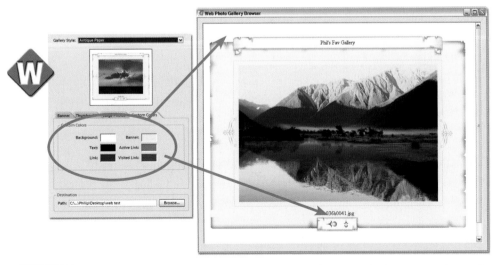

Figure 10.21 The color scheme for the website can be altered using the settings in the Custom Colors section.

FEATURE
SUMMARY

9 Select the Custom Colors tab to set the hues used in the gallery. This option may be grayed
   out as some web styles will not let you alter the colors used in their design. Double-click on
   each of the swatches to activate the Color Picker. Sample the new color from the dialog and
   click OK to set. See Figure 10.21.

10 Click Save to start the site construction process. When completed, the finished website will
   be displayed in the new Web Gallery Browser.

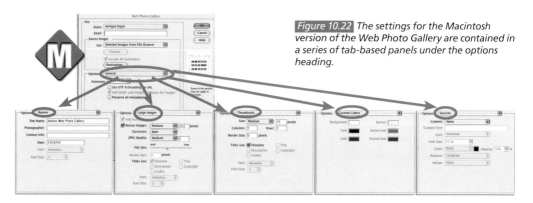

Figure 10.22 *The settings for the Macintosh version of the Web Photo Gallery are contained in a series of tab-based panels under the options heading.*

The Macintosh Web Photo Gallery

Version 3.0: File Browser: Automate > Web Photo Gallery

Mac users can also multi-select the pictures to include in the gallery by opening the file browser
choosing the images and then selecting the Web Photo Gallery from the Automate menu. The
Macintosh version of the Web Photo Gallery contains the same options and settings that were
available in Elements version 2.0. See Figure 10.22.

1 Multi-select the files to include in the gallery from the File Browser then choose Automate >
   Web Photo Gallery.

2 Choose the look that you want for your website from the options available in the Styles
   section of the dialog and input your email address.

3 If you haven't already selected the files to include from the browser you can choose a
   source folder that contains the images that you want to use for the site and then select the
   destination folder that will be used to store the files and folders created during the process.

4 Under the General tab choose the extension and settings favored by your ISP.

5 Select the Banner item from the Options drop-down menu. Input the details for the site using
   the text boxes provided.

6 Select the Large Images item from the Options drop-down menu. Adjust the size and
   compression settings to suit your images. Add a border to your pictures by inputting a border
   size and choose any image-related text to be included.

7 Select the Thumbnails item from the Options drop-down menu. Indicate if you want the File
   Name or File Info included with the thumbnails. Select the font style and size.

FEATURE
SUMMARY

8   Select the Custom Colors item from the Options drop-down menu. Double-click on each of the swatches to activate the Color Picker. Sample the new color from the dialog and click OK to set.

9   In the Security item from the Options drop-down menu nominate the type of security (if any) that you want to use with the site.

10   Click OK to start the site construction process. When completed, the finished website will be displayed in your default browser.

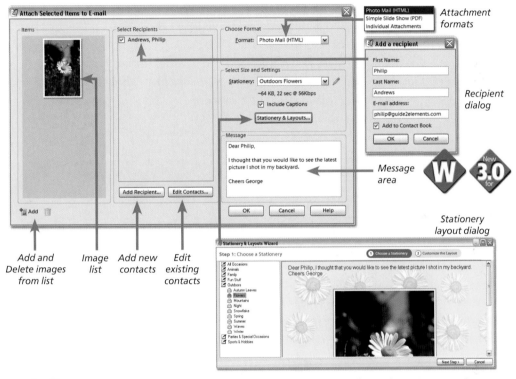

*Attachment
formats*

*Recipient
dialog*

*Message
area*

*Stationery
layout dialog*

*Add and
Delete images
from list*   *Image
list*   *Add new
contacts*   *Edit
existing
contacts*

Figure 10.23 *The new Attach Selected Items to E-mail dialog provides a range of ways that you can attach your pictures to emails. You can also add and remove contacts and type your message directly into the window. Pressing OK opens your email program, adds in your message and recipient details and attaches an optimized version of your picture to the new email document.*

Sending images as email attachments

Version 3.0: Photo Browser: File > Attach to E-mail and Editor: File > Attach to E-mail
Version 2.0: File > Attach to E-mail

For many people, sharing images by sending them as email attachments has become a commonplace activity. Whether you are showing grandparents in another country just how cute their new granddaughter is, or providing a preview look at some holiday property, using email technology to send pictures is both fast and convenient.

Starting with Elements version 2.0 Adobe has included a special Attach to E-mail function designed just for this purpose. The original feature quickly opened your default mail program and attached your current image to a new email document ready for you to address and send. During the attachment process you could choose to send the image 'as is' using its current settings or allow Elements to auto convert the picture to file with medium JPEG compression. For pictures with large pixel dimensions, selecting the Auto Convert option ensured that the attached image was small enough to be able to be sent, received and opened by most email users.

Attach Selected Items to E-mail dialog

The Windows version of the feature introduces a brand new Attach Selected Items to E-mail dialog. Unlike in previous versions here you can attach photographs as individual files (the way you do through your email program), as a PDF slide show (that Elements makes on the fly for you) or you can add the photos to an HTML email complete with choice of a range of fancy backgrounds and borders. The images that will be attached to the email can be selected in the Photo Browser before opening the feature or can be added or removed via the thumbnail listing on the left of the dialog. See Figures 10.23 and 10.24.

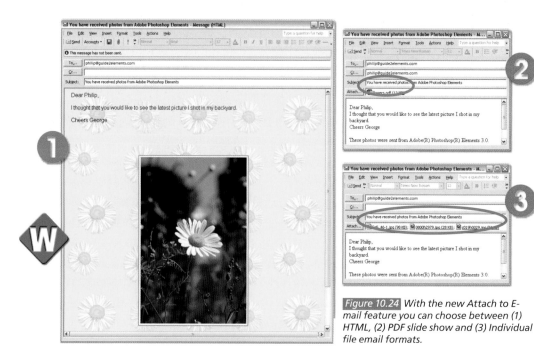

Figure 10.24 *With the new Attach to E-mail feature you can choose between (1) HTML, (2) PDF slide show and (3) Individual file email formats.*

1 You can elect to use a photo that is currently open in the Editor work space or multi-select images from inside the Photo Browser.

2 Select the File > Attach to E-mail to start the feature and display the new dialog.

3 Add or delete photos from the thumbnail list of those to include with the buttons at the bottom left of the dialog.

4 Choose an existing recipient from the contacts list or add a new contact.

5 Choose the format that the pictures will appear in from the drop-down menu.

6 For PDF Slideshow and Individual Attachment options select the size that the pictures will be converted to as part of the attachment process.

7 For the Photo Mail (HTML) option select the stationery to use as a background for the email.

8 Add in your message and click OK.

9 When your email program displays the new message click Send to E-mail in the usual manner.

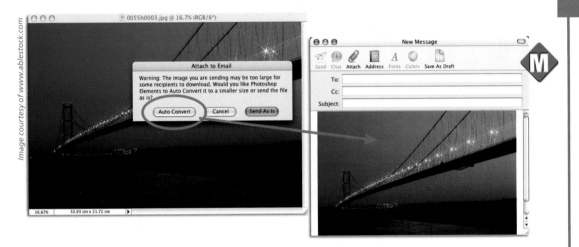

Image courtesy of www.ablestock.com

Figure 10.25 *With the Macintosh version of the Attach to E-mail feature you can choose between Auto Converting the open picture to a format, file size and pixel dimensions suitable for emailing or send the photo As Is with no changes.*

Macintosh Attach to E-mail options M

Editor: File > Attach to E-mail

The Elements 3.0 for Macintosh version of the Attach to E-mail feature works in a very similar way to the feature as it appeared in version 2.0 of the program. The user has two ways of working – you can either choose to allow the program to automatically adjust the size, pixel dimensions and file format of the photograph to suit email use or you can make these adjustments yourself before opening the feature.

If you want to take control of the optimization process yourself then you will need to use commands such as Image Size to resize the picture and Save for Web to convert its file type to JPEG before opening the picture and using the Attach to E-mail feature. See Figure 10.25.

1 Ensure that you have an image opened in Elements before selecting the Attach to E-mail option from the File menu.

2 Select the Auto Convert option to optimize large files to suit web work.

Or

1   Choose Send As Is for pictures whose files size, type and pixel dimensions have already been adjusted.

2   When the new email document appears, input the recipient's address, subject heading and any message you wish to send.

3   Send completed email in the usual manner.

Making simple web animations with Elements

In Chapter 6, we looked at how layers can be used to separate different image parts so that they are easier to enhance and manipulate. Here we will use layers to create simple animations for your website.

Traditional animation

Whether it is the production of a Disney classic or the construction of a small moving cursor for your web page, the basics of making animations remain the same. A series of images, or frames, are created with slight changes recorded from one picture to the next. The sequence is then compiled and each frame is shown in quick succession. As your eye sees a new image, your brain remembers the last, with the result that the still images appear to move.

Historically, the frame images were drawn and painted on a series of acetate cells. Large productions could use thousands of cells, each representing a small slice of movement, to produce just a few seconds of animation on screen. These days, many animation companies use digital versions of this old way of working, but despite all the technological changes, all animation is based on a sequence of still images.

Animation – the Elements method

Adobe has merged traditional techniques with the multi-layer abilities of its PSD file structure to give Elements users the chance to produce their own animations. Essentially, the idea is to make an image file with several layers, the content of each being a little different from the one before. See Figure 10.26. The file is then saved in the GIF format. In the process, each layer is made into a separate frame in an animated sequence. As GIF is a format that is used for small animations on the Net, the moving masterpiece can be viewed with any web browser, or placed on the website to add some action to otherwise static pages.

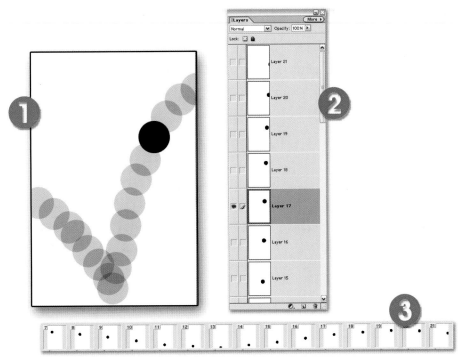

Figure 10.26 *Each layer of a multi-layer Elements file becomes a different frame in a GIF animation. (1) GIF animation. (2) Elements' image layers. (3) Layers as animation frames.*

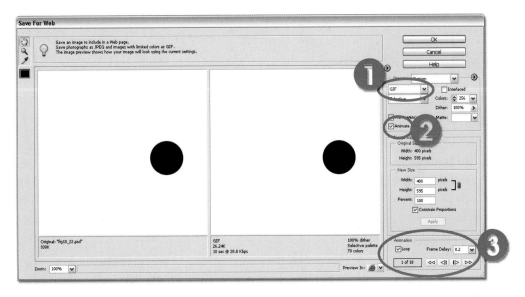

Figure 10.27 *The 'Save for Web' feature provides a series of settings that controls the production of GIF animation files. (1) The GIF file format is used for animation. (2) The animation option must be checked. (3) Use the animation controls to set Frame Delay and loop settings and to preview the individual frames.*

The easiest way to save the GIF file is via the Save for Web feature. See Figure 10.27. The Save for Web dialog contains the original image and a GIF compressed version of the picture. By ticking the Animate checkbox you will be able to change the frame delay setting and indicate whether you want the animation to repeat (loop) or play a single time only. This dialog also provides you with the opportunity to preview your file in your default browser. The final step in the process is to click OK to save the file. See Figure 10.28.

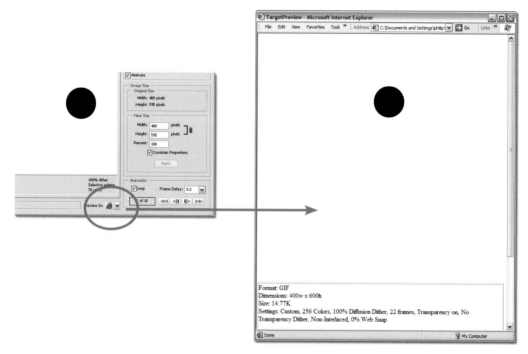

Figure 10.28 *Your animation can be previewed in your default web browser directly from the Save for Web window.*

Animation advice

Keep in mind when you are making your own animation files that GIF formatted images can only contain a maximum of 256 colors. This situation tends to suit graphic, bold and flat areas of color rather than the gradual changes of tone that are usually found in photographic images. So, rather than being disappointed with your results, start the creation process with a limited palette; this way you can be sure that the hues you choose will remain true in the final animation. It is also worth remembering that the Elements animation feature is designed for short, non-complex compositions. If you are planning a major epic made up of large, high-resolution files that when compiled will play for an extended period of time, or even if you just want to add sound to your moving images, it would be best for you to use a dedicated animation package.

FEATURE
SUMMARY

1 Create an Elements file with several layers of differing content.

2 Select File > Save for Web.

3 Ensure that the GIF setting is selected in the Settings section of the dialog.

4 Tick the Animate checkbox.

5 Adjust the Frame Delay option to control the length of time each individual image is displayed.

6 Tick the Loop checkbox if you want the animation to repeat.

7 Preview the animation by clicking the browser preview button. Close the browser to return to the Save for Web dialog.

8 Select OK to save the file.

Creating your own slide shows ⓦ

Version 3.0: Photo Browser: File > New > Slide Show or
Version 3.0: Editor: File > New > Creation then Photo Creations: Slide Show
Version 2.0: File > Automation Tools > PDF Slide Show

Version 2.0 of Elements introduced a PDF slide show making option. The feature proved so popular that version 3.0 for Windows now has two slide show making options – Simple and Custom, both of which are accessible in the Photo Creations work space. As well as a new interface the revised feature contains a host of new options that allow users to create true multimedia slide shows, complete with music, narration, transitions and titles. The finished presentations can be output to PDF files (simple slide shows) or output as a Windows Media Video (custom slide shows) or even burnt to disk as a Video CD (custom slide shows).

Simple slide shows ⓦ

Version 3.0: Photo Browser: File > New > Slide Show then Photo Creation: Slide Show > Simple Slide Show

The PDF (Portable Document Format), or Adobe Acrobat, format has quickly become a favorite way for photographers, graphic designers and printers to share their work. The file format can save text, graphics and photographs in high quality, and can be read by viewers with a wide range of computer systems using the free Adobe Acrobat Reader. With this in mind, the Elements engineers had the great idea of including a slide show creator that output to the PDF format in the program.

Using this feature a selection of images can be ordered, transitions and timing applied between individual slides, and the whole sequence saved as a self-running slide show. The resultant PDF file can be saved to disk or CD or uploaded to the web ready for online viewing. In this way, digital image makers can put together a showcase of their work, which they can then share with a range of viewers, irrespective of the computer system they use. See Figure 10.29.

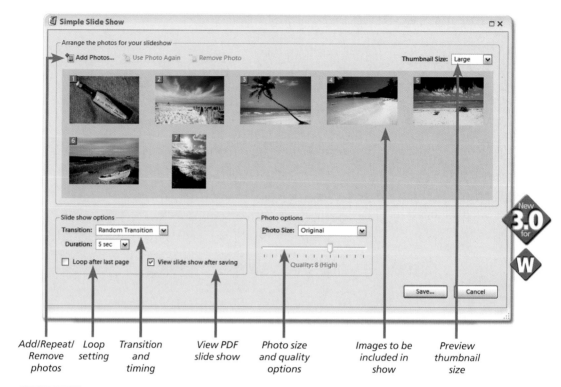

Add/Repeat/   Loop   Transition   View PDF   Photo size   Images to be   Preview
Remove   setting   and   slide show   and quality   included in   thumbnail
photos   timing   options   show   size

Figure 10.29 *The Simple Slide Show option provides a fast and efficient way to create PDF-based self-runing slide shows. Extra images can be added or surplus pictures removed at any time from the thumbnail list. The position of any specific picture in the display sequence can also be adjusted by click-dragging the thumbnail to a new position.*

Putting together a slide show

After selecting the Simple Slide Show option from the Photo Creations work space you are presented with a dialog that contains the main settings for the feature. Selecting the images is the first step in the process. The Add Photos button can be used to locate and add images from a variety of folders on your computer. Alternatively you can multi-select the pictures you wish to include in the Photo Browser first and then open the feature (Photo Browser: File > New Slide Show Photo Creations: Slide Show > Simple).

Any unwanted pictures can be deleted from the list by selecting the individual file and clicking the Remove Photo button. The sequence, numbered from left to right and top to bottom, in which the source files are listed becomes the showing order for the slide show. The order can be changed by selecting and dragging thumbnails to a new position in the list. Clicking the Save button outputs the PDF file to your chosen folder and then displays the finished show in Adobe Acrobat Reader.

The Slide Show Options control the transitions and timings used for the show. The Photo Options section of the dialog contains settings to adjust the dimensions and compression (quality) of the pictures in the final slide show. You may wish to save several versions of the show using different sizes and quality settings before you determine the best match for your needs.

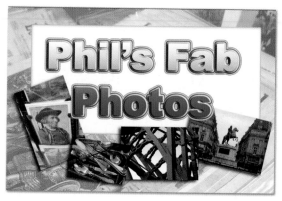

Figure 10.30 *Adding title and graphics pages together with a little preplanning to organize your slide sequence will produce a more professional looking show.*

Adding text or graphic slides to your presentation

You can add a professional look to your simple slide show projects by creating title pages and adding some text or graphical information to the image slides. A little planning covering content, sequencing and the text and graphics you might include will help to present a show that is more enjoyable to your audience. See Figure 10.30.

FEATURE SUMMARY

1 Preselect the photos to include in the show from within the Photo Browser.

2 Select Photo Browser: File > New > Slide Show then Photo Creations: Slide Show > Simple Slide Show

3 Add, Remove or Repeat Photos using the buttons at the top of the dialog.

4 Adjust the sequence of source images to reflect the slide order you want.

5 Adjust the Slide Show Options including Transition type, Duration and Loop and view options.

6 Set the Photo Options, both Size and Quality.

7 Click Save to create your slide show.

Custom Slide Shows Ⓦ

Version 3.0: Photo Browser: File > New > Slide Show then Photo Creation: Slide Show > Custom Slide Show

The new Custom Slide Show option allows the user to create more sophisticated presentations than the Simple Slide Show option offers. Here you can add music, narration and titles along with your images to create a true multimedia experience. The final show is saved as a Windows Media Video (WMV) and can also be burnt as a Video CD. Simple editors for the text and audio added to the show are included and narration can be recorded directly from within the dialog. See Figure 10.31.

The quality of the final WMV file can be adjusted either via the Edit > Slide Show Preferences > Change WMV Output Quality or at the time of outputting the file (File > Output as WMV). Quality settings are included for typical web, VCD and DVD output.

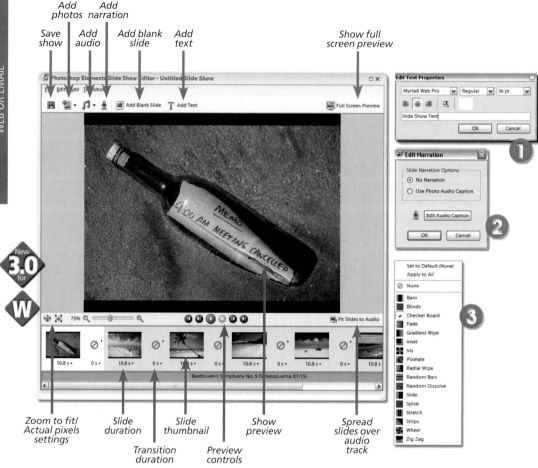

Figure 10.31 The new Custom Slide Show option is a sophisticated presentation editor that includes options for including narration, music and title text to your presentation. The final slide show can be saved in Windows Media Video format or burnt as a Video CD (VCD). (1) Text editor for adding titles to your slides. (2) Narration editor. (3) Transitions menu.

1 Preselect the photos to include in the show from within the Photo Browser.

2 Select Photo Browser: File > New > Slide Show then Photo Creations: Slide Show > Custom Slide Show.

3 Add photos, audio, narration, blank slides and/or text using the buttons at the dialog top.

4 Adjust the sequence of source images by click-dragging the thumbnails to new positions.

5 Add transitions by clicking in between slides and selection transition type from the menu.

6 Adjust the slide and transition durations using the drop-down menus.

7 Click Fit Slides to Audio to adjust slide durations to suit music or narration track.

8 Click the Zoom to Fit or Actual Pixels buttons to determine how each picture is displayed.

9 Save the file and then output the show as a WMV file or burn the show as a VCD.

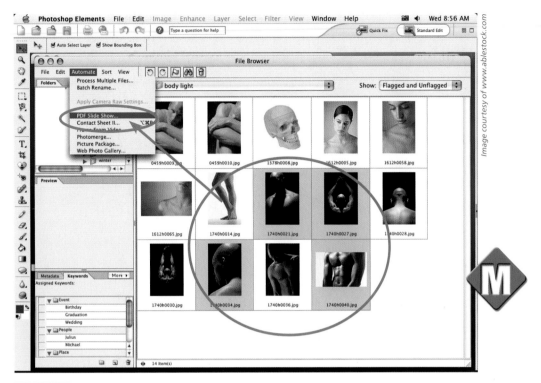

Image courtesy of www.ablestock.com

Figure 10.32 *Macintosh users can multi-select pictures to include in the slide show from inside the file browser.*

Producing slide shows the Macintosh way M

Editor: File > Automation Tools > PDF Slide Show or
File Browser: Automate > PDF Slide Show

Macintosh users do not have access to the Simple and Custom slide show option, instead they are able to create PDF-based slide shows in much the same way as was possible with Elements version 2.0. The feature can be opened via the File > Automation Tools menu or from inside the File Browser using the Automate menu (after selecting the thumbnails of the pictures to include).

Starting with the file browser can make the task of locating and selecting the pictures to include in the show easier as it is possible to multi-select pictures before opening the feature. See Figure 10.32. The chosen photos are automatically passed to the slide show dialog and appear in the add files section. Settings that govern the timing and transitions of the slide show, along with controls that determine if the pictures will advance automatically or manually, are also contained here. See Figure 10.33.

1 Select File > Automation Tools > PDF Slide Show.

2 Add image files to the source list using the Browse button.

3 To include images already open in Elements, tick the Add Open Files checkbox.

4 Adjust the sequence of source images to reflect the slide order you want.

5 For automatic slide advancement, tick the Advance By checkbox and input a timing amount. For manual, or 'mouse click', advancement leave the box unchecked.

6 Select the transition style from the drop-down list.

7 Select the Loop After Last Page option to automatically repeat the slide show when it is finished.

8 Click Save to create your slide show. Set folder and compression options in the succeeding dialogs.

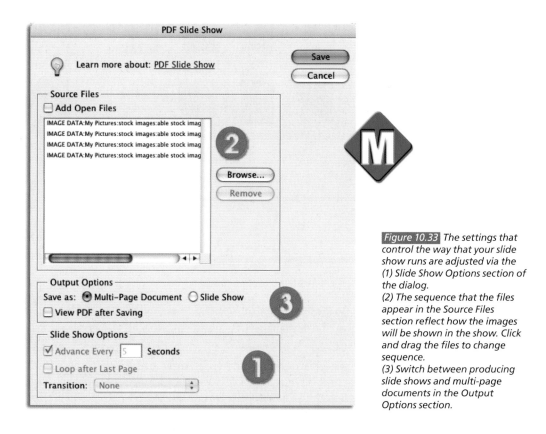

Figure 10.33 *The settings that control the way that your slide show runs are adjusted via the (1) Slide Show Options section of the dialog.*
(2) The sequence that the files appear in the Source Files section reflect how the images will be shown in the show. Click and drag the files to change sequence.
(3) Switch between producing slide shows and multi-page documents in the Output Options section.

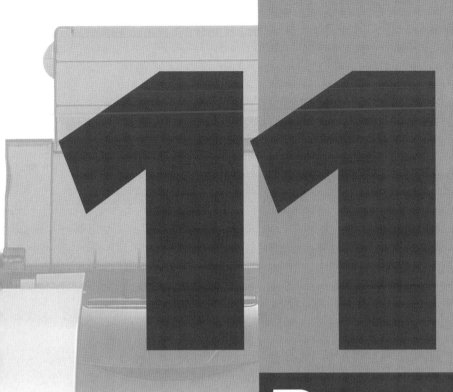

11

Preparing Images for Printing

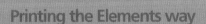

Despite the great rush of some picture makers to 'all things web', most digital images end up being printed at some stage during their existence. Contributing to this scenario is the current crop of affordable high-quality inkjet printers whose output quality is nothing short of amazing. As little as 8 years ago it was almost impossible to get photographic quality output from a desktop machine for under £5000, now the weekend papers are full of enticing specials providing stunning pictures for as little as £150. See Figure 11.1.

Printer manufacturers have simplified the procedure of connecting and setting up their machines so much that most users will have their printer purring away satisfactorily within the first minutes of unpacking the box. Software producers too have been working hard to simplify the printing process so that now it is generally possible to obtain good output from your very first page.

Figure 11.1 Current inkjet printers are capable of providing photographic quality images and cost a fraction of comparative technology just a few years ago.

Elements is a good example of these developments, providing an interactive printing system that previews the image on the paper background 'virtually' before using any ink or paper to output a print. As we have already seen in Chapter 3 the package also includes the ability to print a section of an open image, make a contact sheet of images contained within a folder and produce a print package of different sized pictures optimized to fit on a specific paper stock. See Figure 11.2.

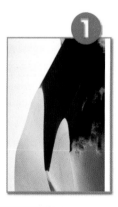
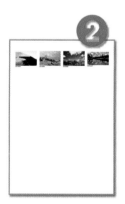
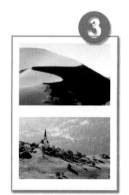
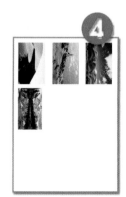

Figure 11.2 Elements contains an interactive print system that can not only produce single image prints, but also contact sheets, picture labels and multi-print packages. (1) Single print. (2) Contact print. (3) Picture package. (4) Picture labels.

Printing the Elements way

Version 3.0: Editor: File > Print, Editor: File > Page Setup, Editor: File > Print Multiple Photos
Version 2.0/1.0: File > Print Preview, File > Page Setup, File > Print

All of the print settings in Elements are contained in three separate but related dialog boxes – Print Preview (Editor: File > Print), Page Setup (Editor: File > Page Setup) and Print Photos (Editor: File > Print Multiple Photos – Windows only). Similar output dialogs were included in previous versions of Elements but the upgraded features in the new release of the program has made the printing process much easier and more flexible. See Figure 11.3.

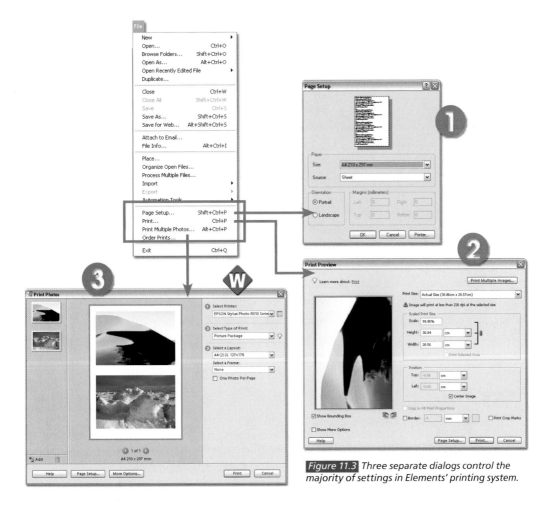

Figure 11.3 *Three separate dialogs control the majority of settings in Elements' printing system.*

The Print Preview dialog is the first stop for most users wanting to make a hard copy of their digital pictures. Here you can interactively scale your image to fit the page size currently selected for your printer. By deselecting the Center Image option and ticking the Show Bounding Box feature, it is possible to 'click and drag' the image to a new position on the page surface. These advanced preview features alone will make a lot of digital photographers very happy. See Figure 11.4.

Book resources at: **www.guide2elements.com**

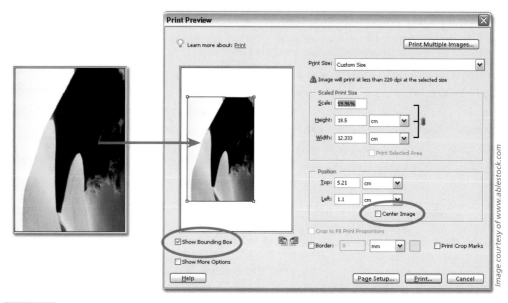

Image courtesy of www.ablestock.com

Figure 11.4 *You can change the size and position of your image on its paper background via the Print Preview (Editor: File > Print) dialog.*

Once you are satisfied with the picture size and position, you can proceed to the Page Setup dialog using the button provided. It is here that you are able to change the settings for the printer, such as paper type, size and orientation, printing resolution and color control, or enhancement. The extent to which you will be able to manually adjust these features will depend on the type of printer driver supplied by the manufacturer of your machine. When complete, click OK to return to the Print Preview dialog. To complete the output process, click the Print button. This step produces a general print dialog where the user has another opportunity to check the printer settings via the Properties button, before sending the image on its way with a click of the OK button. See Figure 11.5.

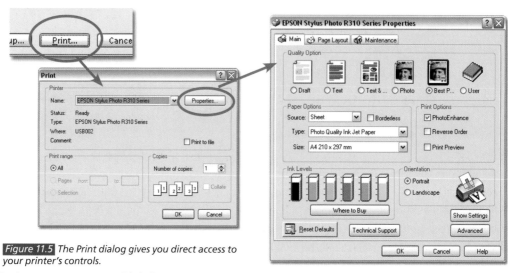

Figure 11.5 *The Print dialog gives you direct access to your printer's controls.*

Book resources at: **www.guide2elements.com**

Printing from the Photo Browser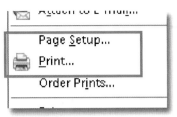

Photo Browser: File > Print, File Page Setup

As we have already seen in our brief introduction to printing in Chapter 3, you can output your pictures directly from the Photo Browser. In fact with the exception of the Print Preview dialog the print options available from the Organizer work space are the same as those available via the editor. For quick printing tasks the Photo Browser: File > Print option takes you directly to the same multi-print dialog that is available in the editor (File > Print Multiple Photos) and there is no practical difference between outputting your files from either space. See Figure 11.6.

Figure 11.6 The Photo Browser offers similar printing options to those found in the Editor work spaces.

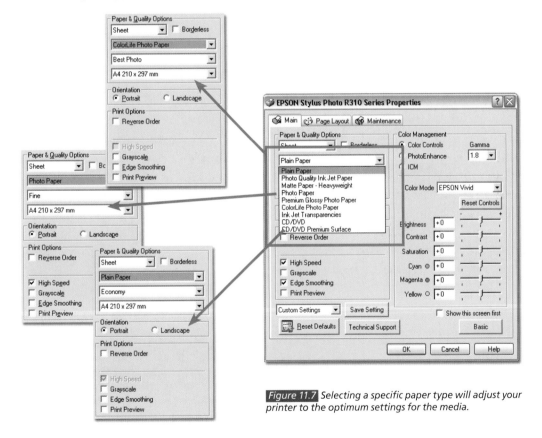

Figure 11.7 Selecting a specific paper type will adjust your printer to the optimum settings for the media.

The link between paper type and quality prints

When you first start to output your own images, the wide range of printer settings and controls can be confusing. To start with it is best to stick to a standard setup and allow the built-in features of the driver to adjust the printer for you. For most printing tasks, selecting the media type in the Print Properties dialog will be sufficient to ensure good results. The manufacturers have determined the optimum ink and resolution settings for each paper type, and for 90% of all printing tasks, using the default settings is a good way to ensure consistently high-quality results. So if you are using gloss photographic paper, for example, make sure that you select this as your paper type in the printer settings dialog. See Figure 11.7.

Making your first print

Editor: File > Print
Version 2.0/1.0: File > Print Preview

With an image open in editor work space, open the Print Preview dialog (File > Print). Check the thumbnail to ensure that the whole of the picture is located within the paper boundaries. To change the paper's size or orientation, select the Page Setup and Printer Properties options. Whilst here, adjust the printer output settings to suit the type of paper being used. Work your way back to the Print Preview dialog by clicking the OK buttons. See Figure 11.8.

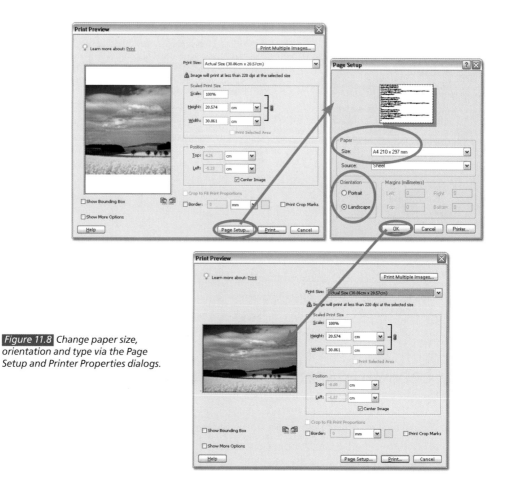

Figure 11.8 Change paper size, orientation and type via the Page Setup and Printer Properties dialogs.

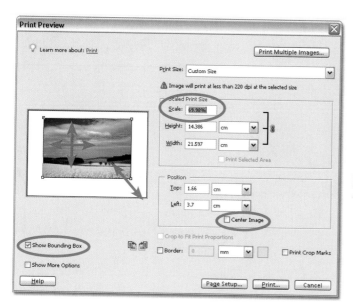

Figure 11.9 Change the size and position of the image on the page with the Print Preview dialog.

To alter the position or size of the picture on the page, deselect the Center Image option, and then select the Show Bounding Box feature. Change the image size by clicking and dragging the handles at the edge and corners of the image. If you can't see the handles try inputting a number smaller than 100% in the scale box until the edge of the picture is visible. Move the picture to a different position on the page by clicking on the picture surface and dragging the whole image to a different area. See Figure 11.9. To print, select the Print button and then the OK button.

1 Select Print Preview (File > Print).

2 Click the Page Setup button.

3 Pick the Printer option to set the paper type, page size and orientation and print quality options.

4 Click OK to exit these dialogs and return to the Print Preview dialog.

5 At this stage you can choose to allow Elements to center the image automatically on the page (tick the Center Image box) and enlarge, or reduce, the picture so that it fits the page size selected (choose the Fit on Page option from the Print Size menu).

6 Alternatively, you can adjust the position of the picture and its size manually by deselecting these options and ticking the 'Show Bounding Box' feature. To move the image, click inside the picture and drag to a new position. To change its size, click and drag one of the handles located at the corners of the bounding box.

7 With all the settings complete, click Print to output your image.

FEATURE SUMMARY

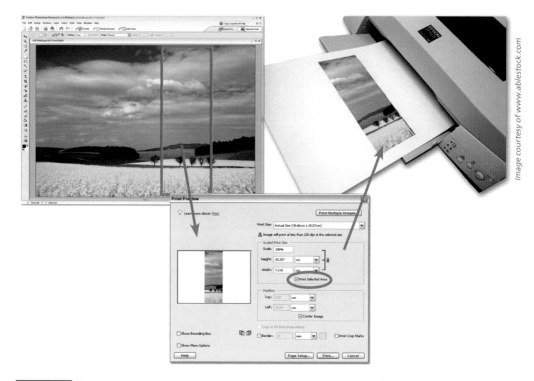

Image courtesy of www.ablestock.com

Figure 11.10 *The Elements printing system allows the user to output a section of a full image.*

Printing a section of a full image

One very convenient feature of the Elements printing system is its ability to output a section of an image without having to modify the original picture itself. Simply pick the Rectangular Marquee tool and make a selection on the picture surface. Proceed to the Print Preview dialog and select the Print Selected Area option. See Figure 11.10.

This feature is very useful for performing spot tests of important sections of large prints. The smaller prints will output faster than a full image and as long as the test areas are selected carefully, this process can be used to economically proof large and difficult images.

FEATURE SUMMARY

1 Select the area to be printed using the Rectangular Marquee tool.

2 Open the Print Preview dialog (File > Print).

3 Tick the Print Selected Area option.

4 Click Print to output the selection.

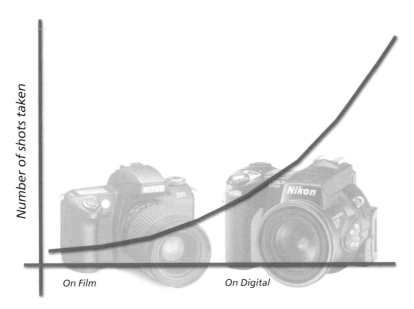

Figure 11.11 *As there is no cost associated with shooting, digital camera users now take more pictures than when they were using film-based cameras.*

Making multiple prints

In the last few years the digital camera market has exploded. Now digital camera sales easily outstrip their film-based counterparts over the same selling period. And with the onslaught of these new silicon shooters has come a change in the way that people take pictures.

Users are starting to alter the way they shoot to accommodate the strengths of the new technology. One of these strengths is the fact that the act of taking a picture has no inherent cost. In comparison, film-based shooting always involves a development cost associated with the production of negatives and prints, as well as the initial purchase of the film – digital picture taking is essentially costless. Yes, there is the outlay for the camera and the expense associated with the storage, manipulation and output of these images, but the cost of shooting is zero. Hence, it seems that the typical digital camera user is shooting more pictures, more often, than they were when capturing to film. See Figure 11.11.

Contact sheets

Editor: File > Print Multiple Photos > Contact Sheet or Editor: File > Contact Sheet II (Macintosh)
Version 2.0: File >Print Layouts > Contact Sheet
Version 1.0: File > Automate > Contact Sheet II

Digital photographers are not afraid to shoot as much as they like because they know that they will only have to pay for the production of the very best of the images they take. Consequently, hard drives all over the country are filling up with thousands of pictures. Navigating this array of images can be quite difficult and many shooters still prefer to edit their photographs

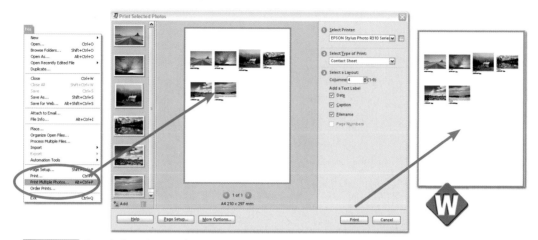

Figure 11.12 *The Windows Contact Sheet option in the Print Selected Images or Print Photos dialog creates thumbnail versions of all the images from the thumbnail list.*

as prints rather than on screen. The people at Adobe must have understood this situation when they developed the Contact Print feature for Photoshop and Elements. Elements 3.0 for Windows contains a completely revised version of the feature that is part of the Print Multiple Photos dialog. Macintosh users have the same dialog (File > Contact Sheet II) that was present in version 2.0.

From within one feature, the imaging program creates a series of small thumbnail versions of all the images in a catalog or those that were multi-selected before opening the tool. These small pictures are arranged on pages and can be labeled with file name, captions and dates. From there it is an easy task to print a series of these contact sheets that can be kept as a permanent record of a folder's images. The job of selecting the best pictures to manipulate and print can then be made with hard copies of your images without having to spend the time and money to output every image to be considered. See Figure 11.12.

The options contained within the Contact Sheet dialog allow the user to select the number of columns of image thumbnails and the content of the text labels that are added. The page size and orientation can be chosen via the Page Setup button. See Figure 11.13.

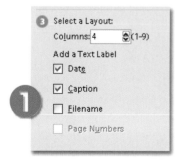
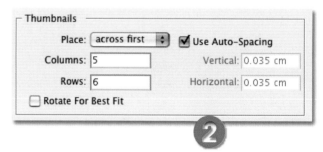

Figure 11.13 *The options in the Contact Sheet dialog allow the user to select the number of thumbnails per page by adjusting the columns value as well as what text will be included as labels. (1) Windows. (2) Macintosh.*

1 If working in the editor work space open the images to be printed, otherwise multi-select the pictures from inside the Photo Browser (or from the file browser for Mac users).

2 Select File > Print Multiple Photos and choose Contact Sheet from the Select Type of Print menu. From the Photo Browser select File > Print and then choose contact print. Mac users select File Browser: Automate > Contact Sheet II.

3 Use the Add and Remove Photos buttons to adjust the list of pictures to be included in the contact sheet.

4 Select the printer from the drop-down list in section one of the dialog. If need be, click the Printer Preferences button next to the printer selection to adjust the hardware settings to suit your output.

5 In section two of the dialog select Contact Sheet from the drop-down list of print types.

6 In the final section (3) choose the number of columns to use (and therefore the total number of thumbnails to place on a single sheet) and select the content of the label text to be included.

7 Click Print to output the contact sheet.

Picture packages

Editor: File > Print Multiple Photos > Picture Package or Photo Browser: File > Print > Picture Package
Version 2.0: File > Print Layouts > Picture Package
Version 1.0: File > Automate > Picture Package

At some stage in your digital imaging career you will receive a request for multiple prints of a single image. The picture might be the only shot available of the winning goal from the local football match, or a very, very cute picture of your daughter blowing out the candles on her birthday cake, but whatever the story, multiple requests mean time spent printing the same image. Adobe included the Picture Package feature in its Elements and Photoshop packages to save you from such scenarios. Originally located in the Print Layouts section of the File menu where the Contact Sheet command was placed, the revamped version 3.0 Picture Package has now been integrated into the Print Multiple Photos dialog. The feature allows you to select one of a series of predesigned, multi-print layouts that have been carefully created to fit many images neatly onto a single sheet of standard paper. Macintosh users can access the feature via the File menu in the editor or under the Automate menu in the file browser.

There are designs that place multiples of the same size pictures together and those that surround one or two larger images with many smaller versions. The feature provides a preview of the pictures in the layout. You can also choose to repeat the same image throughout the design by selecting the One Picture per Page option. There is no option to add labels as there was in version 2.0 of the feature but you can select a frame from one of the many listed to surround the photos you print.

Whichever layout and frame design you pick, this feature should help you to keep both family members and football associates supplied with enough visual memories to make sure they are happy. See Figure 11.14.

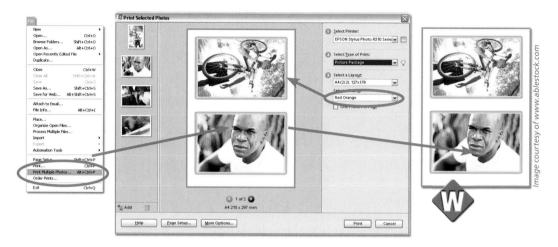

Image courtesy of www.ablestock.com

Figure 11.14 *The Picture Package option lays out multiple versions of the same image or several different pictures on a single sheet of paper and includes an option for surrounding the photos with a fancy frame.*

1 If working in the editor workspace open the images to be printed, otherwise multi-select the pictures from inside the Photo Browser.

2 Select File > Print Multiple Photos and choose Picture Package from the Select Type of Print menu. From the Photo Browser select File > Print and then choose Picture Package.

3 Use the Add and Remove Photos buttons to adjust the list of pictures to be included in the contact sheet.

4 Select the printer from the drop-down list in section one of the dialog. If need be, click the Printer Preferences button next to the printer selection to adjust the hardware settings to suit your output.

5 In section two of the dialog select Picture Package from the drop-down list of print types.

6 In the final section (3) choose the Layout and Frame design to be included.

7 To repeat a single image on a page click the One Photo per Page option. To add many different pictures to the same page leave this item unchecked.

8 Click Print to output the Picture Package pages.

FEATURE SUMMARY

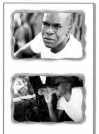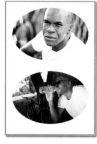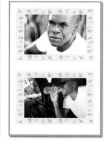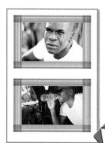

Figure 11.15
There are many different layout and frame designs included in the revised Picture Package feature.

The Picture Package for Macintosh users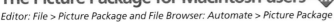

Editor: File > Picture Package and File Browser: Automate > Picture Package

Macintosh users can choose the pictures to include in the Picture Package by multi-selecting thumbnails in the file browser. These files are transferred to the Picture Package dialog by selecting the feature from the Automate menu in the file browser. The layout, page size, and resolution of the final print can be set in the document section of the dialog, whilst the accompanying text options can be adjusted in the label section below. By clicking onto the thumbnail preview area different photos can be substituted for those already selected and the layout itself can be adjusted using the Edit Layout dialog accessed via the Edit Layout button. See Figure 11.16.

1 Select File > Picture Package or multi-select photos from the file browser and then choose Automate > Picture Package.

2 In the Source Image section of the dialog box, select the location of your source images from the drop-down menu.

3 Choose page size and layout design from the Document section of the dialog.

4 Also specify a Resolution and color mode to suit the package.

5 Select the content, style, size, color and positioning of your label text from the next box.

6 Click OK to make the Picture Package.

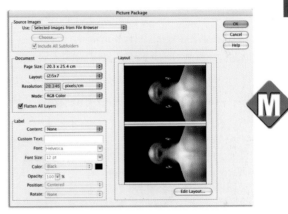

Figure 11.16 *Macintosh users create picture packages via a different dialog that is similar to the one that was included in version 2.0 of Elements.*

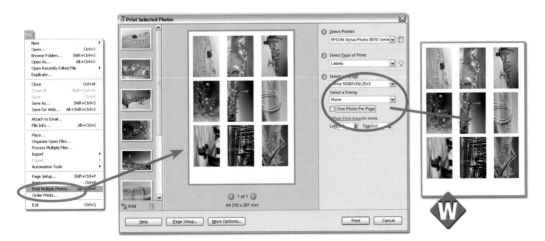

Figure 11.17 *The Labels option lays out multiple versions of the same image or several different pictures in a format to suit commercially made sheets of adhesive labels.*

Picture labels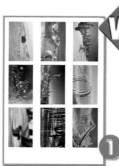

Editor: File > Print Multiple Photos > Labels or Photo Browser: File > Print > Labels

Completely new for Elements 3.0 for Windows is the additional multi-photo printing option that lays out and sizes the images to suit the design of commercially available sheets of adhesive labels. The layout box contains a variety of label sheet designs and just as with the Picture Package feature you can add frames to your label photos. To help with precise aligning of the print to the label sheet Adobe has also included an offset print settings box. Here you can make slight adjustments of where the pictures print on the paper surface. If the print is misaligned to the left then add a positive number to the settings, if the error is to the right then you will need to add a negative number to the dialog. See Figures 11.17 and 11.18.

1 If working in the editor work space open the images to be printed, otherwise multi-select the pictures from inside the Photo Browser.

2 Select File > Print Multiple Photos and choose Labels from the Select Type of Print menu. From the Photo Browser select File > Print and then choose Labels.

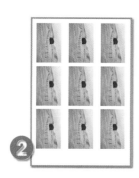

Figure 11.18 As with the other Print Multiple Photos options, the Picture Labels feature allows you to print a page of labels with different images (1) or by selecting the One Photo per Page setting, produce a whole sheet with multiple copies of the one picture (2). The picture label feature is not available for Macintosh users.

3 Use the Add and Remove Photos buttons to adjust the list of pictures to be included in the labels sheet.

4 Select the printer from the drop-down list in section one of the dialog. If need be, click the Printer Preferences button next to the printer selection to adjust the hardware settings to suit your output.

5 In section two of the dialog select Labels from the drop-down list of print types.

6 In the final section (3) choose the Layout and Frame design to be included.

7 To repeat a single image on a page click the One Photo per Page option. To add many different pictures to the same page leave this item unchecked.

8 Click Print to output the label pages.

9 If the label print doesn't quite match the perforations on the sheet then adjust the print position using the Offset Print Area settings.

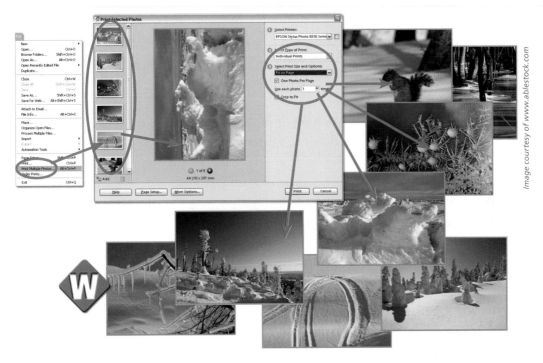

Image courtesy of www.ablestock.com

Figure 11.19 *At first glance the Individual Print option in the Print Multiple Photos feature might seem like a simplified version of the Print Preview dialog but this new addition in Elements 3.0 comes into its own when you want to produce a series of prints of single images quickly and easily.*

Individual Prints Ⓦ

Editor: File > Print Multiple Photos > Individual Prints or
Photo Browser: File > Print > Individual Prints

Also new for Elements 3.0 for Windows is the ability to set up and print several individual photographs at one time. Until this release of the program the traditional Print Preview dialog (Editor: File > Print) was the only way you could print one photo on a page. This approach is fine if all you want to do is print a single photo, but what if you have 10 pictures that you want to print quickly and easily? Well this is where the Individual Print option in the Print Multiple Photos feature comes into play. This options allows the user to 'batch' a variety of one-image-to-one page photos at the same time.

Though you don't have as many options when ouputting your picture with this feature you can still choose the size of the photo on the page and whether it will be cropped in order to fill the paper size fully. And for those times when you need a couple of prints of a group of pictures simply change the number of times the pictures will be used in the print batch. See Figure 11.19.

Book resources at: **www.guide2elements.com**

1　If working in the editor work space open the images to be printed, otherwise multi-select the pictures from inside the Photo Browser.

2　Select File > Print Multiple Photos and choose Individual Prints from the Select Type of Print menu. From the Photo Browser select File > Print and then choose Individual Prints.

3　Use the Add and Remove Photos buttons to adjust the list of pictures to be included in the labels sheet.

4　Select the printer from the drop-down list in section one of the dialog. If need be, click the Printer Preferences button next to the printer selection to adjust the hardware settings to suit your output.

5　In section two of the dialog select Individual Prints from the drop-down list of print types.

6　In the final section (3) select the Print Size you desire. If you are using the Fit on Page option then you can also select the Crop to Fit feature designed to ensure the picture fills the print paper fully.

7　To obtain more than one print of each picture adjust the value in the Use each Photo option.

8　Click Print to output the individual prints.

FEATURE SUMMARY

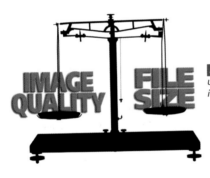

Figure 11.20 *Just as was the case with photos optimized for web usage, good prints are made from files that balance file size and image quality .*

Aiming for the best prints

Balancing image size and picture quality

The printing techniques detailed above can be used for producing good prints for the majority of images, papers, inks and printers. To gain the ultimate in control over your printed output, however, you need to delve a little deeper. Let's start by revisiting the factors that underpin good image quality.

Great prints are made from good images, and we know from previous chapters that digital image quality is based on high image resolution and high bit depth. Given this scenario, it would follow that if I want to make the best prints possible, then I should at first create pictures with massive pixel dimensions and huge numbers of colors. The problem is that such files take up loads of disk space and, due to their size, are very, very slow to work with, to the point of being practically impossible to edit on most desktop machines.

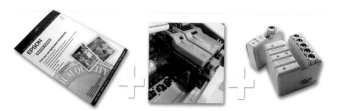

Figure 11.21 The three practical factors that govern all printed output are the printer mechanism, the inks used and the paper or media the image is printed on.

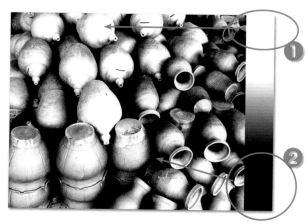

Figure 11.22 Some printers are capable of outputting all tones in an image, others lose delicate highlight and shadow details in the printing process.
(1) Lost highlight.
(2) Shadow detail.

The solution is to find a balance between image quality and file size that still produces 'good prints'. See Figure 11.20. For the purposes of this book, 'good prints' are defined as those that appear photographic in quality and can be considered visually 'pixel-less'. The quality of all output is governed by a combination of the printer mechanism, the ink set used and the paper, or media, the image is printed on. To find the balance that works best with your setup, you will need to perform a couple of simple tests with your printer. See Figure 11.21.

Getting to know your printer

Testing tones

There are 256 levels of tones in each channel (Red, Green and Blue) of a 24-bit digital image. A value of 0 is pure black and one of 255 is pure white. Desktop inkjet machines do an admirable job of printing most of these tones, but they do have trouble printing delicate highlight (230–255) and shadow (0–40) details. Some machines will be able to print all 256 levels of tones, others will only be able to output a smaller subset. See Figure 11.22.

To test your own printer/ink/paper setup, make a stepped grayscale that contains separate tonal strips from 0 to 255 in approximately five tone intervals. Alternatively, download the example grayscale from the book's website. Print the grayscale using the best quality settings for the paper you are using. Examine the results. In particular, check to see at what point it becomes impossible

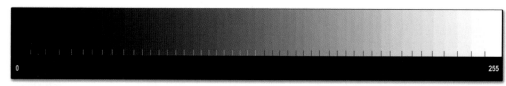

Figure 11.23 *Print the example grayscale, noting down the tones that your machine fails to print.*

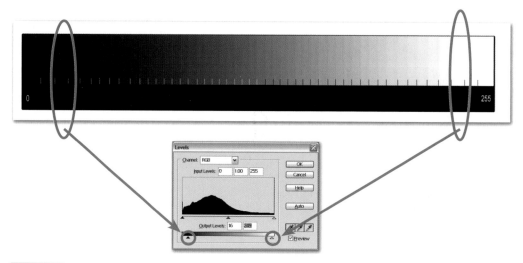

Figure 11.24 *Drag the black and white output sliders till they match the values of those found in the grayscale or tone test.*

to distinguish dark gray tones from pure black and light gray values from white. Note these values down for use later, as they represent the range of tones printable by your printer/paper/ink combination. See Figure 11.23.

When you are next adjusting the levels of an image to be printed, move the output sliders at the bottom of the dialog until black and white points are set to those you found in your test. The spread of tones in your image will now meet those that can be printed by your printer/paper/ink combination. See Figure 11.24.

Testing resolution

Modern printers are capable of incredible resolution. Some are able to output discrete dots at a rate of almost 5000 per inch. Many users believe that to get the utmost detail in their prints they must match this printer resolution with the same image resolution. Although this seems logical, good results can be achieved where one pixel is printed with several printer dots. Thank goodness this is the case, because the result is lower resolution images and therefore more manageable, and smaller, file sizes. But the question still remains – exactly what image resolution should be used?

Again, a simple test can help provide a practical answer. Create a high-resolution file with good sharp detail throughout. Using Image > Resize > Image Size makes a series of 10 pictures from 1000

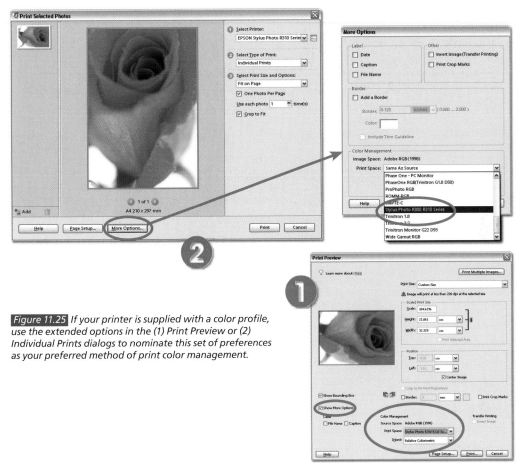

Figure 11.25 *If your printer is supplied with a color profile, use the extended options in the (1) Print Preview or (2) Individual Prints dialogs to nominate this set of preferences as your preferred method of print color management.*

to 100 ppi, reducing in resolution by 100 ppi each time (i.e. 1000, 900, 800, etc.). Alternatively, download the resolution examples from the book's website. Now print each of these pictures at the optimum setting for your machine, ink and paper you normally use. Next, examine each image carefully. Find the lowest resolution image where the picture still appears photographic. This is the minimum image resolution that you should use if you want your output to remain photographic quality.

For my setup, this setting varies between 200 and 300 ppi. I know if I use these values I can be guaranteed good results without using massive file sizes.

Managing color

As computer operating systems have developed, so too have the way that they have handled the management of color, from capture through the manipulation phase to output. A central part of this process is a group of settings, called a color profile, that govern the conversion of an image's color from one device to another. A well-calibrated system will contain a profile for scanner/camera, screen and printer, so that the image is passed from one managed space to another.

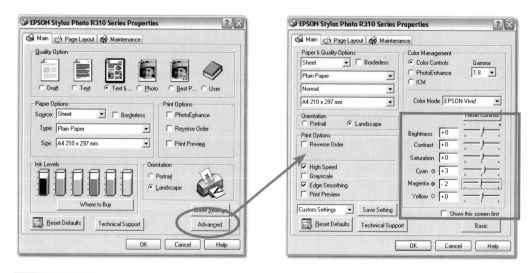

Figure 11.26 *Rid images of persistent casts using the color slider settings built into your printer's driver software.*

When printing with Adobe Elements it is possible to select the type of color management you want to apply to the output. If your printer came supplied with a profile, you can select it in the Print Space area of the Print Preview dialog. You might have to select Show More Options to make this part of the dialog visible. If no profile is supplied, then you can either elect to use the same space the image was captured in or use the printer color management built into the driver. See Figure 11.25.

For the majority of output scenarios these options will provide good results. If you do happen to strike problems where images that appear neutral on screen continually print with a dominant cast, then most printer drivers (the special printer software that manages the activity of printing) include a feature such that individual colors can be changed to eliminate casts. See Figure 11.26.

Figure 11.27 *Surface puddling results from too much ink hitting the paper surface.*

Typical printing problems and their solutions

Surface puddling (pooling)

Prints with this problem show puddles of wet ink on the surface of the paper resulting from too much ink being applied. To help this situation, reduce the cyan, yellow and magenta sliders in the

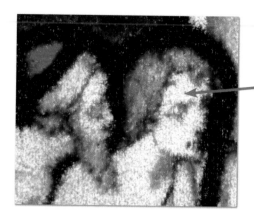
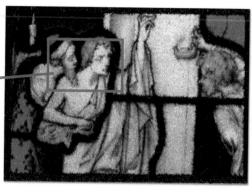

Figure 11.28 *Edge bleeding can result from using an uncoated porous paper.*

printer's dialog box. Make sure that you make the same change to all three sliders, otherwise you will introduce a color cast into the print. Also increase the saturation slider; this will decrease the volume of ink going to the black nozzle. See Figure 11.27.

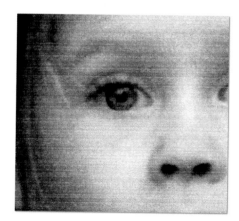

Figure 11.29 *Cleaning the print heads usually solves banding problems.*

Edge bleeding

Edges of the print appear fuzzy and shadow areas are clogged and too dark. This usually occurs when using an uncoated paper. Use the corrective steps detailed in 'puddling' above, as well as choosing a media or paper type such as 'Plain Paper' or 'Backlit Film'. These measures will change the amount of ink being applied and the spacing of the ink droplets to account for the absorbency of the paper. See Figure 11.28.

Banding

This problem usually results from one or more of the print heads being clogged. Consult your printer's manual to find out how to activate the cleaning sequence. Once completed, print a 'nozzle test' page to check that all are working correctly. If banding still occurs after several cleaning attempts, it may be necessary to install a new cartridge. See Figure 11.29.

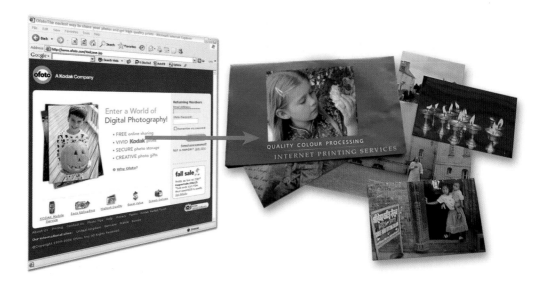

Figure 11.30 The Online Services feature allows you to print digital files photographically direct from your desktop.

Web Based Printing

Version 3.0: Editor: File > Order Prints, Photo Browser: File > Order Prints
Version 1.0/2.0: File > Online Services

In designing Elements, Adobe realized that the web plays, and will continue to play, a large role in the life of most digital image makers. The inclusion of a Web Based Printing option in the package shows just how far online technology has developed.

Although many images you make, or enhance, with Elements will be printed right at your desktop, occasionally you might want the option to output some prints on traditional photographic paper. The Order Prints option, located in the File menu, provides just this utility. See Figure 11.30.

Using the resources of ofoto.com in the USA, Elements users can upload copies of their favorite images to the company's site and have them photographically printed in a range of sizes. The

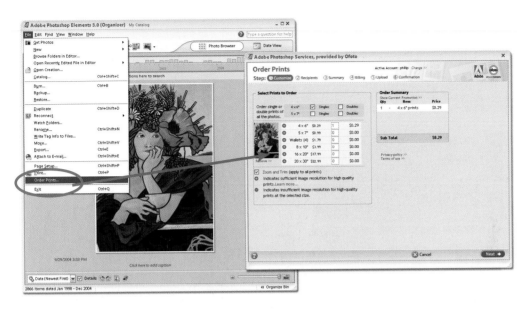

Figure 11.31 *Images that are already opened in Elements can be uploaded directly to the ofoto.com website.*

finished prints will then be mailed back to you. This service provides the convenience of printing from your desktop with the image and archival qualities of having your digital pictures output using a photographic rather than inkjet process.

Making your first web prints

In previous versions of Elements you needed to access the Online Services feature before uploading your pictures to print, but Elements 3.0 for Windows streamlines the process by allowing you to upload directly from the Photo Browser or Organizer work space. The first time you use the feature you will need to register for the service but from that time onwards the feature works seamlessly from inside the Elements package. See Figure 11.31. Although ofoto.com does provide a set of simple online editing and enhancement tools at its main site, I prefer to alter my images in Elements first before uploading. In addition to printing your favorite pictures, ofoto.com also provides album creation and image-sharing services, allowing you and your friends to upload your favorite photos, review them and then print those that you like the most. See Figure 11.32.

If you like the look of true photographic quality prints, then this online option provides a quick, easy and reliable service to output your digital images from your desktop.

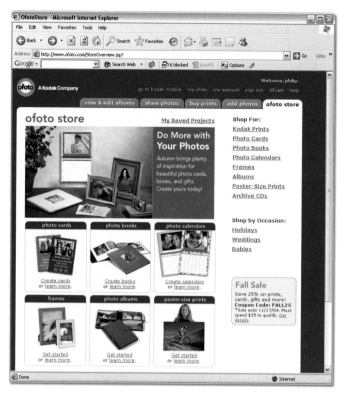

Figure 11.32 The uploaded pictures can be stored in a series of photo albums on the ofoto.com website ready for sharing and printing. The online service can also be used for creating and printing cards, calendars and photo books.

To web print

1 Select or multi-select pictures from Photo Browser.

2 Choose File > Order prints.

3 Choose print numbers and size from the Customise section of ofoto.com. Click Next.

4 Select the recipient of the prints from the list or add new contact details and then click Next.

5 Review print and shipping charges at the next screen and then click Next.

6 At the Billing section insert your credit card information and add the billing address. Click Place Order which will upload your pictures and then display an order confirmation.

To upload files for sharing

1 Select or multi-select pictures from Photo Browser.

2 Choose the Share Online option from the Share button in the Shortcuts bar.

3 Choose the person you want to share the pictures with from the list or add new contact details for a new recipient. Click Next.

4 The files will now be uploaded and an invitation to share the pictures will be sent to the recipients selected in the previous step.

Book resources at: **www.guide2elements.com**

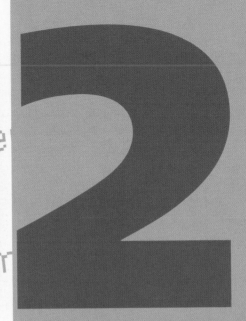

12 New Photo Creations

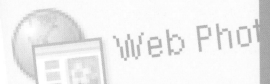

As we have already seen in previous chapters, Photoshop Elements 3.0 (Windows version) now combines much of the great technology that previously existed in the Photoshop Album product, with its own powerful image-editing structure. One standout feature of the marriage is the Photo Browser, another is the inclusion of the Photo Creations work space. Here at last is a common place to house a range of sophisticated imaging projects that enables users to quickly and easily produce and share their pictures in a range of project forms. A few years ago it would have been sufficient for a good image-editing package to include a print command and maybe a way to export pictures in a variety of different file formats, but these days photos are compiled, shared, distributed and displayed in a much broader range of ways. With the inclusion of the Photo Creation work space in Elements 3.0 you too can start to use your pictures in forms that you may never have thought possible.

The Photo Creation projects Ⓦ

Photo Browser: File > New > Creation
Editor: File > New > Creation

The Photo Creation work space can be accessed from the Photo Browser and the Editing spaces by selecting the option from the File > New menu or the Create button in the shortcuts bar. In addition, browser users can also select each of the Creation projects individually from this menu. All these actions will take you to the main Photo Creations dialog. See Figure 12.1.

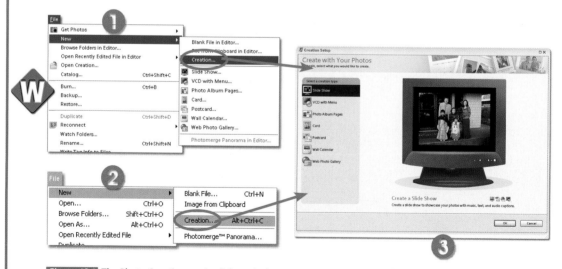

Figure 12.1 *The Photo Creations main dialog window can be accessed from either the Photo Browser or editor work spaces via the Creation option on the File > New menu. (1) Photo Browser. (2) Editor. (3) Main dialog for the Photo Creations feature.*

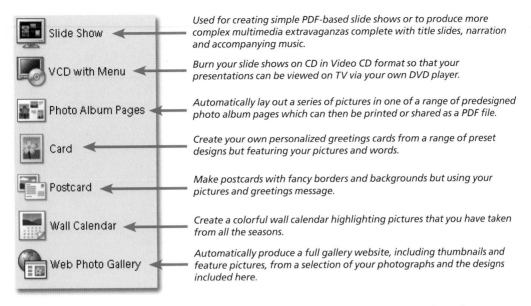

Slide Show — Used for creating simple PDF-based slide shows or to produce more complex multimedia extravaganzas complete with title slides, narration and accompanying music.

VCD with Menu — Burn your slide shows on CD in Video CD format so that your presentations can be viewed on TV via your own DVD player.

Photo Album Pages — Automatically lay out a series of pictures in one of a range of predesigned photo album pages which can then be printed or shared as a PDF file.

Card — Create your own personalized greetings cards from a range of preset designs but featuring your pictures and words.

Postcard — Make postcards with fancy borders and backgrounds but using your pictures and greetings message.

Wall Calendar — Create a colorful wall calendar highlighting pictures that you have taken from all the seasons.

Web Photo Gallery — Automatically produce a full gallery website, including thumbnails and feature pictures, from a selection of your photographs and the designs included here.

Figure 12.2 The Photo Creations main dialog window contains a variety of project options to choose from.

The Photo Creations main screen contains a range of project options that you can feature your pictures in. Some projects, like the Slide Show and Web Photo Gallery, will be familiar to previous users of Elements as basic forms of these features were contained in previous editions of the program, but others such as the Wall Calendar and VCD with Menu items create new and exciting ways to share you pictures with others. See Figure 12.2.

Each project requires you to have some basic resources prepared before starting out. For the most part this means that you should have selected, enhanced and edited any pictures you wish to include before commencing the creation process. In the case of the VCD with Menu option you will need to create the slide shows that you want to feature on the disk as well. For this reason it is a good idea to follow the workflow detailed below when making your Photo Creations. See Figure 12.3.

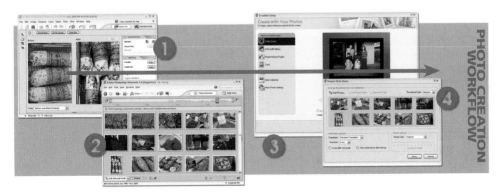

Figure 12.3 As you need to have all your pictures edited and enhanced before adding them to your Photo Creation projects start by enhancing your pictures (1) then save the finished file back to the browser (2). Now select the pictures to include and open the Photo Creations dialog (3) and select the project from the options listed. The selected images will now appear in the project dialog (4).

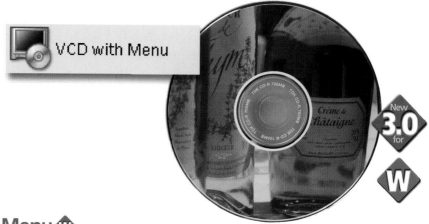

VCD with Menu W

Photo Creation: VCD with Menu

I'm sure that it wouldn't take too much prompting for readers to recall the dreaded family slide shows that seem to occur regularly on lazy Sunday evenings in many households around the country. Everyone's favorite uncle would present a selection of the family archives and we would all sit around amazed at how much we had changed and try not to make rude comments about clothing styles and receding hairlines.

Well the days when most photographers recorded the family history on slide film have long gone but the slide show events that accompanied these images are starting to make a comeback. Thanks to in part the ease with which we can now organize and present our treasured digital photos on new media like CD and DVD. Gone too are the dusty projectors being replace instead by DVD players hooked to widescreen 'tellies'. This project converts your Elements slide shows to VCD format ready for viewing on most DVD players or computers with a DVD drive, but to be sure that your machine is compatible, check the equipment manual first.

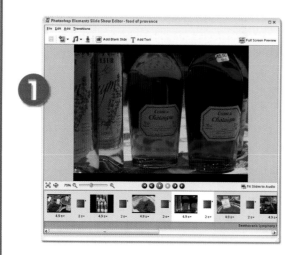

Before you can create a VCD with a menu you must have at least one slide show saved into the Photo Browser. If you don't have a candidate slide show then, start the process by selecting the Custom Slide Show option and creating a multimedia presentation complete with sound. Save the project to the Photo Browser.

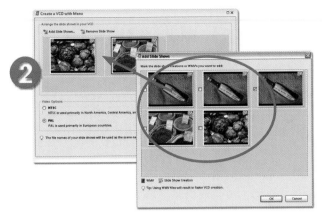

Select the slide shows that you want to include in the VCD from the Photo Browser and then pick VCD with Menu from the Photo Creations main screen. Add or Remove slide shows from the thumbnail list if you are unhappy with your selection. Click and drag slide shows to new positions in the list to adjust where they will be placed in the menu of the VCD. The small number in the top left of each thumbnail indicates the sequence. Click Burn when you are happy with the arrangement.

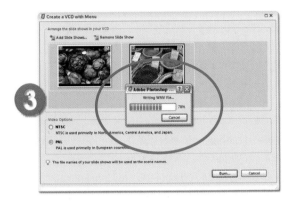

The burn step is a two part process. First any slide show not in the Windows Media Video file will be converted to that format. The conversion can be quite lengthy if you are burning slide shows containing many high-resolution files. If you want to speed up this section of the process, convert your shows to WMV beforehand from inside the slide show project dialog.

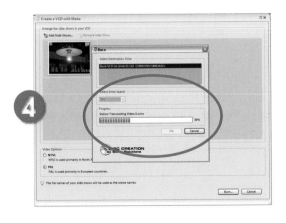

The second part of the burn process is writing the CD itself. After converting the slide shows to WMV files a burn dialog will appear. Make sure that a new blank CD is inserted into the CD writer and click the OK button to create the VCD.

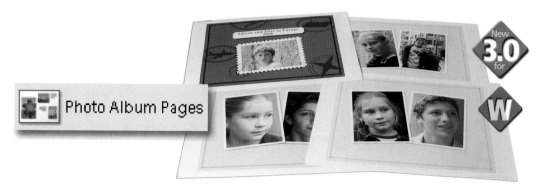

Creating Photo Album Pages Ⓦ

Photo Creation: Photo Album Pages

'Scrapbooking' is fast becoming one of the most popular ways to collate and share your photographs with friends and relatives and the Photo Album Pages feature in the Photo Creations work space is a terrific way to produce the scrapbook pages. Using the step-by-step wizard, your own images and one of the many template designs in the feature you can quickly and easily produce a series of pages (yes including a title page) that look like they have been professionally laid out. The finished pages can be printed, output as a PDF file or sent as an email attachment.

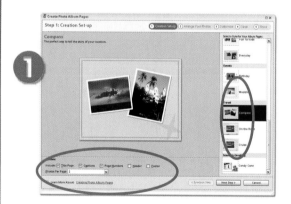

Select the pictures that you want to include from the Photo Browser and then choose the Photo Album Pages option from the Photo Creations main screen. Determine the number of pictures you want per page and the text to include via the options at the bottom of the screen. Finally choose a page style from the template thumbnails on the right of the screen. Click the Next Step button to continue.

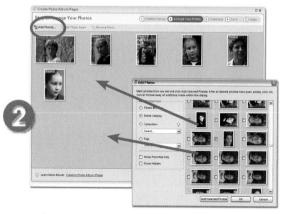

Add or Remove photos from the thumbnail list if you are unhappy with your selection. Click and drag pictures to new positions in the list to adjust where they will be placed in the book. The small number in the top left of each thumbnail indicates which page the picture will be printed on. To use the same image again, select its thumbnail and click the Use Photo Again button. Click the Next Step button.

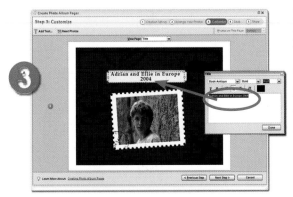

In this step you will see a preview of the pictures laid out in each of the album pages. You can add titles or descriptive text by double-clicking the caption text that is automatically placed next to each picture or by clicking the Add Text button. Adjust the number of pictures per page by selecting an option from the Photos on this Page menu. Move backwards and forwards between pages using the side arrows. Click the Next Step button.

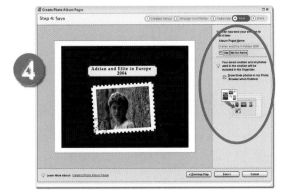

Saving the Photo Album Pages means that it will be possible to edit your settings later. Select the option to include the Photo Album Pages project in the Photo Browser and then click the Save button.

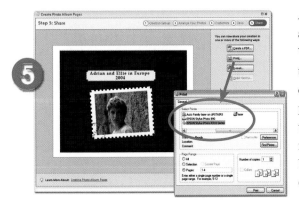

As with most Photo Creation projects you have a choice of the way that it will be produced. With Photo Album Pages you can elect to print the pages out (and bind them into a book form) or you can create a PDF file or even send the project as an email attachment. Depending on the online services available in your area you may also be able to have the pages printed and bound as a book via the Order Online option. Click the Done button.

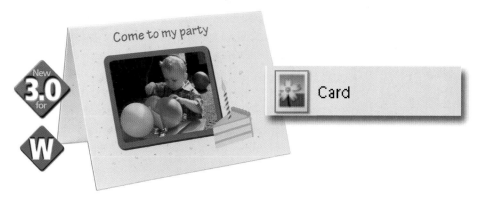

Make your own birthday cards Ⓦ

Photo Creation: Card

Creating greetings or birthday cards customized with your own pictures and heart-felt message is a good way to make the card giving experience a little more personal. The Photo Creations Card project contains many different styles ranging from formal, season's greetings, valentine and baby cards. Most have decorative borders, appropriate color schemes and places for you to add your message. But the best part of this feature is the way that the front and inside faces of the project are automatically rotated and arranged so that when it is printed, the card is ready for folding. No more having to turn the paper around to print on the opposite side or having to guess which way to rotate the inside face to ensure it ends up the right way. The program manages all this for you.

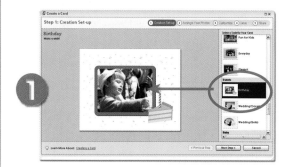

Select the picture you want to feature on the card from the Photo Browser. Select the Card option from the Photo Creations main screen. Choose a card style from the template thumbnails on the right of the screen. Click the Next Step button to continue.

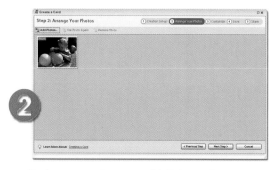

If you are unhappy with your choice then substitute a different photo for the one that you have selected using the Add or Remove Photos buttons. Click the Next Step button.

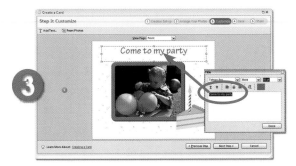

In this step you will see a preview of the picture laid out on the front of the card and on the second page, the greeting that will be printed on the inside of the card. Double-click on any of the text to change it. Move backwards and forwards between inside and outside the card using the side arrows. Click the Next Step button.

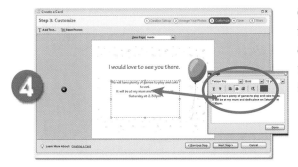

Clicking once on the text will allow you to move the writing around on the card surface. Double-clicking will open a text window which can be used for changing the text's font, color and size. Click the Next Step button.

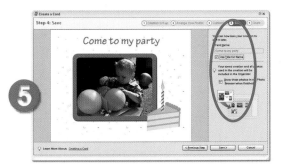

By selecting the 'Use Title for Name' option the project will be saved using the card title as the file name. Saving the project file means that you can return to the card at a later date and make further changes. Select the option to include the Card project in the Photo Browser and then click the Save button.

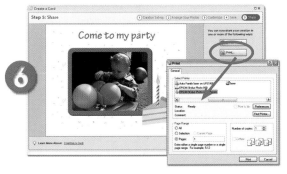

You can choose to print, email your card or create a PDF file of the project. Click the Done button.

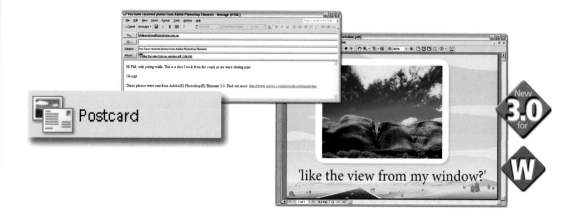

'like the view from my window?'

The Elements Postcard project ⓦ

Photo Creation: Postcard

In Chapter 7 we looked at how to create your own picture postcards and email them to your friends using the Elements' Attach to E-mail feature. The Photo Creations Postcard project provides you with a quick and easy alternative to this more manual technique. What's more this approach also has the advantage of being able to select from a range of predesigned styles as well as the ability to output the final design to print, email or PDF. So that you have a direct comparison of the two workflows the postcard created here is also emailed rather than printed.

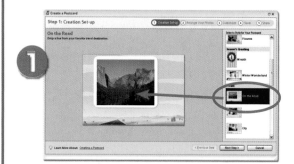

Make your selection of a picture to feature on your postcard. Now pick the Postcard option from the Photo Creations main screen. Select a postcard style from the template thumbnails on the right of the screen. Click the Next Step button to continue.

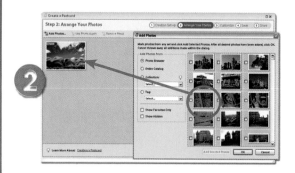

You can swap the selected photo for a different one by using the Add or Remove Photos buttons. Click the Next Step button.

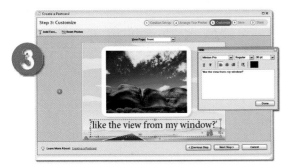

This screen will show you a preview of the picture laid out in the postcard template. Double-click on the text to open the text window where you can change the font, size and color of the text as well as the content of the message. Click the Next Step button.

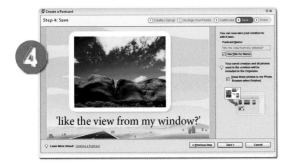

By selecting the 'Use Title for Name' option the project will be saved using the postcard title as the file name. Saving the project file means that you can return to the postcard at a later date and make further changes. Select the option to include the Postcard project in the Photo Browser and then click the Save button.

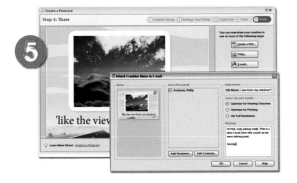

As with the other projects that we have looked at you can choose to print, email your card or create a PDF file of the project. Here we elect to email the postcard and the Attach to E-mail dialog is displayed. Select the Recipient from the Contacts list, add a message and choose a size and quality option from the three provided. Click OK to confirm to pass the email onto your mail program and then click the Done button to exit the project.

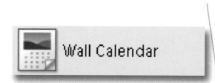

Producing a wall calendar Ⓦ

Photo Creation: Wall Calendar

Next Christmas why don't you make and give your very own wall calendars rather than buying the commercially made variety. The Wall Calendar project takes all the manual labor out of the process by not only providing some great templates for you to add your photos to but also including a date calculator built into the dialog. Simply insert the start and end dates for your calendar and Elements works out the days and dates for whatever year you choose. The hardest task you have to perform in the whole process is choosing which pictures to include and which to leave out.

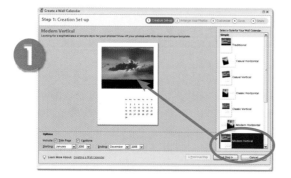

Multi-select the pictures that you want to include from the Photo Browser and then choose the Wall Calendar option from the Photo Creations main screen. Pick the starting and ending date for the period to be covered by the project and choose whether to include captions or a title. Now select a calendar style from the template thumbnails. Click the Next Step button to continue.

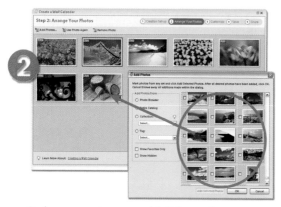

Add or Remove photos from the thumbnail list if you are unhappy with your selection. Click and drag pictures to new positions in the list to adjust where they will be placed in the calendar. The small month label in the top left of each thumbnail indicates which page the picture will be printed on. To use a picture more than once in the project, select its thumbnail and click the Use Photo Again button. Click the Next Step button.

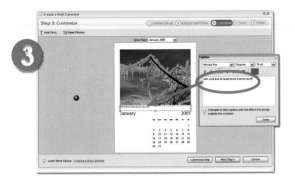

In this step you will see a preview of the pictures laid out in each of the months of the calendar. You can add titles or descriptive text by double-clicking the caption text or by clicking the Add Text button. Move backwards and forwards between months using the side arrows. Click the Next Step button.

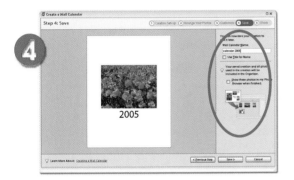

Saving the wall calendar means that it will be possible to edit your settings later. Select the option to include the project in the Photo Browser and then click the Save button.

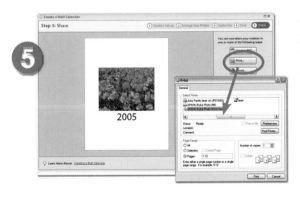

As we have seen with the other projects, here you are provided with the opportunity to print the wall calendar, send it as an email or save the whole project as a PDF file. After printing click the Done button to exit the project.

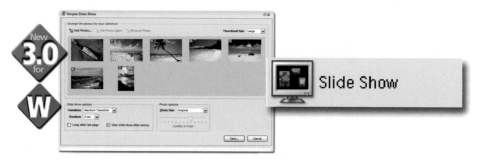

Slide shows on your computer or TV W

Photo Creation: Slide Show

As we have already seen in Chapter 10 there are two new Slide Show options in Photoshop Elements 3.0. The Simple Slide Show creates PDF-based presentations quickly and easily, whereas the Custom Slide Show feature is more suited to multimedia extravaganzas complete with music, narration and title slides. The Custom Slide Show writes its files to Windows Media Video (WMV) format which can be viewed in most computer media players. Both slide show types can be burnt to VCD disks enabling them to be shown on most home TV/DVD systems. For fuller details about how to use the Slide Show feature see Chapter 10.

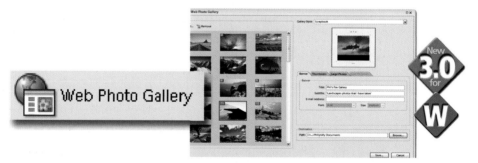

The new improved Web Photo Gallery feature W

Photo Creation: Web Photo Gallery

Photoshop Elements 3.0 ships with a new and improved Web Photo Gallery feature. Located in the Photo Creations work space, not in the Automation menu of the editor as it was in version 2.0, the new design consolidates all the options that were available previously into a single streamlined dialog. But it is not just the interface that has changed, the way that you use the feature has altered also. Now instead of having to copy all your photos into a common folder ready for the web creation process you can now multi-select your favorite pictures direct from the photo browser and then open the feature. The selections are passed to the dialog and show up as thumbnails alongside your options settings. For more details on using the Web Photo Gallery feature see Chapter 10.

Step-by-step guides for Slide Show and Web Photo Gallery features
Don't forget that the guides for using these features are contained in Chapter 10 as they both have options for web distribution.

13

Theory into Practice: Real Life Elements Projects

Projects 1–12

Now that you have an understanding of the program and many of its great features use the following projects to build your skills. You can download all the resources you need to complete the tasks from the book's website (www.guide2elements.com) and once you are feeling confident you can move onto the next step and start to substitute your own pictures for the ones I supplied.

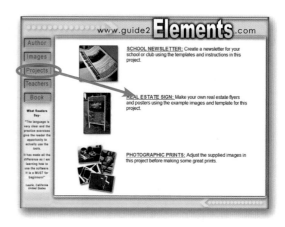

Project 1: Slide shows from your home videos

Skill Level – 1
Version – 3.0, 2.0

The new range of digital video cameras has made the process of capturing and using frames from your home movies easier than ever. As the data is actually stored in a digital format there is no longer the need to buy expensive capture cards when you want to feature a few moments from your latest cinematic efforts. Elements 3.0 is particularly well suited to this task as you can not only grab the 'Frame From Video' (Editor: File > Import > Frame From Video) but you can also compile the captured still moments in a self-contained slide show created using the Slide Show feature (Browser: File > New > Slide Show).

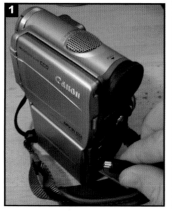

Attach your video camera to your computer and download a few segments of footage to your hard drive using the capture software supplied with the camera.

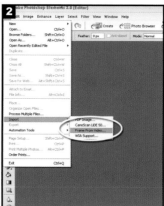

Select Editor: File > Import > Frame From Video to open the Elements video capture dialog.

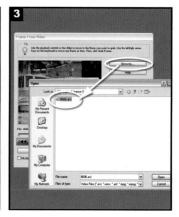

Click the Browse button and search for your video files.

Book resources at: **www.guide2elements.com**

4

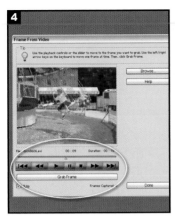

Use the VCR type buttons to navigate the video clip and click the Grab Frame button to capture still images.

5

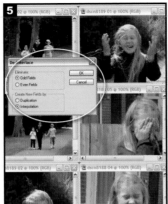

The nature of most video capture means that applying a de-interlace filter (Editor: Filter > Video > De-interlace) will help improve the sharpness of the still frames. Apply the filter to the captured pictures.

6

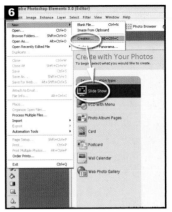

With all the frames still open in the Elements editor select the Slide Show feature (Editor: File > New Creation > Slide Show) and then select the Simple Slide Show option.

7

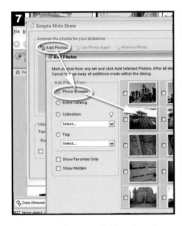

Your open files should be already included in the slide show thumbnail area. To insert more frames use the Add Photos button.

8

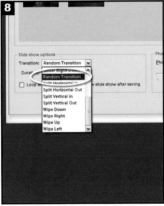

Set the Duration and transition values and then choose the photo size and quality.

9

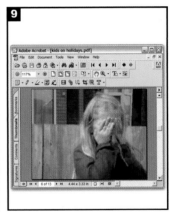

Click Save to create the slide show which you can then preview with the Adobe Acrobat reader/viewer available free from www.adobe.com.

Project 2: Stitching big paintings together

Skill Level – 1
Version – 3.0, 2.0, 1.0

Sometimes it simply isn't possible to get back far enough to capture the whole of a subject in a single shot. A good example of this scenario is when I was trying to make a digital copy of a large painting in a small room. Not being able to move the painting I photographed the artwork four times moving the camera slightly each time and then stitched the files together using the Photomerge feature in Elements.

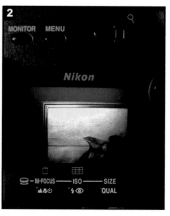

Set up your camera on a tripod in front of the painting.

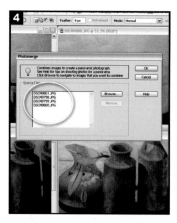

Shoot several images of the picture making sure to overlap side as well as top and bottom edges. Be sure to keep the camera to subject distance, exposure, zoom and white balance settings consistent.

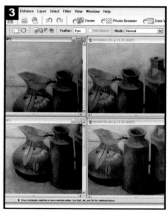

Import all images into Elements. Perform any slight editing alterations such as straightening, brightness and contrast and color cast removal to each image before saving.

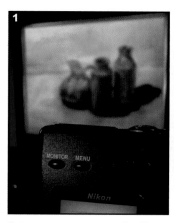

Select Photomerge from the File menu (Editor: File > New > Photomerge) to start a new panorama. The open images should be automatically listed in the Source Files area of the dialog.

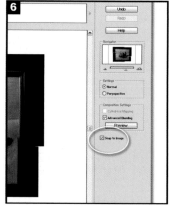

Version 1.0 users only – Set the Image Size Reduction amount to reduce source file sizes. If you are using images greater than 2 megapixels then a setting of 50% or more should be used. To get Elements to lay out the selected images check the 'Attempt to Automatically Arrange Source Images' box, for manual layout control leave the box unchecked. If you are using the 'Automatic Arrange' option then you can also choose to apply perspective correction across the whole of the composition. Do not use this feature for this project.

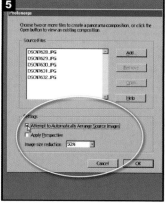

Select OK to open the Photomerge dialog box. Edit the layout of your source images. Turn the Snap to Image function on so that Photomerge will match the like details of the different images when they are dragged over each other.

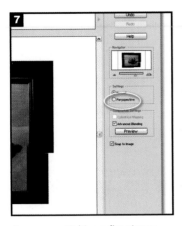

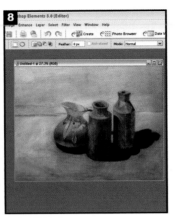

As you are stitching a flat picture make sure that you don't tick the Perspective box.

The final panorama file is produced by clicking the OK button. Crop excess wall area to reveal the full picture.

Project 3: Professional folio of images on CD-ROM

Skill Level – 2
Version – 3.0, 2.0

The picture folio is the photographer's main marketing tool. It wasn't that long ago that all serious image makers owned, and maintained, a black multi-leaf folder of their best prints. With the onset of the digital imaging revolution more and more professionals are converting their weighty and cumbersome image collections to a more easily handled format – the CD-ROM or VCD.

Now well and truly 'as cheap as chips', the humble CD has become the preferred transport medium for photographers worldwide. By combining the great pictures that already reside on your hard drive, with the Elements Slide Show feature and a handy CD burner you can have your own 'virtual' folio produced in no time at all. Don't restrict yourself to just images, use the built-in text abilities of Elements to quickly add biographical and contact details to the presentation.

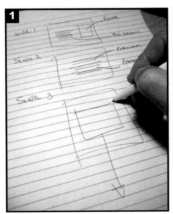

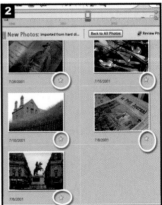

Consider what images and information you should include and how it should be presented. A few quick sketches will help organize your ideas.

Use the Photo Browser to tag the pictures that are to be included in the presentation.

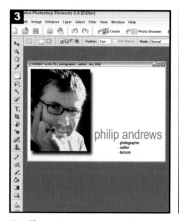

Use Elements to create any text-based heading and biographical slides and tag them and then save them to the Photo Browser.

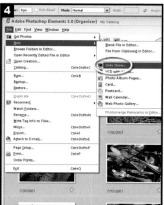

Display the Tagged files in the Photo Browser and then select File > New > Slide Show then Custom Slide Show.

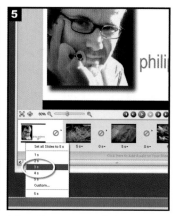

Adjust the sequence of source thumbnails to reflect the slide order you want and choose the duration that each picture will be on screen.

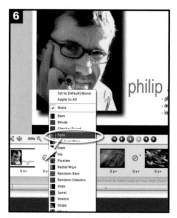

Select the transition style from the drop-down list and add an audio/narration track if you desire.

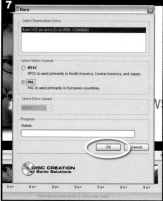

Click File > Save to store your slide show and its settings and then choose File > Burn a Video CD to create the disk.

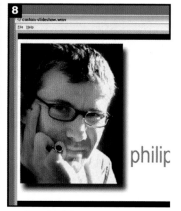

Preview the folio VCD with a DVD and television or on a computer with VCD player software.

Project 4: The school newsletter

Skill Level – 1
Version – 3.0, 2.0, 1.0

Part of the job of running a busy school is maintaining the communications between staff, students and parents. In recent years many schools have found that producing a regular newsletter helps to keep everyone informed. With the advent of lower priced cameras and scanners the humble single page text document has grown into a publication that is full of photographs of students, staff and the school activities.

Wade Haynes, a principal of Wynum North State High School, regularly uses digital images in his school's newsletter. 'It provides the school community with the opportunity to review the week's activities. The students love looking for themselves and their friends in print. Parents also appreciate the extra insight it gives them into school life.'

The staff and students at the school source their images either directly from digital cameras or from prints that have been scanned. Next they are imported directly into an image-editing program where they are cropped, straightened and resized. It is also at this point that the brightness and contrast of the images are improved. From here the pictures are placed into a word processing package containing a template of the magazine. The finished product is then printed out using a high quality inkjet printer before being copied and distributed to school families.

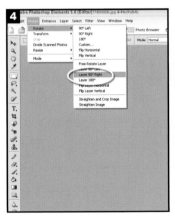

Students and staff shoot images using a digital camera at school activities during the week.

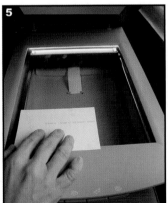

Back in the office or classroom the camera is connected to a computer.

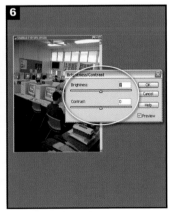

The images are viewed as thumbnails and then downloaded from the camera into image-editing software.

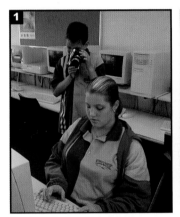

The best photographs are sized, rotated, their contrast and brightness adjusted and then they are saved to disk.

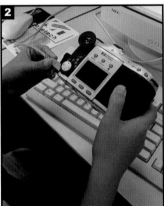

On occasions where the digital cameras are not available traditional film cameras are substituted. The prints from the camera are then converted to digital files using a flatbed scanner.

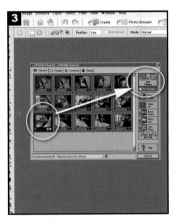

The images from the scanner are then sized, rotated, their contrast and brightness adjusted and saved to disk.

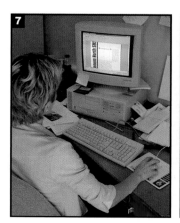 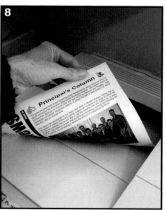 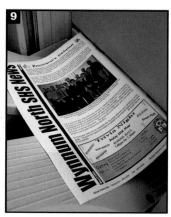

With the pictures now complete, the template for the school's newsletter is opened in a word processing package. The images are imported into the software and positioned in the layout of the page.	A high-quality master print of the completed newsletter is made on an inkjet printer or laser printer.	The school office staff then use a photocopier to duplicate the newsletter ready for distribution.

Project 5: Real estates go digital

Skill Level – 1
Version – 3.0, 2.0, 1.0

Adam Djordjevic is a busy real estate agent in an inner city firm. A lot of his business is based on communicating ideas and images with his clients. He finds that good photos of properties are crucial for establishing common ground and understanding what style and type of dwelling his customers are looking for.

For this reason taking pictures of houses and apartments is an integral part of the selling process. The images can then be used in a range of marketing activities including the show case in the office window, advertisements in local and national papers and on the company's website.

Adam feels that acquiring the images digitally makes it easier to use them in a range of formats. 'We can print them for the window, use them in "open house" literature, send them to the papers for ads and also pop them onto the website. No problems! Before we had to muck around with negatives and prints, the same digital file can be used for all our marketing needs.'

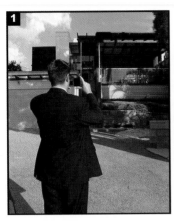

One of the real estate team photographs the property making sure that all the important features of the house are clearly shown. As there is no film or processing costs involved many pictures can be taken and the best selected for use.

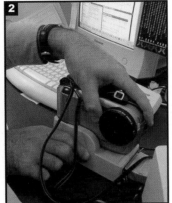

Back at the office the images from the camera are downloaded onto the computer. In this case the camera is connected to the computer using a special cradle.

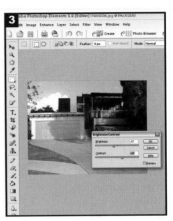

The brightness, contrast and color of the photographs are adjusted. The image is saved at the full resolution that it was captured. This file will be used for all print applications. A further copy is then saved at a resolution suitable for web and email distribution.

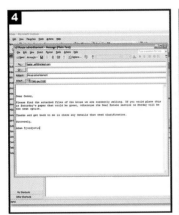

Emails with attached images and text are sent to the papers, printers and sign makers. Each of these companies will use the digital files for layingout of advertisements, brochures and signs.

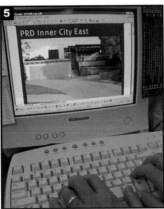

The task of updating the website to include the new listing is handled in-house. A template of the new page is automatically produced and the images and text are pasted into position. After checking the new page is uploaded to the website.

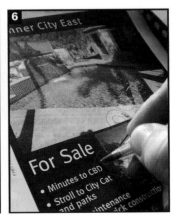

Meanwhile the sign maker has faxed back a draft of the proposed sign. Adam checks the details and sends and corrections back to be fixed.

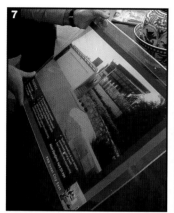

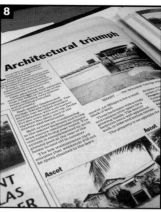

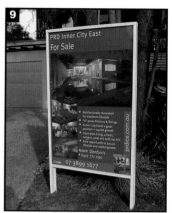

The printed window card arrives and is placed in a plastic mount, which is then hung in the display window.

Later that week the local newspaper features an editorial about the property using details and the digital images supplied online by Adam.

The day the paper is distributed the sign arrives and is hurriedly put in place in front of the property to make the most of the publicity.

Project 6: Photographic print display

Skill Level – 2
Version – 3.0, 2.0, 1.0

A regular activity undertaken by many photographers, both amateur and professional alike, is the production of a series of images for presentation. This group of photographs might be centered on a single idea or theme or it might represent a summary of skills and techniques. Whatever the case, a lot of time and effort is put into the production of a photographic folio. On the one hand the images must be able to be viewed as a series, each separate piece linked with, and contributing to, the next. But each individual picture must also be strong enough to standalone.

In the past photographers would spend long hours in the darkroom trying to ensure that all the variables of chemistry, time, exposure and paper were consistent so that each of the prints in the series would 'feel' similar. More recently imagemakers have started to use the 'digital darkroom' to give their pictures a unified look. Even if the photographs start life as a slide or negative, the enhancing and printing stages are being handled digitally rather than traditionally.

Kathryn Lyndsey is a photographer whose recent images are a good example of this new way of working. When producing a recent series of photographs she chose to shoot the images using a film-based camera and then complete the production process digitally. She says 'Working digitally gives me more freedom to be creative. I can work and rework an image making small adjustments that are not as easy to achieve in the darkroom. I feel less restricted and more in control.'

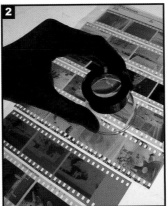

Kathryn's images are shot using traditional film cameras.

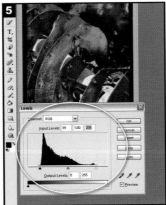

When processed she searches through the negatives to find the most suitable images.

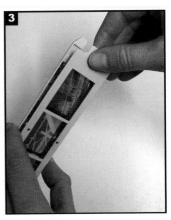

The candidate photographs are then converted to digital using a film scanner.

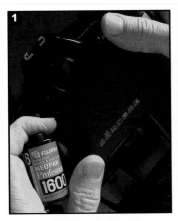

The unenhanced files are previewed on screen and examined carefully to identify areas that need adjusting.

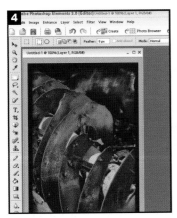

Basic manipulations such as changing orientation and altering brightness and contrast are made first.

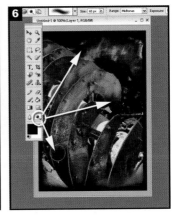

Next parts of the image are darkened and lightened using the Dodge and Burn tools.

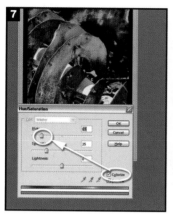

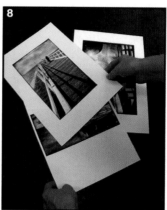

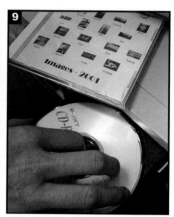

In some images Kathryn adds color and texture to black and white pictures using the Hue/Saturation feature and Texture filters. See Chapter 5 for more details of these techniques.

As a proofing step Kathryn outputs her work to an inkjet printer first to check color and how each of the images appears.

The final step is to burn the files to CD and send them off to a local professional photographic laboratory who will print the folio images on color photographic paper.

Project 7: Business manager presentation
Skill Level – 2
Version – 3.0, 2.0, 1.0

Gone are the days when business presentations are made up of a few sheets of columns of dry figures all neatly contained in a plan manila folder. Now managers of all types of companies are expected to deliver their reports with a little more pizazz and certainly more graphical content. Most of these presentations are put together in slide show type packages like Microsoft PowerPoint and consist of a combination of written information and graphical content. Though very sophisticated in themselves most slide show programs contain no, or very limited, image-editing abilities. Although Elements 3.0 now contains its own slide show maker technology savvy managers who want a few more controls are using Elements in conjunction with their presentation software to produce interesting and dynamic business reports.

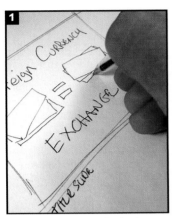

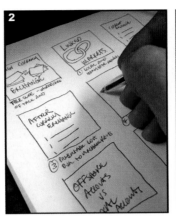

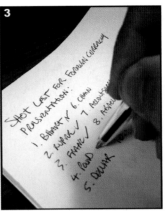

When generating quality business graphics it is important to make sure that the image component supports the business ideas and does not distract from them. For this reason a lot of managers start the process with a few design drawings.

As the presentation process involves the delivery of a series of 'electronic' slides, putting together a story board, similar to those used in the film industry, is the next step in the design process.

With the design complete a list of visual elements, or props, that need to be photographed, or scanned, is compiled.

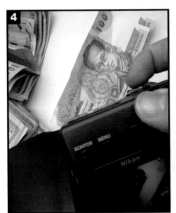

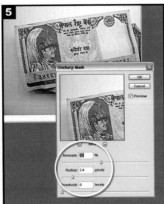

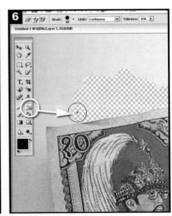

The props are then captured being sure to take several images from different directions or angles so that there is more choice later in the process.

Next the images are downloaded to the computer and imported into Elements. Brightness, contrast, color and sharpness are adjusted.

The background is removed from the objects using the Background Eraser tool and a Cutout filter (Filters > Artistic > Cutout) applied to give the props a more graphic appearance.

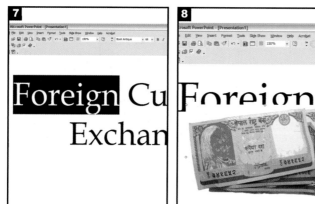

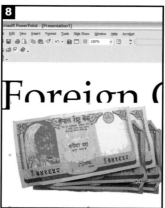

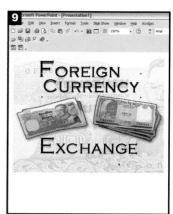

The presentation program is started and the background and text and graph components of the slide composed.

The finished graphic components are then copied in Elements (Select > All, then Edit > Copy) and pasted (Edit > Paste) into the presentation program.

The graphics are then resized and arranged to fit the background and text content. The final slide is saved as part of the full presentation.

Project 8: Restoration of a family heirloom

Skill Level – 3
Version – 3.0, 2.0, 1.0

Stored away in the lofts of many homes is a collection of family history documents. Usually contained in boxes, or old suitcases, they are a mixture of photographs and letters. One of the first tasks that a family member with a new interest in digital imaging inherits is the restoration of some of these heirlooms to their former glory. Suffering from a mixture of scratches, stains and fading these images can be improved and repaired using a combination of the techniques introduced in previous chapters.

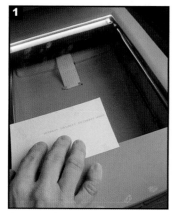

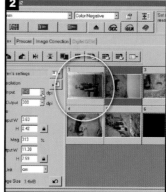

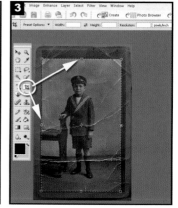

Open up the scanner plug-in either from within Elements or via the Acquire option in the Quick Start screen.

Capturing the photograph to be restored is a critical part of the process. Make sure that the scanner's contrast and brightness settings are adjusted to capture all the highlight and shadow details contained in the original.

With the image imported into Elements rotate and crop the image using the Straighten and Crop Image selection from the Rotate section of the Image menu. For manual control you can use the Crop tool from the toolbox.

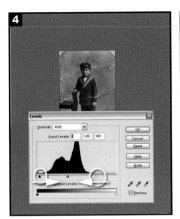

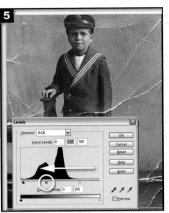

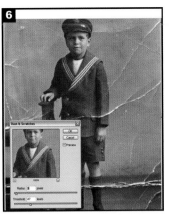

Use the finer tone control of Levels (Enhance > Adjust Lighting > Levels) to peg the white and black points in the image.

Adjust the midtone value in Levels to darken or lighten middle value tones in the image.

Use the Dust & Scratches filter (Filter > Noise > Dust & Scratches) to eliminate some of the marks on the image surface. For more difficult areas or those sections that need reconstruction use the Clone Stamp or Spot Healing Brush tools to copy and paste new tones and textures.

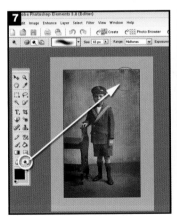

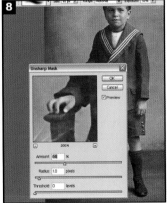

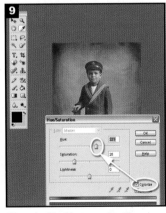

Darken or lighten selected areas of the picture using the Dodging or Burning tools.

Sharpen the image by using the Unsharp Mask filter (Filter > Sharpen > Unsharp Mask). Ensure that the preview thumbnail is set to 100% to gauge the strength of the filter effect.

Tone the final image using the Colorize option from within the Hue/Saturation feature (Enhance > Adjust Color > Hue/Saturation).

Project 9: Menu for restaurant

Skill Level – 3
Version – 3.0, 2.0, 1.0

Updating a restaurant menu to keep track with the seasonal availability of ingredients can be a long-winded and costly affair. Each time a dish is replaced the menu has to be redesigned and printed to account for the changes. However, if the menu is created digitally using a package like Elements and the different dishes and their descriptions stored in different layers, then changing the food list at short notice can be as simple as switching off one layer and turning on another. The new-look menu can then be printed and displayed.

The selection tools and layer techniques we looked at earlier in this book are central to the production of this quick change menu.

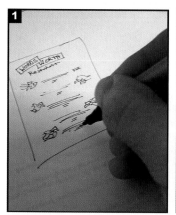

The general design for the menu was sketched roughly on paper taking into account that the layout would not change, but particular menu items might be added or taken away depending on ingredient availability.

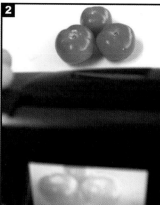

The image content was then shot making sure that each component had similar lighting and angle of view. These settings were noted down so they could be repeated later for new dishes.

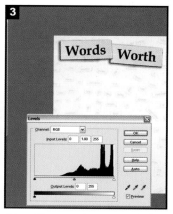

A base Elements document was then created with all the static elements compiled on the background layer.

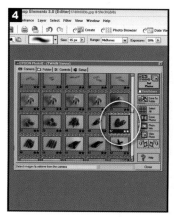

The pictures were then imported as separate documents into Elements.

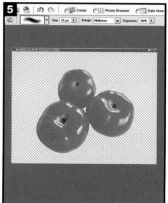

Each image was adjusted and cut from its background. The image parts were then copied and pasted as new layers into the base menu file.

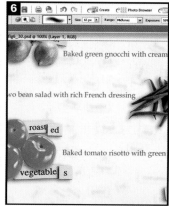

The description and pricing for each dish were then added as a text layer. The text layer and its associated image layer were then linked so that they could be moved together.

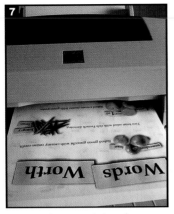

With the layout complete the menu was printed and was ready for display.

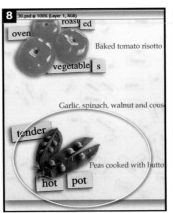

With changing availability of ingredients new dishes were added to the menu. Older items were kept in the stack but were removed from view by clicking their Eye icons.

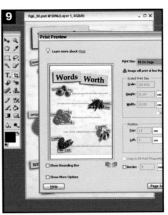

With the changes complete the new version of the menu was printed and displayed.

Project 10: Advertisement optimized for black and white

Skill Level – 2
Version – 3.0, 2.0, 1.0

Advertising in the local newspaper is a good way to attract new custom to small businesses, but often the task of putting together a design can seem to be a little overwhelming. Using the text features in Elements and a few imaging tricks you can produce a simple but effective advertisement, which can be supplied to the paper's classifieds department on disk for inclusion in the next edition.

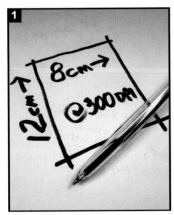

Find out from your local newspaper the exact size and resolution that you need to submit to them. These details will usually be supplied in terms of centimeter or inch dimensions together with a figure for resolution in dots per inch or dpi. For our example we will construct an advertisement that is 12 × 8 cm (h × w) at 300 dpi.

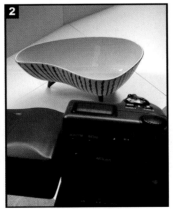

Photograph some images that represent your business or the products that you sell. Shoot a range of different photographs so that you have a few to choose from. Keep in mind that the advertisement is in a vertical or portrait format and that horizontal images might need to be cropped to fill the space.

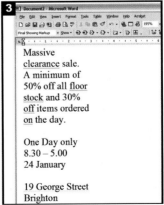

At the same time as shooting, use a word processor to organize and input the text that will be included in the advertisement. At this stage keep the typeface and style simple, as enhancements will be made in Elements.

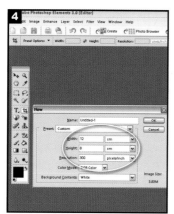

Open Elements and select the New File option from the Welcome screen. Input the size and resolution values directly into the New Image dialog.

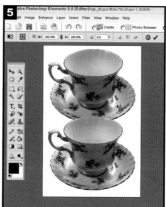

Open and select one of the images that you have photographed using the Select All command from the Select menu. Copy (Edit > Copy) and Paste (Edit > Paste) the picture into the advertisement document. With the new layer selected adjust its size using the Image > Transform > Free Transform command.

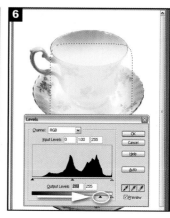

Using the Marquee tool make a rectangular selection in the middle section of the image. Feather the selection by 20 pixels (Selection > Feather) and then open the levels dialog (Enhance > Adjust Lighting > Levels). Move the black output slider to the right to lighten the selection.

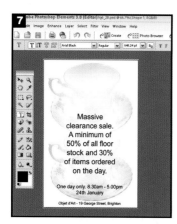

Switch to the word processing package and highlight and copy the advertisement text. Switch back to Elements and with the text tool selected click onto the canvas in the lightened area. Paste the copied text here. End of line breaks can be added by inserting the cursor in the correct position and hitting the return or enter key.

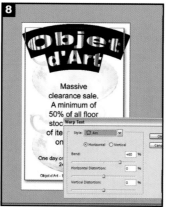

To add a bold heading, insert another text cursor and type directly onto the canvas altering the size and font to suit. Use the Warp and Layer Styles features to make the type stand out from the background.

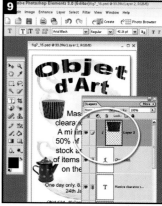

Finally to add some more interest to the heading open a second image from those photographed earlier. Select and copy the picture. Switch back to the advertisement and paste the picture onto a layer directly above the heading text. Next insert this new image into the heading text by selecting Group With Previous from the Layer menu.

Project 11: Company logo, letterhead, business card

Skill Level – 3
Version – 3.0, 2.0, 1.0

The Eastside Community Support Group is a small network of volunteers who regularly give their time to help settle new migrants in their local area. The group runs many orientation activities that require a great deal of organization and communication with the participants, small businesses and the local authorities. Presenting a professional face is an important aspect of reassuring all parties that despite the volunteer nature of the network, the group is committed and organized. They found that 'for some people you have to look the part before they give you a chance'. Part of looking the part is having simple but effective stationery.

The first task was to produce a logo that was not too complex, represented the group's concerns, was easy to understand and was cheap to reproduce. The 'Helping Hands' image met most of these criteria but needed to be simplified so that it could be reproduced using low cost printers or photocopiers. A basic black and white design seemed to be the solution.

A digital picture of two hands was photographed against a white background and then imported into Elements. The image was then cropped and straightened. The background was erased using the Background Eraser tool. Now that the hands had been isolated from the surrounding detail the Threshold feature was applied to the whole image. This converted all picture tones to either black or white, giving a stark graphic image. The edges of the hands were then stroked and any gray areas were either erased or brushed to black. To complete the logo the image was cropped again and some inverted text added to a black rectangle at the bottom. The whole image was then selected and stroked with black. The finished logo was then 'Inserted' into word processing software to produce the required stationery.

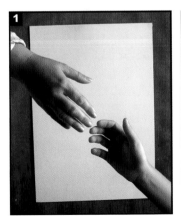

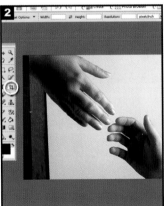

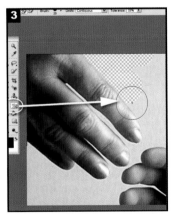

A piece of white card was used as a background for the photograph. This simple step helped when it came to isolating the hands from the background later.

The digital picture was downloaded from the camera and cropped and straightened in Elements using the Crop tool.

The Background Eraser tool is designed to eliminate unwanted detail from around a subject. The tool was used here to erase the white background so that only the hands were left.

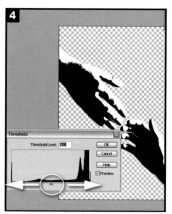

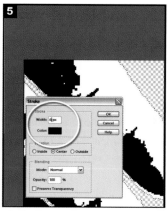

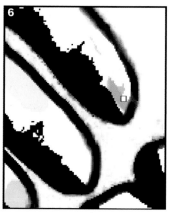

The Threshold feature (Filter > Adjustments > Threshold) was used to convert the image to just black and white. The slider in the dialog controls the point at which image parts are changed to white or black.

The background was selected using the Magic Wand tool and the selection was then inverted (Select > Inverse) so that only the hands were selected. The selection was then stroked (Edit > Stroke) with a black six pixel line.

With the major manipulations complete the Eraser tool was used to clean up any fuzzy or gray areas. The tool was changed from block to paint brush mode to erase smaller details.

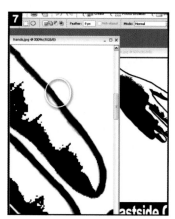

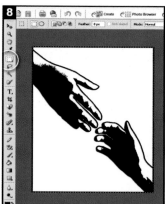

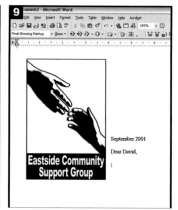

Next the lines were cleaned up and some areas reshaped using the paint brush. To check progress a second view (View > New) of the image was opened. Changes were made on the magnified view and the effects of these changes checked on the full view.

With the retouching complete, the image was cropped and stroked again. A black rectangle was added to the bottom and the name of the group was laid out in white type.

The completed image was then saved as a TIFF file and used in a desktop publishing or word processing package to produce the stationery item masters. As the design is just black and white the items could then be reproduced using photocopy or cheap printing services.

Project 12: Holiday panoramic posters

Skill Level – 2
Version – 3.0, 2.0, 1.0

Seeing new and different places can be a real 'eye opening' experience. The culture, people, architecture and clothing can vary so much from country to country that trying to take it all in, or worse, remember it, can be a difficult proposition. Most people prompt their memories with loads of photographs that, for many, spend more time in the drawer in the living room than being admired. Some pictures are framed and make it to the walls but it is only occasionally that these few pictures can sum up all of what the holiday traveler experienced. With stitching programs like Photomerge it is now possible to document a much wider view of the environment and all its differences. Hanging a few of these vistas on the wall will certainly bring back the sights and possibly even the sounds and smells of those distant shores.

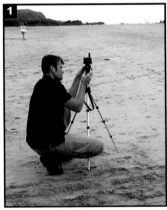

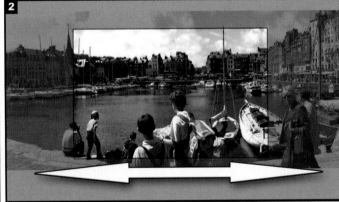

Find a suitable scene that contains interesting and memorable details in fore, mid and background areas. Set up your tripod or position yourself so that it is possible to record the action around you.

Rotate the camera looking through the viewfinder but not taking any images, checking that the horizon is level and the zoom setting you have selected captures the main features of the scene.

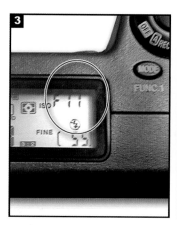

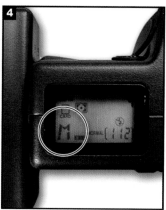

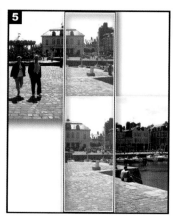

Set the aperture of the camera to a high f-stop number to ensure the sharpness of each picture extends from the foreground right into the distance.

Set the exposure manually on an average between that needed for the brightest part of the scene and what is required for the dark areas.

Start to photograph a sequence of images from left to right overlapping each sequential picture by a minimum of 30% and a maximum of 50%.

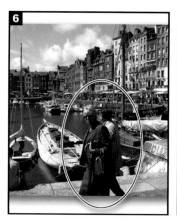

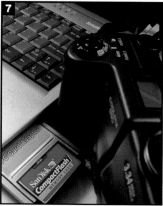

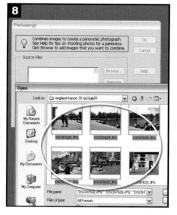

Watch and wait for moving details to be positioned in the center of each shot. If this isn't possible take extra reference pictures so that the important details can be cut and pasted into the main composition later.

Back at the hotel download the images onto your laptop and import them into Elements using the Photomerge option in the File menu.

Browse for the panorama images using the Add button in the initial Photomerge dialog. Once found select all the pictures in the sequence and click the Open and then Add buttons.

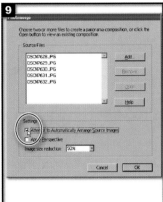

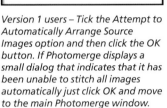

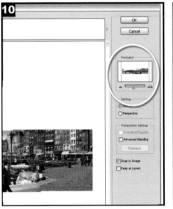

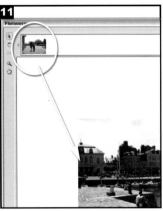

Version 1 users – Tick the Attempt to Automatically Arrange Source Images option and then click the OK button. If Photomerge displays a small dialog that indicates that it has been unable to stitch all images automatically just click OK and move to the main Photomerge window.

Adjust the view of the image using the Navigator control so that the whole composition can be seen.

Drag and 'Snap to Image' any of the pictures that are still contained in the light box section of the dialog.

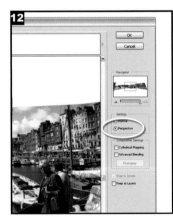

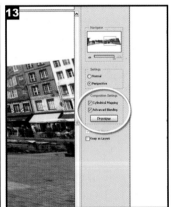

Apply perspective correction to the image if needed by checking the box in the dialog.

Tick the Cylindrical Mapping feature to help compensate for the bow tie effect that is caused by the perspective corrections. Use the Advanced Blending option to help disguise exposure changes.

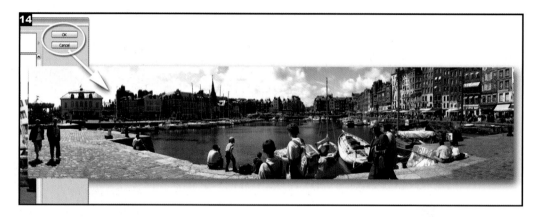

Produce the final panorama by clicking the OK button. Use the cropping tool if necessary to trim the top and bottom of the image.

14

Where to From Here?

The differences between Elements and Photoshop

Who can guide me further?

started this book by applauding Adobe for their foresight in releasing Elements, because in doing so they had obviously realized the importance of a huge group of users who wanted the power of Photoshop but didn't need all the features. I hope that the last few chapters have demonstrated that for 95% of your digital imaging needs Elements should be your first port of call.

Most users will find that this package more than covers their entire image-editing requirements, but as you develop your skills and understanding some of you will arrive at a point where you need some of the sophisticated professional features contained in Photoshop. To help you decide when this day has arrived, this chapter will look at the differences between Elements and the Adobe image-editing flagship – Photoshop.

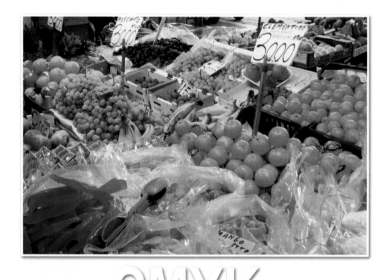

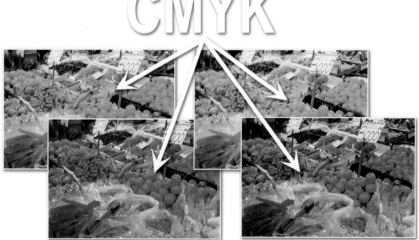

Figure 14.1 *Images destined for publication in magazine or book form are separated into Cyan, Magenta, Yellow and Black (or CMYK) components.*

The differences between Elements and Photoshop

From the outset it is important to understand that Photoshop is a professional imaging tool. In the current industry climate, this means that not only does the software contain 'bullet-proof' editing and enhancement features, but it also must allow users to output files that are customized for high-quality offset printing and web production. For this reason, Photoshop contains many features dealing with these areas.

Offset printing

Although Elements is more than sufficient for making prints with most desktop inkjet machines, Photoshop can also create and edit images in the CMYK (Cyan, Magenta, Yellow and Black) press format. See Figure 14.1.

This four-color separation mode is the basis of most offset printing and Photoshop's ability to work with these files is the reason why it has become a favorite software tool of printers all over the world. Unlike Elements, the mode section in Photoshop contains extra options for the conversion of images to CMYK and Duotone, as well as specialist LAB and Multi-channel formats. The options in the Info feature also reflect the different modes available in each package. In addition, Photoshop provides the ability to output the separation images needed to make printing plates directly. See Figures 14.2 and 14.3.

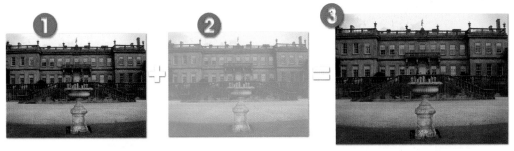

igure 14.2 *Duotone is a special printing mode that colors a monotone image by using two separate printing inks. (1) Ink color 1. (2) Ink color 2. (3) Duotone image combining both ink colors.*

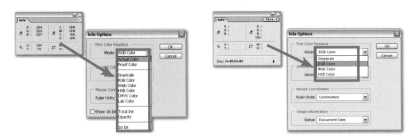

Figure 14.3 *Photoshop's Info palette contains more display and sampling options than the reduced set found in the Elements version.*

Web-based production

Adobe has deemed quality output to the Net to be so important that a few years ago they created a totally new product call ImageReady. Supplied free with Photoshop, ImageReady is a dedicated image-editing package designed to produce web components such as animations, rollovers, image slices and maps. See Figures 14.4 and 14.5.

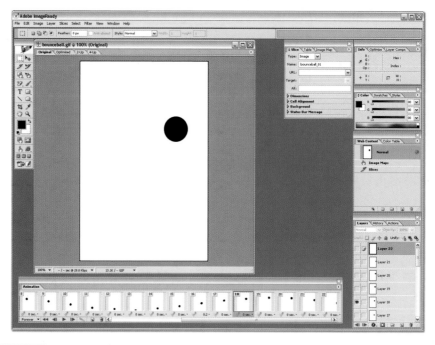

Figure 14.4 *ImageReady is a stand-alone editing program that is used to optimize and create web images.*

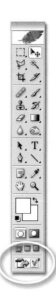

Figure 14.5 *You can jump between Photoshop and ImageReady by using the extra button located at the bottom of the tool bar.*

The animations features extend the basic abilities found in Elements and provide more creative control over how each individual frame fits within a GIF animation. Rollovers are a specialist button type that has gained in popularity over the last few years. ImageReady not only allows the user to set up the pictures that will be used for the button, but the program also writes the special code that is needed to make the button function. See Figure 14.6.

Some advance features in web imaging require an image to be sliced into smaller image segments. Photoshop and ImageReady contain advanced features for editing of web images and their sliced components.

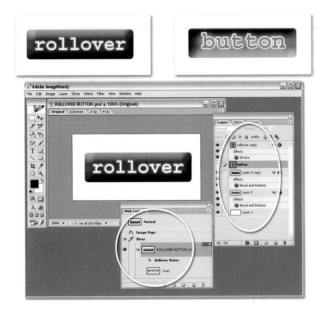

Figure 14.6 The main image in a rollover button changes when the mouse pointer moves over it.

Image maps allow users to allocate different button features and web links to small sections of a large image, and also allow areas of an image that contain more or less detail to be compressed by differing amounts. ImageReady provides a toolset designed to construct, edit and maintain the image maps within a website. Through the use of these special features, users can optimize their existing images for the web or create totally new web elements not possible in Photoshop or Elements alone.

The other main differences revolve around features that allow finer control of images, their tones and hues. In particular, Photoshop contains advanced color management settings, curves functions, extended selection capabilities and special paths features.

Color management

It is assumed that most Photoshop users will be professional imaging specialists. As such, the program contains sophisticated color management controls that can be customized to suit a myriad of output scenarios. This level of color organization makes Photoshop the pivot point for digital image creation, manipulation and output. Professionals who are involved at different points in the process can pass image files to each other, being secure in the knowledge that Photoshop will adjust picture data to suit their imaging setup. See Figure 14.7.

In contrast, Elements' color management is designed for use with a single digital setup – a camera connected to a computer linked to a printer. It performs this job admirably, but if your business involves inputting and outputting files from a range of sources to a variety of destinations with the best color management available, then there is no other choice than to use Photoshop.

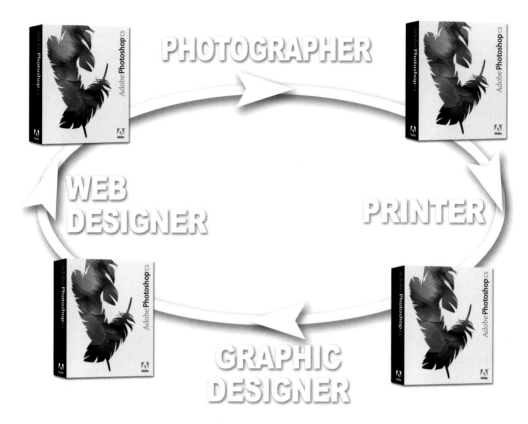

Figure 14.7 *The advanced color management features in Photoshop provide a common base for conversion of color images as they are passed from one person to another along the production line.*

Automated functions

A feature that was introduced to Photoshop a few versions ago was the ability to record a series of actions, which could be replayed later. For those users whose daily work involves repetitive image changes, this feature was a godsend. To some extent the Layer Styles in Elements is a more basic version of the technology. Here the repeated actions that would need to take place to make a drop shadow, for instance, have been collated and are performed at the push of a single button. The 'Actions' feature in Photoshop takes this idea further by allowing users to record and organize their own series of steps. See Figure 14.8.

There are now dedicated websites that house thousands of Photoshop actions that are designed to make the professional's day-to-day imaging tasks much simpler. Unlike Elements, the Photoshop batch is able to apply any action to a group of images within a specific folder.

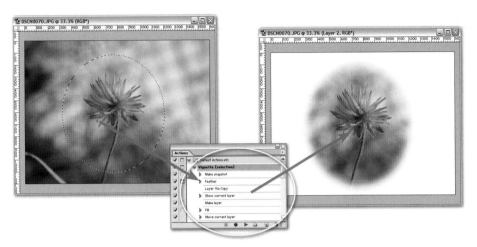

Figure 14.8 *Photoshop's Actions feature allows the recording and playback of a series of production steps.*

Paths

Photoshop includes a series of tools designed to create and edit paths. Creating a path is similar to making a selection. The Pen is used to make the path outline around image parts. Like the Polygonal Lasso, the Pen lays down anchor points, between which a straight line is drawn. When complete, the path can be saved as part of the image file. Anchor points can be added to and removed from the path at any time. The position of any point can be moved and the line that stretches between two points can be adjusted to fit image curves.

And if all these features didn't impress you, a saved path can be converted to an active selection at any time. See Figure 14.9. In addition, any path can be converted to and saved as a custom shape ready for later use. See Figure 14.10.

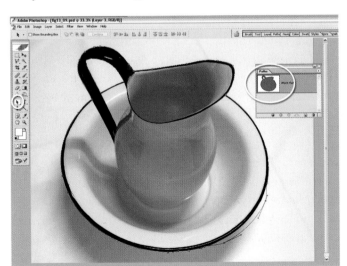

Figure 14.9 *Path tools offer a more sophisticated and editable pathway to making selections.*

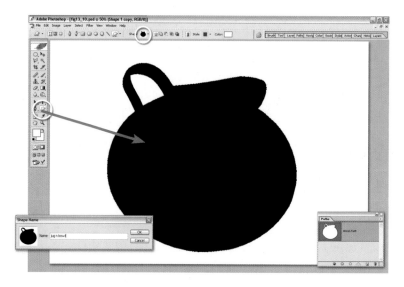

Figure 14.10 *Converting paths to custom shapes allows them to be selected from the shape palette and used later.*

The extra editing abilities of paths make this tool a more sophisticated way to select areas within your image than the selection options available in either Photoshop or Elements.

Curves

The characteristic curve is a familiar sight to many photographers. It is used to describe how the tones in the shadow, highlight and midtone areas are spread throughout an image. In effect, it is another way to represent the information contained in the Levels dialog, with the difference that Curves allows you to interact and change very specific groups of tones. Dedicated Photoshop users often use this feature to make very slight but visually important corrections to areas such as the shadow details of a picture. See Figure 14.11.

Color Balance

Many Photoshop users have a background in traditional photography; Adobe included a hue control in Photoshop that works in a similar way to the sliders or dials of a color enlarger. The Color Balance feature contains three sliders – yellow/blue, magenta/green and cyan/red. The dominant color of any image can be changed by adjusting the mix of these three spectra. It is also possible to alter the cast of highlights, midtones and shadows independently.

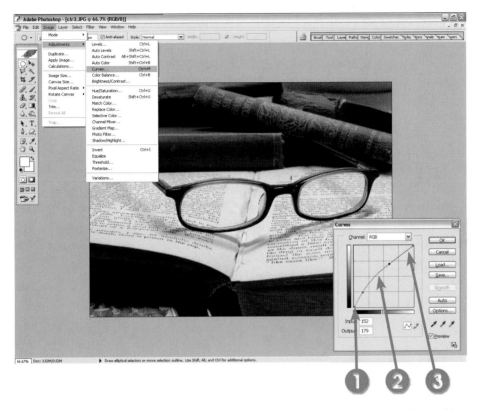

Figure 14.11 *Curves provides advanced tonal control of delicate areas such as shadows and highlights. (1) Shadows. (2) Midtones. (3) Highlights.*

16-bit support

The 24-bit (8 bits per red, green and blue channel) mode provides a color gamut that is suitable for most imaging needs, but occasionally, when the highest quality pictures are required, the image files need to be captured at a higher bit depth. Many professional cameras and good quality scanners can now capture images in 16 bits per channel (48-bit mode) as either a TIFF or RAW file. Even though Photoshop Elements 3.0 can now open and, in a very limited way, enhance 16-bit files with Photoshop CS you have a much larger range of tools and features available for the manipulation of these files. Features like adjustment layers, adding text, paint brush, advanced selection options, clone stamp and healing brushes are all available in 16-bit mode in Photoshop CS.

Who can guide me further?

If you are wanting to switch over to Photoshop and need a text that will give you a good grounding in the basic skills and techniques then *Photoshop CS: Essential Skills* is a great place to start. Written by myself and Mark Galer, the text provides the same highly visual approach as this book uses and contains plenty of terrific examples of how to improve your pictures using Photoshop.

Wanting something a little more substantial? Well with the previous versions of this book never straying from the top 10 digital imaging publications for photographers at Amazon.com, Martin Evening's *Adobe Photoshop for Photographers* is the book to introduce you to the sophistication of this powerful program. The current edition is updated to include the new features and functions contained in the latest release of the industry-leading, image-editing software. Evening's style is ever practical, as he provides step-by-step guides and tutorials loaded with real life examples and pragmatic advice.

Windows

Ctrl + O

Shift + Ctrl + O

Ctrl + W

Ctrl + S

Ctrl + Z

Ctrl + Y

Ctrl + T

Shift + Ctrl + L

Alt + Shift + Ctrl + L

Shift + Ctrl + B

Ctrl + U

Ctrl + L

Ctrl + A

Ctrl + F

Ctrl + R

Ctrl + H

F1

Ctrl + P

Ctrl + Q

Ctrl + D

Appendices

Jargon buster

Keyboard shortcuts

Elements/Photoshop feature equivalents

Jargon buster

A >>

Aliasing The jaggy edges that appear in bitmap images with curves or lines at any angle other than multiples of 90°. The anti-aliasing function in Elements softens around the edges of images to help make the problem less noticeable. See Figure A.1.

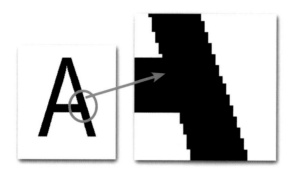

Figure A.1 Aliasing is most noticeable on the edges of text and objects with diagonal or curving edges.

Aspect ratio This is usually found in dialog boxes concerned with changes of image size and refers to the relationship between width and height of a picture. The maintaining of an image's aspect ratio means that this relationship will remain the same even when the image is enlarged or reduced. See Figure A.2.

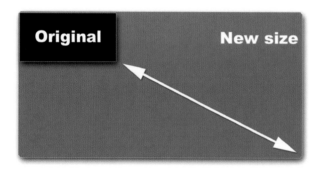

Figure A.2 Mantaining the aspect ratio of your photograph when you enlarge or reduce sizes will help guarantee that all your picture elements remain in proportion.

B >>

Background printing Is a printing method that allows the user to continue working whilst an image or document is being printed.

Batch processing or **Process Multiple Files** as it is known in Elements 3.0. Refers to a function or a series of commands being applied to several files at one time. This function is useful for making the same changes to a folder full of images. In Elements this function is found under the File menu and is useful for converting groups of image files from one format to another. See Figure A.3.

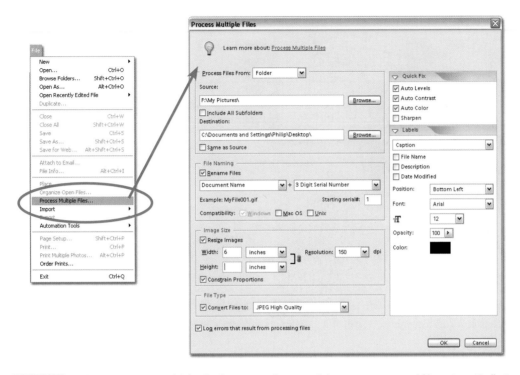

Figure A.3 *The batch or Process Multiple Files feature applies a set of changes to a group of files automatically. In version 3.0 of Elements the feature can be used to change file types, image sizes, rename, apply quick fixes or even add labels.*

Bit Stands for 'binary digit' and refers to the smallest part of information that makes up a digital file. It has a value of only 0 or 1. Eight of these bits make up one byte of data.

Bitmap or **'raster'** Is the form in which digital photographs are stored and is made up of a matrix of pixels.

Blend mode The way in which a color or a layer interacts with others. The most important after Normal are probably Multiply, which darkens everything, Screen, which adds to the colors to make everything lighter, Lighten, which lightens only colors darker than itself, and Darken, which darkens only colors lighter than itself. Both the latter therefore flatten contrast. Color maintains the shading of a colour but alters the color to itself. Glows therefore are achieved using Screen mode, and Shadows using Multiply.

Brightness range The range of brightnesses between shadow and highlight areas of an image.

Burn tool To darken an image, can be targeted to affect just the Shadows, Midtones or Highlights. Opposite to Dodge. Part of the toning trio, which also includes the Sponge.

Byte This is the standard unit of digital storage. One byte is made up of 8 bits and can have any value between 0 and 255. 1024 bytes are equal to 1 kilobyte. 1024 kilobytes are equal to 1 megabyte. 1024 megabytes are equal to 1 gigabyte.

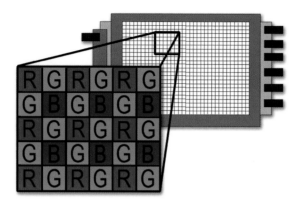

Figure A.4 The CCD sensor is the digital equivalent of film and is used to record the photograph.

C>>

CCD or **Charge Coupled Device** Many of these devices placed in a grid format comprise the sensor of most modern digital cameras. See Figure A.4.

Clone Stamp or **Rubber Stamp tool** Allows a user to copy a part of an image to somewhere else. It is therefore ideal for repair work, e.g. unwanted spots or blemishes. Equivalent to Copy and Paste in a brush.

Color mode The way that an image represents the colors that it contains. Different color modes include Bitmap, RGB and Grayscale. See Figure A.5.

Compression Refers to a process where digital files are made smaller to save on storage space or transmission time. Compression is available in two types – lossy, where parts of the original image are lost at the compression stage, and lossless, where the integrity of the file is maintained during the compression process. JPEG and GIF use lossy compression whereas TIFF is a lossless format.

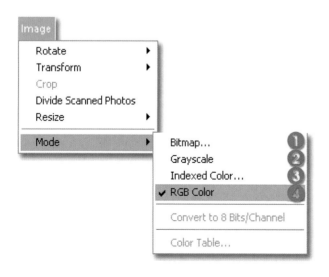

Figure A.5 The mode of a picture determines the numbers of colors that can be used in the photo.
(1) Bitmap uses just black and white tones.
(2) Grayscale consists of up to 256 levels of gray.
(3) The Index color format is restricted to 256 colors in total.
(4) RGB contains up to 16.7 million colors.

D >>

Digitize This is the process by which analog images or signals are sampled and changed into digital form.

Dodge tool For lightening areas in an image. See also Burn.

DPI or **Dots per inch** Is a term used to indicate the resolution of a scanner or printer. See Figure A.6.

Dynamic range Is the measure of the range of brightness levels that can be recorded by a sensor.

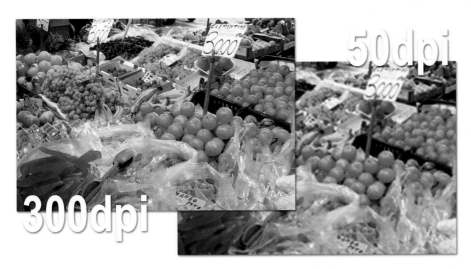

Figure A.6 *The dpi or dots per inch term is used as a measurment of the resolution of a picture. The higher the dpi value the higher the image's resolution will be.*

E >>

Enhancement Is a term that refers to changes in brightness, color and contrast which are designed to improve the overall look of an image.

F >>

File format The way that a digital image is stored. Different formats have different characteristics. Some are cross-platform, others have inbuilt compression capabilities.

Filter In digital terms a filter is a way of applying a set of image characteristics to the whole or part of an image. Most image-editing programs contain a range of filters that can be used for creating special effects. See Figure A.7.

Front page Sometimes called the home or index page, refers to the initial screen that the viewer sees when logging onto a website. Often the name and spelling of this page file is critical if it is to work on the web server. Consult your ISP staff for the precise name to be used with your site.

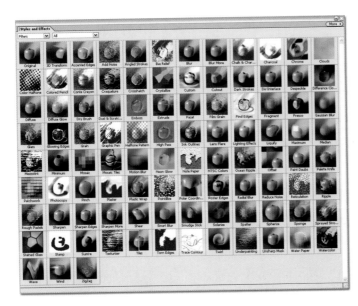

Figure A.7 *Elements contains a host of filters that can change the look of your digital photographs. See the complete collection by displaying the Styles and Effects palette.*

G >>

Gamma Is the contrast of the midtone areas of a digital image.

Gamut The range of colors or hues that can be printed or displayed by particular devices.

Gaussian Blur When applied to an image or a selection, this filter softens or blurs the image.

GIF or **Graphic Interchange Format** This is an indexed color mode that contains a maximum of 256 colors that can be mapped to any palette of actual colors. It is extensively used for web graphics, buttons and logos, and small animated images.

Grayscale A monochrome image containing just monochrome tones ranging from white through a range of grays to black.

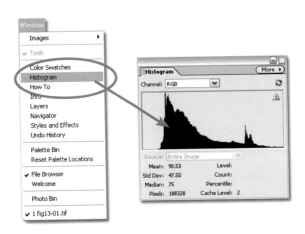

Figure A.8 *The histogram is a visual representation of the pixels that make up your digital photograph.*

H >>

Histogram A graph that represents the tonal distribution of pixels within a digital image. In version 3.0 of Elements the histogram can be found under the Windows menu. See Figure A.8.

History Adobe's form of Multiple Undo.

Hot linked This term refers to a piece of text, graphic or picture that has been designed to act as a button on a web page. When the viewer clicks the hot linked item they are usually transported to another page or part of a website.

HTML The Hyper Text MarkUp Language is the code used to create web pages. The characteristics of pages are stored in this language and when a page file is downloaded to your computer the machine lays out and displays the text, image and graphics according to what is stated in the HTML file.

Hue Refers to the color of the light and is separate from how light or dark it is.

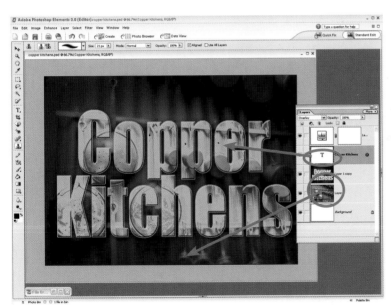

Figure A.9 Layers help keep different parts of a complex image separate. This makes editing and enhancement steps easier.

I >>

Image layers Images in Elements can be made up of many layers. Each layer will contain part of the picture. When viewed together all layers appear to make up a single continuous image. Special effects and filters can be applied to layers individually. See Figure A.9.

Interpolation This is the process used by image-editing programs to increase the resolution of a digital image. Using fuzzy logic the program makes up the extra pixels that are placed between the original ones that were generated at the time of scanning.

ISP The Internet Service Provider is the company that hosts or stores web pages. If you access the web via a dial-up account then you will usually have a portion of free space allocated for use for your own site, others can obtain free (with a small banner advert attached) space from companies like www.tripod.com.

J >>

JPEG A file format designed by the Joint Photographic Experts Group that has inbuilt lossy compression that enables a massive reduction in file sizes for digital images. Used extensively on the web and by press professionals for transmitting images back to newsdesks worldwide. See Figure A.10.

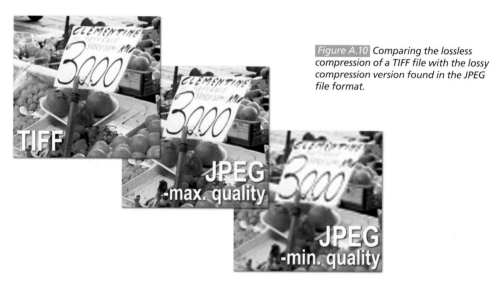

Figure A.10 Comparing the lossless compression of a TIFF file with the lossy compression version found in the JPEG file format.

L >>

Layer opacity The opacity or transparency of each layer can be changed independently. Depending on the level of opacity the parts of the layer beneath will become visible. You can change the opacity of each layer by moving the Opacity slider in the Layers palette.

LCD or **Liquid Crystal Display** A display screen type used in preview screens on the back of digital cameras, in laptop computers and more and more as replacement desktop screens.

Liquify A tool that uses brushes to perform distortions upon selections or the whole of an image.

M >>

Marquee A rectangular selection made by clicking and dragging to an opposite corner.

Megapixel One million pixels. Used to describe the resolution of digital camera sensors.

N >>

Navigator In Elements, a small scalable palette showing the entire image with the possibility of displaying a box representing the current image window frame. The frame's color can be altered; a new frame can be drawn (scaling the Image window with it) by holding the Command/Ctrl keys and making a new marquee. The frame can be dragged around the entire image with the Hand tool. The Zoom tools (mountain icons) can be clicked, the slider can be dragged, or a figure can be entered as a percentage.

O >>

Optical resolution The resolution that a scanner uses to sample the original image. This is often different from the highest resolution quoted for the scanner as this is scaled up by interpolating the optically scanned file.

Options bar Long bar beneath the menu bar, which immediately displays the various settings for whichever tool is currently selected. Can be moved to other parts of the screen if preferred.

P >>

Palette A window that is used for the alteration of image characteristics: Options palette, Layers palette, Styles palette, Hints palette, File Browser, History, etc. These can be docked together vertically around the main image window or if used less frequently can be docked in the Palette Well at the top right of the screen (dark gray area). See Figure A.11.

Pixel Short for picture element, refers to the smallest image part of a digital photograph. See Figure A.12.

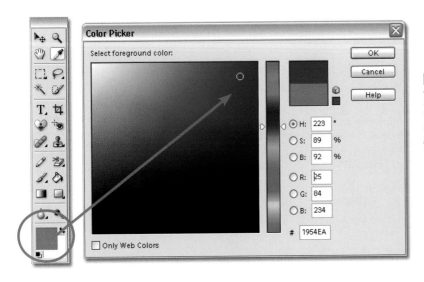

Figure A.11 Palettes are a good way for image-editing software to provide users with a range of options for a particular tool or feature.

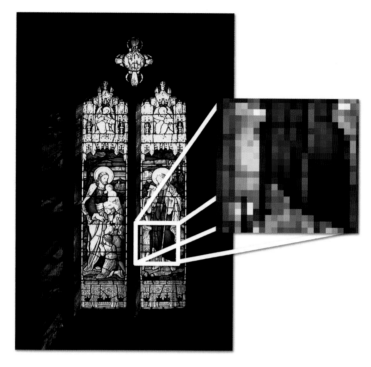

Figure A.12 *The pixel is the digital equivalent of what was called grain for film users.*

Q >>

Quantization Refers to the allocation of a numerical value to a sample of an analog image. Forms part of the digitizing process.

R >>

RGB All colors in the image are made up of a mixture of Red, Green and Blue colors. This is the typical mode used for desktop scanners, painting programs and digital cameras. See Figure A.13.

S >>

Sponge tool Used for saturating or desaturating part of an image that is exaggerating or lessening the color component as opposed to the lightness or darkness.

Status bar Attached to the base of the window (Mac) or beneath the window (PC). Can be altered to display a series of items from Scratch Disc usage and file size to the time it took to carry out the last action or the name of the current tool.

Stock A printing term referring to the type of paper or card that the image or text is to be printed on.

Swatches In Elements, refers to a palette that can display and store specific individual colors for immediate or repeated use.

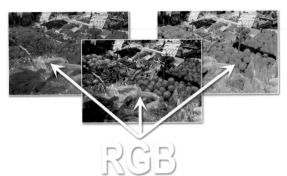

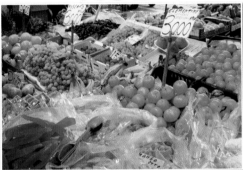

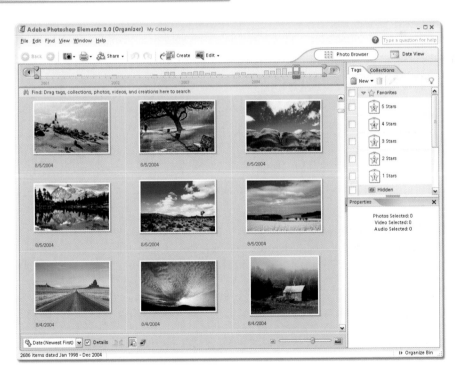

Figure A.13 Digital photographs are typically made of three components – one for the red parts of the image, one for green and one for blue. When combined these three parts form a full color picture.

Figure A.14 Browsing software like the Photo Browser contained in the Windows version of Elements 3.0 makes use of smaller copies of the pictures contained on your hard drive as a way of previewing the contents of the full file quickly and easily.

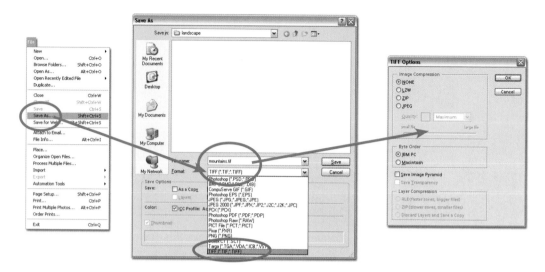

Figure A.15 The TIFF file format uses lossless compression and can be read by both Macintosh and Windows-based machines. This means that this format is a good choice for storing high-quality photos that need to be avaiable on both platforms.

T >>

Thumbnail A low resolution preview version of larger image files used to check before opening the full version. See Figure A.14.

TIFF or **Tagged Image File Format** Is a file format that is widely used by imaging professionals. The format can be used across both Macintosh and PC platforms and has a lossless compression system built in. See Figure A.15.

W >>

Warp tool A means of creating differing distortions to pieces of text such as arcs and flag ripples.

Keyboard shortcuts

General >>

Action	Windows	Macintosh
Open a file	Ctrl + O	Command + O
Open file browser	Shift + Ctrl + O	Shift + Command + O
Close a file	Ctrl + W	Command + W
Save a file	Ctrl + S	Command + S
Step backward	Ctrl + Z	Command + Z
Step forward	Ctrl + Y	Command + Y
Free Transform	Ctrl + T	Command + T
Auto levels	Shift + Ctrl + L	Shift + Command + L
Auto contrast	Alt + Shift + Ctrl + L	Option + Shift + Command + L
Auto Color Correction	Shift + Ctrl + B	Shift + Command + B
Hue/Saturation	Ctrl + U	Command + U
Levels	Ctrl + L	Command + L
Select All	Ctrl + A	Command + A
Apply last filter	Ctrl + F	Command + F
Show/Hide rulers	Ctrl + R	Command + R
Show/Hide selection	Ctrl + H	Command + H
Help	F1	Command + ?
Print Preview	Ctrl + P	Command + P
Exit Elements	Ctrl + Q	Command + Q
Deselect	Ctrl + D	Command + D
Feather a selection	Alt + Ctrl + D	Option + Command + D

Viewing >>

Action	Windows	Macintosh
Fits image on screen	Ctrl + 0	Command + 0
100% magnification	Alt + Ctrl + 0	Option + Command + 0
Zoom in	Ctrl + +	Command + +
Zoom out	Ctrl + -	Command + -
Scrolls image with hand tool	Spacebar + drag mouse pointer	Spacebar + drag mouse pointer
Scrolls up or down 1 screen	Page Up or Page Down	Page Up or Page Down

Selection/Drawing tools >>

Action	Windows	Macintosh
Adds to an existing selection	Shift + selection tool	Shift + selection tool
Subtracts from an existing selection	Alt + selection tool	Command + selection tool
Constrain marquee to square or circle	Shift + drag selection tool	Shift + drag selection tool
Draw marquee from center	Alt + drag selection tool	Option + drag selection tool
Constrain shape tool to square or circle	Shift + drag shape tool	Shift + drag shape tool
Draw shape tool from center	Alt + drag shape tool	Option + drag shape tool
Exit cropping tool	Esc	Esc
Enter cropping tool selection	Enter	Return
Switch magnetic lasso to lasso	Alt + drag tool	Option + drag tool
Switch magnetic lasso to polygonal lasso	Alt + drag tool	Option + drag tool
Switch from selection to move tool	Ctrl (except hand tool is selected)	Command

Painting >>

Action	Windows	Macintosh
Change to eyedropper	Alt + painting or shape tool	Option + painting or shape tool
Cycle through blending modes	Shift + + or -	Shift + + or -
Set exposure or opacity for painting	Painting tool + Number key (% = number key × 10)	Painting tool + Number key (% = number key × 10)
Display Fill dialog box	Shift + Backspace	Shift + Delete
Perform Fill with background color	Ctrl + Backspace	Command + Delete

Type editing >>

Action	Windows	Macintosh
Selects word	Double-click	Double-click
Select line	Triple-click	Triple-click
Decrease font size by 2 points/pixels	Selected text + Shift + <	Selected text + Shift + <
Increase font size by 2 points/pixels	Selected text + Shift + >	Selected text + Shift + >

Elements/Photoshop feature equivalents

Activity	Elements	Photoshop
Lighten shadow areas in an image	Fill Flash feature (ver.1.0/2.0)	Curves feature
Darken highlight areas in an image	Backlighting feature (ver.1.0/2.0)	Curves feature
Transformation	Image > Transform	Edit > Transform
Rotate Layer	Image > Rotate > Layer 90 deg left	Edit > Transform > Rotate 90 deg CCW
Rotate Canvas	Image > Rotate > 90 deg left	Image > Rotate Canvas > 90 deg CW
Resize image	Image > Resize > Image Size	Image > Image Size
Resize canvas	Image > Resize > Canvas Size	Image > Canvas Size
Batch dialog	File > Batch Processing	File > Automate > Batch
Web Photo Gallery	File > Create Web Photo Gallery	File > Automate > Web Photo Gallery
Contact Sheet	File > Print Layouts > Contact Sheet	File > Automate > Contact Sheet II
Picture Package	File > Print Layouts > Picture Package	File > Automate > Picture Package
Auto Levels	Enhance > Auto Levels	Image > Adjustments > Auto Levels
Auto Contrast	Enhance > Auto Contrast	Image > Adjustments > Auto Contrast
Auto Color Correction	Enhance > Auto Color Correction	Image > Adjustments > Auto Color
Hue/Saturation	Enhance > Adjust Color > Hue/Saturation	Image > Adjustments > Hue/Saturation
Color Variations	Enhance > Adjust Color > Color Variations	Image > Adjustments > Variations
Brightness/contrast	Enhance > Adjust Brightness/Contrast > Brightness/Contrast	Image > Adjustment > Brightness/Contrast
Levels	Enhance > Adjust Brightness/Contrast > Levels	Image > Adjustments > Levels

Index

Index

INDEX